SLAVERY AND PUBLIC HISTORY

ALSO BY JAMES OLIVER HORTON AND LOIS E. HORTON

Slavery and the Making of America

*In Hope of Liberty: Culture, Community, and Protest
Among Northern Free Blacks, 1700–1860*

*Black Bostonians: Family Life and Community Struggle
in the Antebellum North*

*A History of the African American People: The History,
Traditions and Culture of African Americans*

Hard Road to Freedom: The Story of African America

SLAVERY AND PUBLIC HISTORY

The Tough Stuff
of American Memory

EDITED BY
JAMES OLIVER HORTON AND
LOIS E. HORTON

THE NEW PRESS

NEW YORK
LONDON

Published in the United States by The New Press, New York, 2006
Distributed by W. W. Norton & Company, Inc., New York

Library of Congress Cataloging-in-Publication data is available.

ISBN-13 978-1-56584-960-0
ISBN-10 1-56584-960-4

The New Press was established in 1990 as a not-for-profit alternative to the large,
commercial publishing houses currently dominating the book publishing
industry. The New Press operates in the public interest rather than for private
gain, and is committed to publishing, in innovative ways, works of educational,
cultural, and community value that are often deemed insufficiently profitable.

www.thenewpress.com

Composition by dix!
This book was set in Granjon

Printed in the United States of America

10   9   8   7   6   5   4   3   2   1

CONTENTS

INTRODUCTION

James Oliver Horton and Lois E. Horton

This book is a collection of essays that focus on public history and the difficulty that public historians encounter in dealing with the nation's most enduring contradiction: the history of American slavery in a country dedicated to freedom. From its inception, the United States of America was based upon the principle that human freedom was a God-given right, but it also tolerated and was shaped by human slavery. By the time Virginia planter Thomas Jefferson penned the words announcing the colonies' intention to seek independence from Britain, slavery had existed in British North America for more than a century. It held a firm grip on each of the original thirteen British colonies. Ironically, when Jefferson wrote, "We hold these truths to be self-evident, that all men are created equal," referring to basic human rights including freedom, he held at least 150 human beings in slavery. Jefferson personified the paradox of the new and emerging United States.

Many in Britain believed that this blatant inconsistency discredited the American cause, and said so directly. Granville Sharp, England's most famous antislavery advocate, believed that slavery in America "weakens the claim [of] natural Rights of our American Brethren to Liberty." English writer Samuel Johnson posed a pointed question calculated to underscore the hypocrisy of the situation: "How is it that we hear the loudest yelps [for] liberty among the drivers of negroes?" Other English critics were more direct. One observed, "If there be an object truly ridiculous in nature, it is an American patriot, signing resolutions of independency with the one hand, and with the other brandishing a whip over his frightened slaves." [1]

Sale of Estates, Pictures and Slaves in the Rotunda, New Orleans.

This engraving by J.M. Starling depicts slaves being sold as part of an estate settlement in New Orleans. The image appeared in James S. Buckingham's *The Slave States of America,* published in London in 1842. COURTESY OF THE UNIVERSITY OF VIRGINIA LIBRARY SPECIAL COLLECTIONS

Americans too understood the hypocrisy. As John Adams was in Philadelphia attending to the business of nation building in Philadelphia, his wife, in Massachusetts, worried about the contradiction slavery posed for the revolutionary actions of a freedom-loving people. "I wish most sincerely," Abigail Adams wrote to her husband, that "there was not a slave in the province." She agonized over the injustice of it all: "It always seemed a most iniquitous scheme to me to fight ourselves for what we are daily robbing and plundering from those who have as good a right to freedom as we have."[2]

Indeed, throughout the Revolutionary era and beyond, slavery remained America's fundamental contradiction. To explain or justify their tolerance of slavery, some Americans drew on new secular or scientific theories of race developing during the mid- to late eighteenth century. Whereas the Bible indicated a single origin for the human race, some Americans speculated that Africans were a lesser race of people. Although Jefferson seemed uncertain that Africans were a lower order of human, his writings strongly suggested this belief. "I advance it therefore as a suspicion only," he wrote in 1781, "that the blacks, whether originally a distinct race, or made distinct by time and circumstances, are inferior to the whites in the endowments both of body and mind." More specifically, Jefferson speculated, "in reason [blacks are] much inferior, as I think one could scarcely be found capable of tracing and comprehending the investigations of Euclid; and that in imagination they are dull, tasteless, and anomalous." Despite his later favorable review of the almanac (a scientific journal) produced by Benjamin Banneker, a free black man from Baltimore, Jefferson remained unconvinced that blacks were intellectually equal to whites. Further, he suggested that this inequality could not be explained by the degrading effects of slavery. "It is not their condition then," he reasoned, "but nature, which has produced the distinction." Although he believed that further observation and study were needed to verify his suspicions concerning African intellectual ability, perhaps his relationship with his slave Sally Hemings, mother of at least one of his children, encouraged Jefferson to speculate on some measure of black equality: "I believe that in [endowments] of the heart [nature] will be found to have done [blacks] justice."[3]

In Jefferson's time some ethnologists were beginning to think of human beings as part of the natural world, subdividing them into distinct races and considering them variations of a single human species. By the early nineteenth century, however, an increasing number of writers, especially those committed to the defense of slavery, argued that different races constituted separate species. This theory conveniently addressed the disjunction between America's values and its slave reality, supporting a selectively democratic society in which white skin became the mark of membership. Indeed, the presence of enslaved black Americans facilitated the ideal of freedom among white Americans. As English diplomat Sir Augustus John Foster argued in the early nineteenth century, Americans could feel free to "profess an unbounded love of liberty and of democracy in consequence of the mass of the people, who in other countries might become mobs, being there nearly altogether composed of their own Negro slaves." Slavery provided a racial floor below which no white person could fall. All whites, regardless of social and economic standing, were encouraged to feel a common racial bond. Each had a vital interest in maintaining an orderly society that could control the slaves. Under these circumstances the rich seemed to have less to fear from the unruly masses at the bottom of white society so long as the presence of black slavery emphasized their common commitment to white supremacy.[4]

Racial theories fostering the notion of white supremacy developed over the decades before the Civil War. They bolstered an increasingly militant defense of the slave system then fading from northern states and becoming more isolated in the South, though becoming more economically and politically powerful nationally. The need to justify slavery in a free nation, then, was the impetus for the modern American racist theory that continued to develop after the Civil War and the abolition of slavery. During the final decades of the nineteenth century the old proslavery arguments took on new life under the guise of scientific theory. These theories were used to justify the Jim Crow system of racial segregation for the better part of the twentieth century.

Thus, what we understand today as racism is largely a legacy of the slavery that formally ended nearly a century and a half ago. The history of American slavery is a shameful tale of inhumanity and human exploitation and of the attempt to hide national hypocrisy behind tortured theories of racial inequality. The history of slavery continues to have meaning in the twentieth century—it burdens all of American history and is incorporated into public interpretations of the past. This book tells about some of the struggles of historians and public history presentations to deal with race, slavery, and the public memory of slavery.

In the lead essay, Ira Berlin notes that books and articles on slavery in America's history have recently found a substantial readership and films a receptive TV audience. He reviews the development of slavery and the changing nature of race in early America, linking it to many familiar historical milestones and suggesting lessons for our national present and future. David W. Blight continues this theme with a thought-provoking essay on the subject of public memory and its relationship to history. The clash between memory's ownership and history's interpretation often takes place in the public arena of historic museums, memorials, and historical sites. During the twentieth century the struggle for control of the memory of America's past has been central to debates over national identity and significant for concerns about modern civil rights. Blight argues, as do all in this book, that contemporary debates must be grounded in a knowledge of history. This is especially true of debates over American identity, which are often characterized by issues of race and shaped by the urge to forget slavery's long and critically influential history.

James Oliver Horton explores the teaching of slavery's history in the public schools and the importance of the presentation of that history in museums and historic sites, places where most of the public confronts this fundamental but little-understood aspect of the national story. From park rangers at national historic parks to costumed historical interpreters at Virginia's Colonial Williamsburg, historians encounter a public often unwilling to hear a story that calls into question comfortable assumptions about the nation's past. There is no more striking example of this than public reaction, most often but not limited to the South, to any suggestion that slavery was a major cause of the Civil War. Anticipating essays in the final section of this book, this essay discusses recent examples of this heated controversy.

Although, as Horton argues, white Americans and African Americans may react to the story of slavery in different ways, that history can be painful for both. John Michael Vlach's essay tells the story of the Library of Congress's cancellation of "Back of the Big House," an exhibition on slavery that he created. The institution came under substantial pressure from many of its African American employees who found the subject very uncomfortable. In the context of the Library of Congress, the thought of daily confronting the visual images of slavery was apparently too distressing for those black workers who protested their exhibition. Different reactions by other African Americans in Washington, D.C., provided other opportunities for displaying this exhibition and exploring its themes.

The National Park Service encountered a similar controversy in its planning of an exhibition for its new Liberty Bell Center in Philadelphia. Gary B. Nash examines the controversy that arose over the interpretation of slavery at the site and slavery's connection to George Washington, many of the other founding fathers, and the Revolution itself. The fierce debate that resulted extended from city politics to the Park Service and the nation. This essay tells us much about the continuing culture wars over historical interpretation that have extended into the public education system and shaped a national controversy.

Joanne Melish continues the discussion with an analysis of efforts to interpret slavery at historic sites in New England, a region of the country seldom associated with that institution. Her essay explores the links among slavery, the Atlantic slave trade, and the fortunes of prominent New England families, particularly the Browns of Rhode Island, whose family members were both proslavery and antislavery advocates. The presence and importance of slavery in New England's history poses special challenges for historical interpretation at the museums and historical societies of that region, and for Brown University as it seeks an honest look back at its history. There is also the opportunity to educate and explore complex issues of identity, as with the creation of a memorial to Rhode Island's black Revolutionary War regiment. The effort to deal with the history of slavery at a historic house in the border state of Kentucky provides a particularly interesting comparison.

The next two essays focus on Virginia and tell the story of the Old Dominion and its heroes. Lois E. Horton sets forth a fascinating study that utilizes interviews at Monticello to explore the public reaction to DNA findings concerning the relationship between Thomas Jefferson and his slave Sally Hemings. This two-hundred-year-old controversy is clarified by modern science but still disputed by those who refuse to believe that such a historical icon as Jefferson could have fathered children by an African American slave woman. Strangely, the controversy compelled visitors to come to terms with Jefferson as a slaveholder. Marie Tyler-

McGraw traces the efforts of the City of Richmond to deal with the racially charged history of the old capital of the Confederacy, now a site of heritage tourism. From the placement of a portrait of Confederate commander Robert E. Lee to statues of President Abraham Lincoln and African American tennis star Arthur Ashe, Richmond's history has complicated its municipal landscape and its political debates.

The next two essays take on the highly volatile issues of race, slavery, and the Civil War. Dwight T. Pitcaithley relates the story of National Park Service endeavors to deal with issues of race at historic sites and especially its attempts to interpret the history of slavery at Civil War battlefield parks. His discussion of the opposition to these efforts, particularly selected quotes from the hundreds of protest letters received by the Park Service, bears witness to the controversy still raging about the role of race and slavery in the South's decision to leave the United States in the mid-nineteenth century.

Continuing and broadening this discussion, Bruce Levine takes on the fascinating recent neo-Confederate claims of voluntary black military support for the southern cause during the Civil War. He argues that this is an attempt to vindicate the Confederate cause, disconnecting it from the human exploitation of slavery and linking it firmly to issues of independence and states' rights. In this way modern-day supporters of the Confederate cause can honor their ancestors without having to deal with the thorny issue of slavery for which the Confederate South fought. This provocative essay sets out the irony of the adoption of the issue of race by those who defend the actions of the proslavery forces who sought the dismemberment of the United States.

Finally, Edward T. Linenthal reflects on the issues raised by the preceding essays. His comparisons move the discussion beyond national bounds and beyond those of the history of slavery to the question of a society's effort and need to memorialize the past. He poses a critical question: how does a nation deal with its historical sites of shame? The answer to this question reveals much, not only about the history of any particular site or subject but also about the nature, values, and culture of a nation and its people. The critical question is not simply how people remember their past but how they deal with and ultimately learn from the "tough stuff" of their history and how they apply the lessons learned to the challenges of their present and their future.

We are indebted to numerous friends who listened patiently to our ideas for this book as they unfolded over years of formulation. Our students Kevin Strait, Stephanie Ricker, and David Kieran worked tirelessly on project administration and picture research. We thank them all.

SLAVERY AND
PUBLIC HISTORY

Five generations of a black family born in slavery on the J.J. Smith plantation in Beaufort, South Carolina, taken by Civil War photographer Timothy H. O'Sullivan, who visited the plantation in 1862. COURTESY OF THE LIBRARY OF CONGRESS

I

Coming to Terms with Slavery in Twenty-First-Century America

Ira Berlin

A merican racial history is marked by unexpected twists and turns, and the latest bend in the road is no more surprising than most. Interest in African American slavery—an institution put to rest in a murderous civil war almost a century and a half ago—has reappeared in a new guise. The last years of the twentieth century and the initial years of the twenty-first have witnessed an extraordinary engagement with slavery, sparking a rare conversation on the American past—except, of course, it is not about the past. The intense engagement over the issue of slavery signals—as it did in the 1830s with the advent of radical abolitionism and in the 1960s with the struggle over civil rights—a search for social justice on the critical issue of race.

The new interest in slavery has been manifested in the enormous place of slavery in American popular culture as represented in movies (*Glory, Amistad,* and *Beloved*), TV documentaries (PBS's *Africans in America,* HBO's *Unchained Memories,* WNET's *Slavery and the Making of America*), radio shows (*Remembering Slavery*), monuments, indeed entire museums, along with hundreds of roadside markers and thousands of miles of freedom trails—and, of course, Web sites, CDs, and books. Slavery has been on the cover of *Time* and *Newsweek,* above the fold in the *Washington Post,* and the lead story in the "Week in Review" section of the Sunday *New York Times.*[1]

All of this marks the entry of slavery into American politics, as with arguments over apologies, the establishment of federal and state commissions on race, the filing of numerous lawsuits, and presidential visits to slave factories on the west coast of Africa. Slavery has sparked debates over flags and songs in some half dozen states, transformed a graveyard in New York and the site of the Liberty Bell in Philadelphia into contested terrain, and made the paternity of Sally Hemings's children a subject of national interest. The names of scores of schools and highways have become as much a matter of concern as the vexed matter of reparations. Without question, slavery has a greater presence than at any time since the end of the Civil War.[2]

On one level, the reason for this is not too difficult to discern. Simply put, American history cannot be understood without slavery. Slavery shaped America's economy, politics, culture, and fundamental principles. For most of the nation's history, American society was one of slaveholders and slaves.

The American economy was founded upon the production of slave-grown crops, the great staples of tobacco, rice, sugar, and finally cotton, which slave owners sold on the international market to bring capital into the colonies and then the young Republic. That capital eventually funded the creation of an infrastructure upon which rests three centuries of American economic success. In 1860, the four million American slaves were conservatively valued at $3 billion. That sum was almost three times the value of the entire American manufacturing establishment or all the railroads in the United States, about seven times the net worth of all the banks, and some forty-eight times the expenditures of the federal government.[3]

The great wealth slavery produced allowed slave owners to secure a central role in the establishment of the new federal government in 1789, as they quickly transformed their economic power into political power. Between the founding of the Republic and the Civil War, the majority of the presidents—from Washington, Jefferson, Madison, Monroe, and Jackson through Tyler, Polk, and Taylor—were slaveholders, and generally substantial ones. The same was true for the justices of the Supreme Court, where for most of the period between the ratification of the Constitution and the Civil War a slaveholding majority was ruled over by two successive slaveholding chief justices, John Marshall and Roger Taney. A similar pattern can be found in Congress, and it was the struggle for control of Congress between the slaveholding and nonslaveholding states around which antebellum politics revolved.

The power of the slave-owning class, represented by the predominance of slaveholders in the nation's leadership, gave it a large hand in shaping American culture and the values central to American society. It is no accident that a slaveholder penned the founding statement of American nationality and that freedom became central to the ideology of American nationhood. Men and women who drove slaves understood the meaning of chattel bondage, as most surely did the men and women who were in fact chattel. And if it is no accident that the slaveholder Thomas Jefferson wrote that "all men are created equal," then it was most certainly no accident that some of the greatest spokesmen for that ideal, from Richard Allen and Frederick Douglass through W.E.B. Du Bois and Martin Luther King Jr., were former slaves or the descendants of slaves. The centrality of slavery in the American past is manifest.[4]

It would be comforting, perhaps, to conclude that a recognition of slavery's importance has driven the American people to the history books. But there is more to it than that. There is also a recognition, often back-handed and indirect, sometimes subliminal or even subconscious, that the United States' largest, most pervasive social problem is founded on the institution of slavery. There is a general, if inchoate, understanding that any attempt to address the question of race in the present must also address slavery in the past. Slavery is ground zero of race relations. Thus, in the twenty-first century—as during the American Revolution of the 1770s, the Civil War of the 1860s, and the civil rights movement of the 1960s—the history of slavery mixes with the politics of slavery in ways that leave everyone, black and white, uncomfortable and often mystified as to why.

Perhaps that is because most Americans do not know what slavery was. Beyond the obvious, who were the slaves and what exactly did they experience? Who were the slaveholders, the white majority who did not own slaves, and the black men and women who were not slaves? Are the slaves of American history represented by Pharaoh Sheppard, who in 1800 was rewarded with freedom for informing on the slave rebel Gabriel? Are the descendants of Pharaoh Sheppard to be accorded the same consideration as Gabriel's descendants? Does Pharaoh Sheppard, once free, represent the free black experience, or might that better be appreciated in the person of the rebel Denmark Vesey? Should the descendants of the white boatman who assisted Gabriel in his failed escape be given a special dispensation from the burden of slavery's sordid history? If the evil of slavery was unambiguous, the lives of the men and women—

both black and white—who lived through the era were as complicated as any.

But there is much to learn from those complications, not the least of which is the perplexing connection between slavery and race and the relation of both to the intractable problems of race and class in the twenty-first century. Nothing more enrages black and white Americans than the race-based policies that aggravate class inequities and the class-based policies that expose deep-seated racism. The award of an equal-opportunity scholarship to the daughter of a wealthy black cardiologist angers members of the white working class, just as working-class black men and women are infuriated by the supposedly color-blind school entrance exam that excludes people of color. Conflicts of this sort stem from a system that once elevated a few white slave owners into positions of extraordinary power. It continues to shape American society today.

The lines of class do not only cross those of race between white and black. Within an increasingly diverse America—where blacks are no longer the largest minority and where many whites are foreign-born—new complexities have arisen. Whereas once the descendants of white immigrants questioned what slavery had to do with them when their fathers or even grandfathers arrived in the United States after slavery had been abolished, now the same question is broached by newly arrived black men and women. "Barack Obama claims an African American heritage," declared Alan Keyes, the black Republican candidate for an Illinois Senate seat in 2004, about his equally dark-skinned Democratic opponent. But, he contends, "we are not from the same heritage. My ancestors toiled in slavery in this country. My consciousness, who I am as a person, has been shaped by my struggle, deeply emotional and deeply painful, with the reality of that heritage."[5] In a similar if less publicized controversy in the District of Columbia, one longtime African American leader condemned his foreign-born if equally dark-skinned challengers, noting disdainfully that "they look like me, but they don't think like me."[6]

All of which is to say that what is needed are not only new debates about slavery and race but also a new education—a short course in the historical meaning of chattel bondage and its many legacies. The simple truth is that most Americans know little about the three-hundred-year history of slavery in mainland North America with respect to peoples of African descent and almost nothing of its effect on the majority of white Americans.

Some Americans believe slavery was foisted upon unknowing and sometimes unwilling European settlers and unfortunately entwined itself around American institutions until it could be removed only by civil war. While it burdened white Americans, this basically benevolent institution tutored a savage people in the niceties of civilization. Such a view still has some adherents, perhaps more than we would like to admit, but it is on the wane and in some places totally discredited, as it should be.

It has been replaced by the view that slavery was an institution of suffocating oppression, so airtight that it allowed its victims little opportunity to function as full human beings. Slavery robbed Africans and their descendants of their culture and denied their language, religion, and family life, reducing them to infantilized ciphers. Slavery, in short, broke Africans and African Americans.

Recent studies of slavery suggest that neither view correctly represents the experience of enslaved people in the United States.

In January 1865, General William Tecumseh Sherman and Secretary of War Edwin S. Stanton met in Savannah to query an assemblage of former slaves and free people of color on precisely these subjects. The response of Garrison Frazier, a sixty-seven-year-old Baptist minister who served as spokesman for the group, offers about as good a working definition of chattel bondage as any and as clear an understanding of the aspirations of black people as can be found. "Slavery," declared Frazier, "is receiving by the *irresistible power* the work of another man, and not by his *consent.*" Freedom, Frazier continued, "is taking us from the yoke of bondage, and placing us where we could reap the fruits of our own labor, take care of ourselves and assist the Government in maintaining our freedom."[7]

Frazier's last remark—calculated to reassure the general and the secretary—spoke to the minister's appreciation of the political realities of the moment. But his definition of slavery—irresistible power to arrogate another's labor—drew on some three hundred years of experience in bondage in mainland North America. Slavery, of necessity, rested on force. It could only be sustained when slave owners—who, with reason, preferred the title "master"—enjoyed a monopoly on violence backed by the power of the state. Without irresistible power, slavery quickly collapsed—an event well understood by all those who came together at that historic meeting in Savannah.

Frazier also correctly emphasized the centrality of labor to the history of slavery. African slavery did not have its origins in a conspiracy to dishonor, shame, brutalize, or otherwise reduce black people on some perverse scale of humanity—although it did all of those at one time or another. The stench of slavery's moral rot cannot mask the design of American captivity: to commandeer the labor of the many to make a few rich and powerful. Slavery thus made class as it made race, and, in entwining the two processes, it mystified both.

No understanding of slavery can avoid these themes: violence, power, and the usurpation of labor for the purpose of aggrandizing a small minority. Slavery was about domination, and of necessity it rested on coercion. The murders, beatings, mutilations, and humiliations, both petty and great, were an essential, not incidental, part of the system. To be sure, one could dwell upon the wild, maniacal sadism of some frenzied slave owners who lashed, traumatized, raped, and killed their slaves; the record of such lurid tales is full. But perhaps it would be more instructive to underscore the cool, deliberate actions of, say, Robert "King" Carter, the largest slaveholder in colonial Virginia, who petitioned and received permission from the local court to lop the toes off his runaways; or William Byrd, the founder of one of America's great families, who forced an incontinent slave boy to drink a "pint of piss"; or Thomas Jefferson, who calmly reasoned that the greatest punishment he could inflict upon an incorrigible fugitive was to sell him away from his kin. Without question, the history of slavery is the story of victimization, brutalization, and exclusion; it is the story of the power of liberty, of a people victimized and brutalized.[8]

But there is a second theme, for the history of slavery is not only that of victimization, brutalization, and exclusion. If slavery was violence and imposition, if it was death, slavery was also life. Former slaves did not surrender to the imposition, physical and psychological. They refused to be dehumanized by dehumanizing treatment. On the narrowest of grounds and in the most difficult of circumstances, they created and sustained life in the form of families, churches, and associations of all kinds. These organizations—often clandestine and fugitive, fragile and unrecognized by the larger society—became the site of new languages, aesthetics, and philosophies as expressed in story, music, dance, and cuisine. They produced leaders and ideas that continue to inform American life, so much so that it is impossible to imagine American culture without slavery's creative legacy.

What makes slavery so difficult for Americans, both black and white, to come to terms with is that slavery encompasses two conflicting ideas— both with equal validity and with equal truth, but with radically different implications. One says that slavery is one of the great crimes in human history; the other says that men and women dealt with the crime and survived it and even grew strong because of it. One says slavery is our great nightmare; the other says slavery left a valuable legacy. One says death, the other life.

Mastering that contradiction is difficult, but even when it is accomplished there is more to be done. The lives of slaves, like those of all men and women, changed over time and differed from place to place. Thus slavery was not one thing but many. Like every human being who ever lived, the slave was a product of his or her circumstances, only one part of which—to be sure, a significant part—was that he or she was owned. Knowing that a person was a slave does not tell us everything about him or her. It is the beginning of the story, not its end.

What were these circumstances that shaped slaves' lives? Ask most Americans and they would probably say three things: cotton, the deep South, and African Christianity. Like most such conventional wisdom, this is not wrong, as there was a moment—an important moment—when most slaves grew cotton, lived in the deep South, and embraced Christianity. But that moment—the years immediately prior to the American Civil War—was just a small fraction of slavery's history in the United States. For the most part, Americans have read the history of slavery backward, freezing slavery in its death throes. This perhaps is a tribute to the abolitionist movement and its ability to shape popular understandings of the history of slavery, but it is a disservice to the experience of the slaves and to those who try to come to terms with ground zero of American race relations.

During the last two decades, historians have worked hard to detach slavery from its Civil War nexus and to explore its larger history—that is, the full three hundred years of African and African American bondage. They have shown that for most of its history in what becomes the United States, slavery was not a southern institution but a continental one—as much at home in the North as in the South, in New York and Philadelphia as fully as in Charleston or New Orleans. They have demonstrated how slavery in the United States was part of a larger world system—

indeed, beginning in the sixteenth century, slavery more than anything else linked Africa, Europe, and the Americas.[9]

Historicization of slavery does not deny the exceptional character of the North American experience. Indeed, slavery's globalization revealed with ever greater precision what made slavery in the United States unique: the early emergence of an indigenous slave population, the rapid development of a Creole culture, the peculiar definitions of race, and the particularly bloody and destructive emancipation. But the historicization of slavery countered a static and transhistorical vision of slavery, and in so doing it connects the history of slavery to the rest of American history— the making of classes as well as the making of races.

Viewing slavery in the United States not as a status that remains forever unchanged but as history that is forever being made and remade, five "generations" of slaves can be identified: a Charter Generation, a Plantation Generation, a Revolutionary Generation, a Migration Generation, and finally—and triumphantly—a Freedom Generation.[10]

The Charter Generation refers to people of African descent who arrived as slaves in mainland North America prior to the advent of the plantation. Drawn disproportionately from the Atlantic littoral, their world focused outward onto the larger Atlantic, not inward to the African interior. They spoke—among other languages—the Creole dialect that had developed among the peoples of the Atlantic in the fifteenth and sixteenth centuries, a language with a Portuguese grammar and syntax but a vocabulary borrowed from every shore of the Atlantic. They understood something about the trading etiquettes, religions, and laws of the Atlantic world. Many were employed as interpreters, supercargoes, sailors, and *compodores*—all-purpose seaboard handymen—for the great sixteenth- and seventeenth-century trading corporations: the Dutch West India Company, the French Company of the West, the Royal African Company, and a host of private traders and privateers. They entered societies in which many people of European descent, although not slaves, were held in servitude of a variety of types. Almost immediately they began the work of incorporating themselves into those societies—taking familiar names, trading on their own, establishing families, accumulating property, and employing their knowledge of the law to advance themselves and secure their freedom in remarkably high numbers. About one-fifth to one-quarter of the Charter Generation would gain their liberty.[11]

Little is known about these men and women, who had telling names such as Paulo d'Angola of New Amsterdam, and Francisco Menéndez of Saint Augustine, and Anthony Johnson of Virginia—names that speak to the larger Atlantic world. The Charter Generation's history can be glimpsed through Anthony Johnson, a man who spent his life on the eastern shore of Virginia and Maryland. Johnson was sold to the English at Jamestown in 1621 as "Antonio a Negro." During the dozen years following his arrival, Antonio labored in Virginia, where he was among the few who survived the 1622 Indian raid that all but destroyed the colony, and where he later earned an official commendation for his "hard labor and known service." His loyalty and his industry also won the favor of his owner, who became Antonio's patron as well as his owner, perhaps because worthies such as Antonio were hard to find among the rough and hard-bitten, if often sickly, men who comprised the mass of servants and slaves in the region. Whatever the source of his owner's favors, they allowed Antonio to farm independently while still a slave, to marry, and to baptize his children. Eventually, he and his family escaped bondage. Once free, Antonio anglicized his name, transforming "Antonio a Negro" into Anthony Johnson, a name so familiar to English-speakers that no one could doubt his identification with the colony's rulers.[12]

Johnson, his wife, Mary, and their children—who numbered four by 1640—followed their benefactor to the eastern shore of Virginia and Maryland, where the Bennett clan had established itself as a leading family, and where the Johnson family began to farm on its own. In 1651, Anthony Johnson earned a 250 acre headright, a substantial estate for any Virginian, let alone a former slave. When Anthony Johnson's eastern-shore plantation burned to the ground in 1653, he petitioned the county court for relief. Reminding authorities that he and his wife were longtime residents and that "their hard labors and knowne services for obtayneing their livelihood were well known," he requested and was granted a special abatement of his taxes.[13] Like other men of substance, Johnson and his sons farmed independently, held slaves, and left their heirs sizable estates. As established members of their community, they enjoyed rights in common with other free men and frequently employed the law to protect themselves and advance their interests.

The Johnsons were not unique in the Chesapeake region. As elsewhere in mainland North America, the Charter Generation ascended the

social order and exhibited a sure-handed understanding of the social hierarchy and the complex dynamics of patron-client relations. Although still
in bondage, they began to acquire the property, skills, and social connections that became their mark throughout the Atlantic world. Men of the
Charter Generation worked provision grounds, kept livestock, traded independently, and married white women as often as they married black.
They sued and were sued in local courts and petitioned the colonial legislature and governor.[14]

At the time of American settlement, African slavery was a long-
established institution. Europeans in the New World identified blackness
with slavery (how could they not, with the Atlantic filled with African
slaves?) and disparaged blackness, to the disadvantage of people of
African descent. Wherever black people alit, whatever their legal status
and whatever skills they carried, they faced hostility and condescension.
But as long as the linkages between slavery and blackness were imperfect,
people of African descent were not denounced as congenitally dull, dirty,
stupid, indolent, and libidinous, even in the eyes of the most Eurocentric
settlers. Rather, Europeans and European Americans condemned them
as sly, cunning, deceptive, manipulative, and perhaps too clever by half,
expressions that at once admitted grudging respect along with utter contempt. It was a mixture of scorn and admiration that was not unlike the
evaluations that Europeans made of one another, as with English stereotypes of the Dutch as mean and narrow but shrewd and knowledgeable,
or portrayals of the French as flippant and oversexed but clever and determined. Such characterizations of black people, moreover, were rarely
joined to animalistic metaphors or doubts that people of African descent
could compete with Europeans and European Americans for wealth,
power, or sexual favor. The daily experience of Europeans and European
Americans in mainland North America—as throughout the Atlantic
world—refuted such a possibility. In fact, it was precisely the presumption of African competence that made black people so dangerous. In
short, the nature of slavery—the relationship of black and white—
determined the character of racial ideas.

The successors to the Charter Generation, the Plantation Generation,
were not nearly as fortunate as their predecessors. The degradation of
black life with the advent of the plantation altered the meaning of blackness and whiteness—the very definition of race.

Members of the Plantation Generation worked harder and died earlier than those of the Charter Generation. Their family life was truncated, and few men and women claimed ties of blood or marriage. They knew little—and probably did not want to know more—about Christianity and European jurisprudence. They had but small opportunities to participate in independent exchange economies, and they rarely accumulated property. Most lived on large estates deep in the countryside, cut off from the larger Atlantic world. Few escaped slavery.

Their names reflected the contempt with which their owners held them. Most answered not to names such as Anthony Johnson, Paulo d'Angola, or Samba Bambara but to such European diminutives as Jack and Sukey. As if to emphasize their inferiority, some were tagged with names more akin to those of animals: Topper, Postilion. Others were designated with the names of some ancient deity or great personage, such as Hercules or Cato, as a kind of cosmic jest; the most insignificant were given the greatest of names. Whatever they were called, they rarely bore surnames, as their owners sought to obliterate marks of lineage and to deny them adulthood. Such names suggest the anonymity of the Plantation Generation. The biographies of individual men and women, to the extent that they can be reconstructed, are thin to the point of invisibility. Less is known about these men and women than about any other generation of American slaves.

The degradation of black life had many sources, but the largest was the growth of the plantation producing staple commodities for an international market, a radically different form of social organization and commercial production controlled by a class of men whose appetite for labor was nearly insatiable. Planters—backed by the power of the state—transformed slavery. The plantation revolution came to mainland North America in fits and starts. Beginning in the late seventeenth century in the Chesapeake, planters moved unevenly across the continent over the next century and a half, first to lowland South Carolina in the early eighteenth century and then, after failing to establish a plantation regime in the colonies north of the Chesapeake, to the lower Mississippi Valley. By the beginning of the nineteenth century, slave societies dedicated to cultivating tobacco in the Chesapeake, rice in low-country South Carolina and Georgia, and sugar in the lower Mississippi Valley had swept away the Charter Generation.

Although the variations in the nature of settlement, the character of the slave trade, and the demands of particular staple crops produced striking differences in the Plantation Generation, the trajectory of the plantation revolution was always the same. The number of slaves lurched upward. No longer did slaves dribble into the mainland from various parts of the Atlantic littoral. Instead, planters turned to the African interior as their primary source of labor and imported slaves by the boatful. The proportion of the population that was African grew steadily, in some places reaching a majority. For many European settlers, it seemed like the mainland would "some time or other be confirmed by the name of New Guinea."[15] As Africans filled the continent, they began to create their own world. Whereas the Charter Generation had beaten on the doors of the established churches to gain a modicum of recognition, the new arrivals showed neither interest in nor knowledge of Christianity—Jesus disappeared from African American life, not to return for most people of African descent until well into the nineteenth century.

The Africanization of American slavery accompanied a sharp deterioration in the conditions of slave life. The familial linkages that bound members of the Charter Generation attenuated, undermining the ability of the slave population to reproduce itself. Just as direct importation drove birthrates down, it pushed mortality rates up, for the transatlantic journey left transplanted Africans vulnerable to New World diseases. Whereas members of the Charter Generation lived to see their grandchildren, few of the newly arrived Africans would even reproduce themselves.[16]

Confined to the plantation, African slaves faced a new harsh work regimen, as planters escalated the demands they placed on those who worked the fields. Slaves found their toil subject to minute inspection, as planters or their minions monitored the numerous tasks that the cultivation of tobacco, indigo, and rice necessitated. Slaves suffered as planters prospered. Living on isolated plantations, the slaves found their world narrowed. Physical separation denied the new arrivals the opportunity to integrate themselves into the larger society, preventing them from finding a well-placed patron and enjoying the company of men and women of equal rank. The planters' intent to strip away all ties upon which the persona of the enslaved individual rested—village, clan, household, and family—and leave slaves totally dependent upon their owners was nearly realized.

Most important, the new regime left little room for free blacks. Planter-controlled legislatures systematically carved away at the free blacks' liberty. In various places, free black people lost the right to hold office, bear arms, muster in the militia, and vote. They were required to pay special taxes, punished more severely for certain crimes, and subjected to fines or imprisonment for striking a white person, no matter what the cause. Having cannibalized the rights of black people, lawmakers closed the door to freedom, constricting manumission. The number of free people of African descent declined, and it became increasingly easy to equate slavery with blackness.

Evidence of the degradation of slave life was everywhere. Violence, isolation, exhaustion, and alienation often led African slaves to profound depression and occasionally to self-destruction. However, most slaves refused to surrender to the dehumanization that accompanied the Plantation Revolution. Instead, they contested the new regime at every turn, answering the planters' ruthless imposition with an equally desperate resistance, as the creation of the plantation regime sparked bloody reprisals. The mainland grew rife with conspiracies and insurrectionary plots. But resistance required guile as well as daring. If the planters' grab for power began with the usurpation of the African's name, slaves soon took back this signature of their identity. Of necessity, slaves answered to the names their owners imposed on them, but many clandestinely maintained their African names—and so began a battle of wits between master and slave.

As the struggle between whites and blacks changed, so did the meaning of race. The coincidence of slavery with African descent became nearly perfect. With few free blacks to contradict their design, planters equated the brutish realities of slave life with blackness. People of African descent became known for their "gross bestiality and rudeness of their manners, the variety and strangeness of their languages, and the weakness and shallowness of their minds." Some speculated those differences placed black people closer to the apes than to man, and others projected their most fanciful ideas upon blackness. The slaveholders' notions were often embraced by white nonslaveholders, free and unfree, many of whom saw in their white skin a mechanism for eluding the terrible fate that had befallen men and women with whom they had once shared much.[17]

While people of European descent had long distinguished themselves from Africans in a manner that disparaged black people, this new under-standing of race gave blackness a different meaning. Unlike members of the Charter Generation, who had been blasted as clever, manipulative, cunning, deceptive, and too smart by half, descriptors that at once ex-pressed grudging admiration mixed with utter disdain, such designations were never extended to the members of the Plantation Generation. They were stereotyped as dull, dirty, stupid, indolent, brutish creatures—the very opposite of white people, whose intelligence, ingenuity, industry, and civilization were celebrated. If the members of the Charter Genera-tion were all too human, members of the Plantation Generation were hardly human at all.[18] The transformation of slavery had changed the meaning of race. It would not be the last time race would change its meaning.

At the end of the eighteenth century, as a new generation of black men and women—many of them American-born—reconstructed African life in mainland North America, a series of dramatic changes again remade slavery. The great democratic revolutions—the American, the French, and the Haitian—marked a third transformation in the lives of black people, propelling some slaves to freedom and dooming others to nearly another century of captivity. The changes that remade the institution of slavery also remade the ideology of race.

The War for American Independence and the revolutionary conflicts it spawned throughout the Atlantic gave slaves in mainland North America new leverage in their struggle with their owners.[19] By shattering the unity of the planter class and compromising its ability to mobilize the metropolitan state to slavery's defense, the war offered slaves new oppor-tunities to challenge both the institution of chattel bondage and the allied structures of white supremacy. The Revolution also gave slaves a new weapon: the idea of universal equality, as promised in the Declaration of Independence and by the evangelical awakenings. Planters recovered their balance, beat back the abolitionist challenge, reopened the transat-lantic slave trade, and created a new internal slave trade, so that by the be-ginning of the nineteenth century there were more slaves in the United States than there were at the beginning of the Revolution. The transfor-mation of both black slavery and black freedom had profound conse-quences for understanding race.

As the reality of worldwide revolution manifested itself, slaveholders retreated and slavery faltered in the new North American republic. In the North—first in areas where slaves were numerically few and economically marginal and then throughout the region—slavery collapsed; one state after another abolished slavery by legislative actions, judicial fiat, or constitutional amendment. In the states of the upper South (Delaware, Maryland, Virginia, and North Carolina), slave owners successfully resisted the emancipationist onslaught but were nevertheless forced to give ground, and the free black population, which had declined for nearly a century, expanded rapidly. As a result, the proportion of black people enjoying freedom increased, so that some 10 percent of the black population in the upper South had gained their freedom by the beginning of the nineteenth century. For the first time since the destruction of the Charter Generation, freedom became the possession of large numbers of black men and women. The link between slavery and blackness was broken.[20]

Once freed, former slaves began reconstructing their lives. Newly freed men and women commonly celebrated emancipation by taking new names (such as Freeman, Newman, and Somerset)[21], new residences (deserting their former owners), and new occupations. They solidified old institutions (family and church) and created new ones (schools, fraternal organizations, debating clubs, insurance societies), with such names as the African Society or the African School that connected their members to their African past. Finally they began to create a new politics and new leaders.

The simultaneous emergence of freedom and nationality dramatically transformed race, creating two different racial traditions that would remain central to American life into the twenty-first century. One drew upon a literal reading of the Declaration of Independence's precept that all were created equal. This new understanding of race demanded the abolition of African slavery, along with the elimination of all the trappings of inequality. From this literalist reading of the Declaration, the movement against slavery and for racial equality would expand in the years that followed. Racial distinctions would have no place in American life.

But the Declaration also spawned a second definition of race, particularly since slavery remained and, indeed, expanded in the Age of Revolution. The presumption that all men were equal by nature and the continued presence of slavery cried for explanation. Those who were not willing to support abolition or embrace equality found a rationale by writing black people out of humanity. In his 1786 *Notes on Virginia,* the slave-owning author of the Declaration of Independence speculated that black people were different from whites, a result not of circumstance but of nature. Thomas Jefferson's speculations were soon followed by others who wrote without the Sage of Monticello's reservations. They maintained black people were a separate species. Racialist clergy broke with the biblical story of a unified creation. Racialist scientists conjured the physical differences between white and black. Others theorized that blacks and whites had different psychologies. Such differences rationalized exclusion, separation, and the projected extirpation of free black people, who were denied the rights of citizens—the vote and the rights to testify in court, sit on juries, and stand in the militia. Likewise, free blacks were denied entry to respectable society, segregated in white churches, and barred from schools with white children. Whites and blacks could not even be buried in the same cemeteries. As earlier, a new understanding of race emerged from transformation of the institution of slavery.

But if the Revolution transformed slavery and race, it did not do so permanently. As the new century began, they were altered yet again. Between the election of Thomas Jefferson in 1800 and Abraham Lincoln in 1860, more than one million black people—enslaved and free—were forced from the homes they and their forebears had created. The Second Middle Passage from the upper South to the lower South dwarfed the initial transatlantic slave trade that had carried black people to mainland North America. Driven by a seemingly insatiable demand for cotton and an expanding market for sugar, the massive migration transported black people across the continent, assigning most to another half century of captivity and providing immediate freedom for a few. Some of the latter reentered the Atlantic from which they or their ancestors had come, completing the diasporic circle. Whatever direction they traveled and whatever the circumstance under which they traveled, this Second Middle Passage forced people of African descent to remake their lives on new terrain.

The lives of men and women ensnared in the Second Middle Passage—the Migration Generation—were changed forever. Tobacco and rice cultivators came to grow cotton and sugar. Southerners became northerners or Canadians. Still others traveled to Africa, Europe, or various other places in the Americas. In the process, some husbands and wives were separated and children orphaned, while other families were reconstructed. Still others found new families, married or remarried, and themselves became parents, creating new lineages. Migrants, voluntary or coerced, came to speak new languages, practice new skills, and find new gods, as thousands of men and women abandoned the beliefs of their parents and grandparents and embraced new ideas.

As slavery was transformed, so too were notions of race. Slaveholders invented distinctions between black and white, rooting their origins in the Bible, antiquity, and the new sciences. But even as some extended the racialist ideas Jefferson had advanced merely "as a suspicion" in the *Notes on Virginia,* others continued to embrace a literal reading of the Declaration. The egalitarian tradition found a home within the radical abolitionist movement, which denounced all racial distinction as invidious. The struggle between slavery and antislavery occupied Americans in the nineteenth century and eventuated in civil war, which also redefined blackness and whiteness, embedding a new relationship between race and citizenship in the Constitution of the United States. But even before the ink was dry on the Fourteenth Amendment, others began to reconstruct race in contrary ways. Building upon Jefferson's racialist remarks, they created a new anthropology and psychology of race that emphasized difference and hierarchy in ways with which slaveholders would have been familiar and comfortable.[22]

The process of race formation, of course, did not end with the passage of the Civil War amendments or the counterrevolution that accompanied the overthrow of Reconstruction and the elevation of Jim Crow segregation. In the twentieth century and down to the twenty-first, notions of race continued to be transformed with the circumstances of American life. What was true in the Charter, Plantation, Revolutionary, and Migration Generations was equally true in the Freedom Generation and those that followed. If the omnipresence of race in American history provided the dismal specter of permanence, race's ever-changing character suggests its malleability. That it could be made in the past argues that it can be remade in the future—a prospect that provides all the more reason to come to terms with slavery.

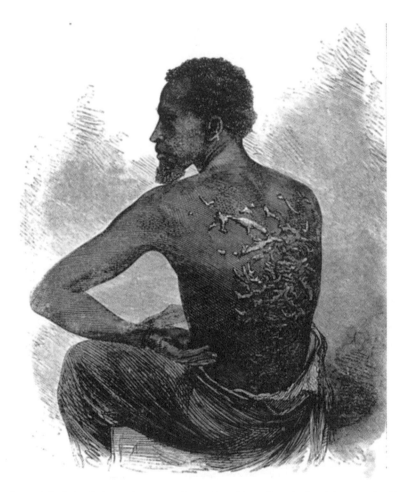

Gordon, a Mississippi slave who escaped to U.S. military lines in Louisiana and enlisted in the army to fight against the Confederacy. This picture of his whip-scarred back, which appeared in *Harper's Weekly* in 1863, encouraged other African American enlistments in the U.S. Army during the Civil War and became ingrained in the nation's memory of slavery. COURTESY OF THE LIBRARY OF CONGRESS

2

If You Don't Tell It Like It Was,

It Can Never Be as It Ought to Be

David W. Blight

In Gabriel García Márquez's epic novel *One Hundred Years of Solitude,* a plague attacks a small village, causing the people to lose, in stages, parts of their memories. First, each person loses the ability to recollect his or her childhood, then names and functions and all manner of objects. Then identities begin to vanish; people do not recognize one another, and some even lose a sense of their own being. A silversmith who is terrified that he cannot remember the word *anvil* for one of his own crucial tools frantically places labels on everything in his house in the hope he will not lose all memory. He labels animals and plants, furniture and windows—a cow, a pig, a banana. "Little by little," writes García Márquez, "studying the infinite possibilities of the loss of memory, he realized that the day might come when things would be recognized by their inscriptions but no one would remember their use." So he begins to write longer and longer descriptions of function: "This is the cow. She must be milked every morning so that she will produce milk," and so on.

Buendía, the silversmith, becomes traumatized by the prospect of living a life of endless labeling to survive with a sense of humanity. He tries to develop a memory machine that will store written entries of all experiences and all knowledge in each villager's life. After placing thousands of entries into his machine, Buendía is mercifully saved from his nightmare by a friend who miraculously cures him of the plague. Buendía recovers his full power of memory. But he has seen this world without memory: a world of despair and incurable confusion, a world where people lost their humanity in an anarchy of ignorance. Personal identity had died, and all forms of symbolic communication had ceased.[1] Memory, this story implies, is at the heart of our humanity; as individuals, and perhaps as societies as well, we cannot function in practical or moral terms without memory.

Memory is one of the most powerful elements in our human constitution. In one of the most interesting meditations on memory ever written, St. Augustine, in the *Confessions,* refers to memory as the "vast court," the "treasury" in the mind. He stands in awe of its force—a great "chamber," he calls it, and no one had "sounded the bottom thereof." "Great is the power of memory," Augustine writes, "a fearful thing. O my God, a deep and boundless manifoldness; and this thing is the mind, and this am I myself."[2] Augustine seems convinced that we are our memories; they dictate to us, we respond to them, and we endlessly revise them. Memory can control us, overwhelm us, poison us. Or it can save us from utter confusion and despair. As individuals, we cannot live without it, but it is part of the agony in the human condition to live with it as well.

Is all of this as equally true of memory when it takes on the collective, social form? Do whole societies or institutions take their very sustenance from memory in ways similar to individuals? How do groups remember? Is Yale University's struggle to face its past relationships to slavery and the slave trade a little like García Márquez's silversmith? Not in some ways, but perhaps in one key way yes. After an apparent inattention to memory (not quite a plague of growing amnesia, more an avoidance), should it as an institution frantically delve into every corner of its past looking for complicity with slavery, and then label or relabel buildings, fellowships, the residential colleges themselves? Should it fear the loss of memory in a wave of constant revision of honorific practices, inscriptions, or institutional identities? The silversmith was desperate over the loss of memory itself, and therefore the loss of his ability to function as a human. An institution faces, preserves, or reconsiders its past for deeper self-understanding, for the meaning and use of its public image, or simply to understand its historical evolution. Yale can worry, if it must, about its Calhoun College in a much more sedate, deliberative way than García Márquez's silversmith. But it must nevertheless take care to examine its losses or resurrections of memory. And perhaps most important, it will want to take care to understand those historical moments in which memory decisions were made. The village silversmith needed labels and increasingly longer inscriptions to survive; the great institution needs to investigate, to study how and why the labels and inscriptions were adopted when they were adopted.

Memory inspires awe for its control over us, but the neuroscientist Daniel Schacter contends that memory operates as a "fragile power," always unstable and changing. "Scientific research," says Schacter, "is the most powerful way to find out how memory works, but artists can best illuminate the impact of memory in our day-to-day lives."[3] With a subject such as slavery and the slave trade, we especially need artists to give us access to the story, and especially to the hold of its memory on us.

In his poem "Middle Passage," the modern American poet Robert Hayden captured the meaning of slave ships:

Shuttles in the rocking loom of history
The dark ships move, the dark ships move,
Their bright ironical names
Like jests of kindness on a murderer's mouth . . .
Weave toward New World littorals that are
Mirage and myth and actual shore.
Voyage through death,
Voyage whose chartings are unlove.

A charnel stench, effluvium of living death
Spreads outward from the hold,
Where the living and the dead, the horribly dying,
Lie interlocked, lie foul with blood and excrement . . .

But, oh, the living look at you
With human eyes whose suffering accuses you,
Whose hatred reaches through the swill of dark
To strike you like a leper's claw.

You cannot stare that hatred down
Or chain the fear that stalks the watches
And breathes on you its fetid scorching breath;

Cannot kill the deep immortal human wish,
The timeless will.

Calculating the costs of such human suffering and loss has always teetered uneasily on the scale of historical justice; clinical statistics, modern moral outrage, tragic sensibility, and horror-filled stories of human commerce and survival have all found their places on the scale. The slave trade has to be assessed for what it was: a massive economic enterprise that helped build the colonial Atlantic world, a story of enormous human cruelty and exploitation that forged one of the foundations of modern capitalism, and a tale of migration and cultural transplantation that brought African peoples and folkways to all New World societies. Hayden offered a poet's simple and timeless definition for the slave trade: a "voyage through death to life upon these shores."[4]

Sometimes history "accuses" us, as Hayden says, and we cannot "stare . . . down" its moral responsibilities. But history also forces us to interpret, explain, and imagine ourselves into the events of the past. In the words of the historian Nathan Huggins, Africans engulfed in the slave trade and transported to the Americas experienced a physical, psychological, and cultural "rupture" from their known universe. They were ripped out of the "social tissue" that gave meaning to their lives and converted into "marketable objects." For so many landing in Brazilian and Caribbean ports, or in Charleston, South Carolina, by 1700, we must imagine them lost, wrote Huggins, "in a process, the end of which was impossible to see from its onset and its precise beginnings lost forever to recall."[5]

But we are responsible for our own recall, and this raises the question of the relationship of history to memory. At the end of his first book, *Suppression of the African Slave Trade* (1896), after two hundred pages of historical analysis, W.E.B. Du Bois ended with a kind of moral statement entitled "The Lesson for Americans." "No American can study the connection of slavery with United States history," wrote Du Bois, "and not devoutly pray that his country may never have a similar social problem to solve, until it shows more capacity for such work than it has shown in the past." Then Du Bois took aim at the dominant way most Americans had come to view slavery. "It is neither profitable nor in accordance with scientific truth to consider that whatever the constitutional fathers did was right," he declared, "or that slavery was a plague sent from God and fated to be eliminated in due time." "We must face the fact," Du Bois continued, "that this problem arose principally from the cupidity and carelessness of our ancestors."[6]

Here, Du Bois's broad strokes are those of a historian, but one appealing to the moral sensibilities of his countrymen and to the idea of a national memory—if by that we mean the master narrative from which people garner a collective sense of definition and destiny. Contrary to the image of America as a progressive, freedom-loving people with a Constitution that welcomes all, Du Bois said the founders and the generations to follow made a "bargain" with "evil." "There began, with 1787, that system of . . . truckling, and compromising with a moral, political, and economic monstrosity," he said, "which makes the history of our dealing with slavery in the first half of the nineteenth century so discreditable to a great people." In this mixture of moral hindsight and foresight about how Americans use the past, the young Du Bois tried to tilt American memory toward a more critical, tragic sensibility—toward confrontation with slavery and its legacies rather than mere celebration that it was gone. "We" Americans, he insisted, "congratulate ourselves more on getting rid of a problem than on solving it." Delay and denial, he implied, were deep American habits when it came to race and slavery. "The riddle of the Sphinx may be postponed," he wrote, "it may be evasively answered now; sometime it must be fully answered."[7]

As scholar, editor, artist, and activist, Du Bois worked both sides of the street in this struggle between history and memory. But what exactly is the relationship between these two ways of seeing the past? For more than a decade, historians from many fields and nations have been studying the past through the lens of "memory." Some say we have veered from our training and subject matter ("gone over to the enemy" of poststructuralism, as one questioner put it to me). But many others have felt the pull to investigate how societies remember, to research the myths that define cultures, to cross over into the realm of public, collective historical consciousness in all its messy manifestations.

The concepts of history and memory can be conflated or discretely preserved in use and meaning; it is important to establish their differences. They are like two attitudes toward the past, two streams of historical consciousness that must at some point flow into each other. Historians are custodians of the past; we are preservers and discoverers of the facts and stories out of which people imagine their civic lives. But we need a sense of both humility and engagement in the face of *public* memory. "The remembered past," warned John Lukacs in 1968, "is a much larger category than the recorded past."[8]

History is what trained historians do, a reasoned reconstruction of the past rooted in research; it tends to be critical and skeptical of human motive and action, and therefore more secular than what people commonly call memory. History can be read by or belong to everyone; it is more relative, contingent on place, chronology, and scale. If history is shared and secular, memory is often treated as a sacred set of absolute meanings and stories, possessed as the heritage or identity of a community. Memory is often owned; history is interpreted. Memory is passed down through generations; history is revised. Memory often coalesces in objects, sites, and monuments; history seeks to understand contexts in all their complexity. History asserts the authority of academic training and canons of evidence; memory carries the often more immediate authority of community membership and experience. In an essay about the slave trade and the problem of memory, Bernard Bailyn aptly stated memory's appeal: "Its relation to the past is an embrace . . . ultimately emotional, not intellectual."[9]

Scholars working on memory are no less devoted to traditional sources than those on any other subject. We assess all manner of individual memories (actual remembered experience) in letters, memoirs, speeches, debates, and autobiography. But our primary concern is with the illusive problem of collective memory—the ways in which groups, peoples, or nations construct versions of the past and employ them for self-understanding and to win power in an ever-changing present. The fierce debates over National History Standards during the early 1990s, as well as many other conflicts in public history (the *Enola Gay* exhibition, the Holocaust Museum, the World War II Memorial in Washington), were not only clinics about the stakes in America's culture wars but a culture-wide lesson in the politics of history's relationship to collective memory.[10] In the past couple of years it seemed that the culture wars had run their course. But it is possible in these tense times of terrorism and war that the reparations debate, as well as the Bush administration's desire to bring more attention to American history, may revive battles over our national memory in ways we have not fully anticipated.

Modern nations have taken their very sustenance at times from the pasts upon which they are built or imagined. In the classic study *The Collective Memory* (1950), the sociologist Maurice Halbwachs's analysis of the relationship of individual and collective memory (what he called "autobiographical" and "historical" memory) was very much aimed at how historians think. Halbwachs's insights into how we remember in groups, associations, frameworks, communities, and institutional spaces serve historians who seek to know how historical consciousness is forged or diminished or controlled in any given culture and at a particular time.[11] In short, historians study memory because it has been such an important modern instrument of power. And what historians have come to understand is simply that the process by which societies or nations remember collectively itself has a history. We're writing histories of memory.

There are risks, of course, as historians shift their gaze to matters of social and public memory. We could become servants of the very culture wars that have given rise to so many struggles over memory. Memory is usually invoked in the name of nation, ethnicity, race, or religion, or on behalf of a felt need for peoplehood or victimhood. It often thrives on grievance, and its lifeblood is mythos and telos. Like our subjects, we can risk thinking *with* memory rather than *about* it.[12] Indeed, the study of memory is fueled in part by the world's post-Holocaust and post–Cold War need to assess the stories of survivors of genocide, trauma, or totalitarian control over historical consciousness. While I agree that the world is riven with too much memory, and that its obsessions can stifle democratizing and universalizing principles, it is precisely because of this dilemma that we must study historical memory. We should know its uses and perils, its values and dark tendencies.

People will develop a sense of the past by one means or another—from schooling, religion, family, popular culture, or demagoguery. Historical consciousness can result from indoctrination or a free market of a hundred blooming interpretations. But the greatest risk, writes Cynthia Ozick, is the tendency for people to derive their sense of the past only from the "fresh-hatched inspiration" of their "Delphic priests." History is often weak in the face of the mythic power of memory and its oracles. But we run the greatest risk in ignoring that weakness, wishing the public would adopt a more critical, interpretive sense of the past. "Cut off from the uses of history, experience, and memory," cautions Ozick, the "inspirations" alone of any culture's Delphic priests "are helpless to make a future."[13] As historians, we are bound by our craft and by our humanity to study the problem of memory and thereby help make a future. We should respect the poets and priests; we should study the defining myths at play in any memory controversy. But then, standing at the confluence of the two streams of history and memory, we should write the history *of* memory, observing and explaining the turbulence we find.

The dilemma of facing our national past of slavery is, of course, not a new one. In my book *Race and Reunion,* I sketch out five different but overlapping forms of memory by which African Americans themselves faced their own past of slavery, emancipation, and the Civil War, and forged stories about their journey in America. First is the slave past as a dark void, a lost or shameful epoch—even as a paralytic burden better left undisturbed. Second is a black patriotic memory, characterized by insistence that the black soldier, the Civil War constitutional amendments, and the story of emancipation ought to be at the center of the nation's remembrance, its master narrative, and its sense of responsibility. Third is a view of black destiny that combined Pan-Africanism, millennialism, and Ethiopianism—the tradition (more a theory of history than a political movement and rooted in the Sixty-eighth Psalm's famous claim that "princes shall come out of Egypt, and Ethiopia shall soon stretch forth her hands unto God") that anticipated the creation of an exemplary civilization, perhaps in Africa or in the New World, and which saw the American emancipation as only one part of a long continuum of Christian development. Fourth is a reconciliationist-accomodationist mode of memory rooted in Booker T. Washington's philosophy of industrial education and the "progress of the race" rhetoric that set in all over American culture by 1900, and fifth is a tragic vision of slavery and the war as the nation's fated but unfinished passage through a catastrophic transformation from an old order to a new one. These five forms of memory are not definitive, and all could flow into one another. They formed the conflicted determination of a people to forge new and free identities and to find the narrative that best fit their hopes and experience in a society spending great energy to forget the story of black freedom.[14]

Let me focus briefly on this problem of the slave past as either burden or inspiration in the late nineteenth century because it anticipates aspects of our current debate over reparations. By the 1880s and 1890s, north or south, in a city or in a sharecropper's shack, where did most African

Americans look for a safe haven in the past? In what narrative did they root their fragile citizenship? What American story could they safely own? It depended on their circumstances, of course, and the relative degree of protection they experienced for their rights and their dreams. For many, looking back into the past forced an encounter with the shame of slavery. In an age that exalted self-made business titans, when Christianity stressed personal responsibility, when many of their leaders preached self-reliant uplift, and in a culture riven with theories of inherent racial characteristics, blacks carried the stigma of slavery. Bondage had left the collective "injury of slavery," said *Christian Recorder* editor Benjamin Tanner in 1878. "The very remembrance of our experience is hideous." In 1887, Tanner's paper ran a poem, "Keep Out of the Past," by Emma Wheeler Wilcox, which had an unmistakable meaning for blacks:

> *Keep out of the past! For its highways*
> *Are damp with malarial gloom.*
> *Its gardens are sere, and its forests are drear,*
> *And everywhere moulders a tomb . . .*
> *Keep out of the past! It is lonely*
> *And barren and bleak to the view,*
> *Its fires have grown cold and its stories are old,*
> *Turn, turn to the present, the new!*

Hence, in a thousand settings, from magazine articles to sermons, from emancipation exhibitions to anniversaries, and in private communication, many blacks tended to consider slavery as an American prehistory that was painful to revisit. As the black sociologist Kelly Miller put it, "In order to measure . . . progress, we need a knowledge of the starting point as well as a fixed standard of calculation. We may say that the Negro began at the zero point, with nothing to his credit but the crude physical discipline of slavery." [15] With this notion of emancipation as the zero point of group development, blacks risked reflection on their past and measured their progress. And we are still caught in this web of calculation—wondering how to balance historical costs with historical inspiration.

Black intellectuals of the late nineteenth century differed, often fiercely, over just how historically minded their people ought to be. A case in point is an encounter between Alexander Crummell and Frederick

Douglass at Storer College, in Harpers Ferry, West Virginia, on Memorial Day, May 30, 1885. Crummell gave a commencement address, entitled "The Need of New Ideas and New Aims for a New Era," at this school founded for freedmen at the end of the war. An Episcopal priest, educated at the abolitionist Oneida Institute in upstate New York and at Cambridge University in England in the 1840s, Crummell had spent nearly twenty years as a missionary and an advocate of African nationalism in Liberia (1853–71). Crummell hoped to turn the new generation of blacks, most of whom would have been born just before or during the war, away from dwelling "morbidly and absorbingly upon the servile past" and toward an embrace of the urgent "needs of the present." As a theologian and social conservative, Crummell was concerned not only with racial uplift—his ultimate themes were family, labor, industrial education, and especially moral improvement—but also with the unburdening of young blacks from what he perceived as the "painful memory of servitude."[16]

Blacks, Crummell believed, were becoming a people paralyzed by "fanatical anxieties upon the subject of slavery." In his stern rebuke, Crummell made a distinction between memory and recollection. Memory, he contended, was a passive, unavoidable part of group consciousness; recollection, on the other hand, was active, a matter of choice, and dangerous in excess. "What I would fain have you guard against," he told the Storer graduates, "is not the memory of slavery, but the constant recollection of it." Such recollection, Crummell maintained, would only degrade racial progress; for him, unmistakably, "duty lies in the future."[17]

Prominent in the audience that day at Harpers Ferry was Frederick Douglass. According to Crummell's own account, his call to reorient African American consciousness away from the past met with Douglass's "emphatic and most earnest protest." No verbatim account of what Douglass said at Harpers Ferry that day survives, but his many anniversary and Memorial Day speeches during the 1880s offer a clear picture of what he may have said. A healthy level of forgetting, said Douglass in 1884, was "Nature's plan of relief." But Douglass insisted that whatever the psychological need to avoid the woeful legacy of slavery, it would resist all human effort at suppression. The history of African Americans, he remarked many times, could "be traced like that of a wounded man through a crowd by the blood."[18] Better to confront such a past, he believed, than to wait for its resurgence.

In his many postwar speeches about memory, Douglass would often admit that his own personal memory of slavery was best kept sleeping like a "half-forgotten dream." But he despised the politics of forgetting that the culture of reconciliation demanded. "We are not here to visit upon the children the sins of the fathers," Douglass told a Memorial Day audience in Rochester in 1883, "but we are here to remember the causes, the incidents, and the results of the late rebellion." Most of all, Douglass objected to the historical construction that portrayed emancipation as a great national "failure." The growing argument (made by some blacks as well as whites) that slavery had protected and civilized blacks, while freedom had gradually sent them "falling into a state of barbarism," forced Douglass to argue for an aggressive vigilance about memory.[19]

Crummell and Douglass had very different personal histories and agendas. Crummell had never been a slave; he achieved a classical education, was a missionary of evangelical Christianity and a thinker of conservative instincts, and had spent almost the entire Civil War era in West Africa. He returned to the United States twice during the war to recruit black emigrants for Liberia, while Douglass worked aggressively as an advocate of emancipation and recruited approximately a hundred members of the Fifty-Fourth Massachusetts regiment. Crummell represented a brand of black nationalism that combined Western, Christian civilizationalism and race pride. He contended that the principal problems faced by American blacks were moral weakness, self-hatred, and industrial primitiveness. Douglass, the former slave, had established his fame by writing and speaking about the meaning of slavery; his life's work and his very identity were inextricably linked to the transformations of the Civil War. The past made and inspired Douglass: he had risen from slavery's prison, and there was no meaning for him without memory. The past also had made Crummell, but his connections to many of the benchmarks of African American social memory were tenuous. For Douglass, emancipation and the Civil War were truly *felt* history, a moral and legal foundation upon which to demand citizenship and equality. For Crummell, they were potentially paralyzing memories—not the epic to be retold, merely the source of future needs.[20]

Remembering slavery and emancipation thus became a forked road. Douglass's and Crummell's differing dispositions toward the past represent two directions black thought could go in the 1880s: both sought racial uplift, but one would take the risk of sustaining a sense of historic grievance against America as the means of making the nation fulfill its promises, while the other would look back only with caution and focus on group moral and economic regeneration. With differing aims, Crummell and Douglass both sought to teach a new generation of African Americans how to understand and use the legacy of slavery and the Civil War era, how to preserve and destroy the past.

The future beckoned, but the past remained a heavy weight to carry. Forgetting might seem wise, but it was also perilous. To face the past was to court the agony of one's potential limitations, to wonder if the rabbits really could outwit the foxes, or whether some creatures in the forest just did have history and breeding on their side. Long before Du Bois wrote of a struggle with the "double consciousness" of being American and black, African American freedmen had to decide how to look backward and forward. Many may have been like the characters Toni Morrison created in her novel *Beloved*—haunted by slavery's physical and psychic tortures, but desperate to live in peace and normalcy. When Paul D says to Sethe, "Me and you, we got more yesterday than anybody, we need some kind of tomorrow," Morrison imagined herself into the heart of late-nineteenth-century black memory. Memory is sometimes that human burden we can neither live comfortably with nor without. Douglass believed that black memory was a weapon, and its abandonment was dangerous to survival. Crummell argued that a people can "get inspiration . . . in the *yesterdays* of existence, but we cannot healthily live in them."[21] The story of black Civil War memory demonstrates that both were right.

That encounter between Douglass and Crummell is indeed a precursor of the reparations debate today between some black leaders. But the idea of reparations itself is not new either. Led by a white southerner, Walter Vaughan, one practical effort was made in the 1880s and 1890s. Vaughan was the son of a slaveholder and a native of Selma, Alabama. Too young to have fought in the Civil War, he migrated to Philadelphia, where he went to business school, and then moved to Omaha, Nebraska, where he edited a newspaper. Vaughan had a passion for the welfare of former slaves, and he founded a movement to secure pensions for freedmen, with Union veterans' pensions as his model. Vaughan began to lobby Congress in the 1880s. Several U.S. senators responded to Vaughan with either incredulity or claims that only education could help the freedmen and that ex-slave pensions would be too large a burden on taxpayers. But the plan had some luck with Republicans in 1890, and the Ex-Slave Pension and Bounty Bill was introduced in Congress, calling for maximum payments of $15 per month and maximum bounties of $500 for each ex-slave. The three sitting black congressmen at the time did not support the measure. John Mercer Langston of Virginia rejected the bill, saying that "what we want is the means of obtaining knowledge and useful information, which will fit the rising generation for honorable and useful employment."[22]

But Vaughan and his friends did not give up. He visited black churches in Omaha and Chicago, founded Ex-Slave Pension Clubs, and charged 10-cent enrollment fees and 25-cent monthly dues. A significant black group formed out of Vaughan's initial movement, led by the Reverend Isaiah Dickerson and Mrs. Callie D. House in Nashville, Tennessee. This National Ex-Slave Mutual Relief Bounty and Pension Association raised dues to pay for its literature, its annual meeting, its preparation of lists of eligible ex-slaves, and lobbying in Washington. Local organizations were charged $2.50 for a charter. The driving force behind this organization seems to have been Callie House, who had been born in a contraband camp in 1865, had grown up desperately poor, and was the mother of four children by the time she began her activism. House traveled all over the South, recruiting an estimated two hundred thousand members and trying to raise interest in a federal slave pension bill. Her organization tried to introduce some five different bills while the movement lasted, sometimes with the support of white southerners who saw it as a net economic benefit to the South's labor force. But the Bureau of Pensions and the U.S. Postal Service began surveillance of the association in about 1902. Ten years of Justice Department and Postal Service surveillance turned up no direct evidence that any federal laws were ever broken, but the association was finally driven out of business in 1916 when the federal government enforced a fraud order against it.[23]

House's movement received little if any support from black editors or from organizations such as the Afro-American League, the National Negro Business League, or the NAACP. According to research by Mary

Frances Berry, a class-action suit instigated and paid for by House was filed in federal court in the District of Columbia by four African Americans claiming that the Treasury Department owed black people $68,073,388.99, which was the amount of taxes collected on cotton between 1862 and 1868. Since the records for that period could apparently be recovered and traced, such a figure was arrived at as the compensation owed blacks for their labor in production. The suit was dismissed, but not before it received favorable support from two black newspapers, the *Washington Bee* and the *New York Age*. In October 1917, in the midst of the U.S. entry into World War I, House was indicted and convicted of mail fraud and sentenced to one year in federal prison in Jefferson City, Tennessee. House died a few years later of cancer with no medical care. Here and there in the Works Progress Administration narratives some remembrance of House's slave pension movement appears. And in 1934 a group of elderly ex-slaves wrote to President Franklin Roosevelt asking, "Is there any way to consider the old slaves?" One asked directly what had happened to the old idea of "giving us pensions in payment for our long days of servitude?"[24]

Was the best chance at slave reparations in American history missed in Callie House's failed or crushed movement? Were those final old slaves alive in the 1930s the last best chance? Were their dreams somehow eventually or partially realized in social security for their children and affirmative action for their grandchildren, or in the Civil Rights Act of 1964? Those questions do not have easy answers, and they drive our current debate—a movement with deep grassroots support and broad staying power.

I offer no solutions to the reparations issue—that is not my task as a historian. But this much I do know: whatever direction our current debate takes, it must go down the path of broader public education and learning about slavery, the deep complicity of the United States government in its growth and power, and the legacies that persisted and poisoned our national memory for so long in its wake. A couple of years ago I was part of a group of historians invited to conduct roundtable discussions with the board members of the new National Underground Railroad Freedom Center in Cincinnati, Ohio. We spent an entire Saturday morning serving as discussion leaders at tables of six to eight people, most of whom were black and very prominent in American business, law, and life. Our charge was to get these thoughtful and successful people to talk about why a museum about slavery was important. The folks at my table, almost to a person, said many of the right things with both knowledge and sincerity, but they did so by demanding that this museum tell a progressive story, one that would, in the end, uplift young people, and especially leave families with pride. After some time, only one person had not spoken. So, in my teacherly way, I called on him—Fred Shuttlesworth, a Baptist minister and the former leader of the Southern Christian Leadership Conference's campaign against Jim Crow in Birmingham, Alabama, during the civil rights revolution. Shuttlesworth's life had been on the line countless times in the struggles of the sixties. We all looked at him, and he broke his silence. He put Frederick Douglass's plea to remember in the simplest terms; hard as it is to do in the public arena, he named the path we had to take. "If you don't tell it like it was," he said, "it can never be as it ought to be." Whatever else we do about the legacies of slavery in our history, our institutions, or our lives, we can do no less than heed Fred Shuttlesworth's plea.

Reenactor Bridgette Houston portrayed a slave during the controversial and provocative 1994 re-creation of a colonial slave auction at Colonial Williamsburg. COURTESY OF THE COLONIAL WILLIAMSBURG FOUNDATION

3

Slavery in American History:

An Uncomfortable

National Dialogue

James Oliver Horton

In mid-June 1997 at the University of California, San Diego, President William Clinton announced an initiative meant to encourage an honest and candid national conversation on race. His call came in the wake of national attacks on affirmative action programs and California's rejection of them in its state institutions of higher education. The president reminded his audience of the corresponding drop in minority enrollment in California's law schools and other graduate programs and urged that the state's higher education system not be resegregated. There was reason for concern. A recent Gallup national survey had found that most white Americans believed that racial discrimination and isolation were no longer barriers to achievement. These unrealistic assumptions illustrated the huge gap between the lives of most whites and the everyday experiences of most African Americans. To facilitate a racial dialogue that might serve to educate Americans on the subject, and to counsel him on race relations policies, the president appointed a seven-member advisory panel headed by Duke University historian John Hope Franklin. The intent was to hold a series of conversations on race that would highlight the issues Americans must address en route to national racial reconciliation.

This White House effort helped launch several private attempts at national racial dialogue, but what emerged most clearly from such efforts was a picture of a people without a sufficient historical context for such conversation. Americans see themselves as a freedom-loving people, but historical scholarship over the last two generations has clearly shown that too often national actions did not reflect a commitment to human liberty. The little national history that most remember from public school, however, seems to reinforce the romanticized notion of America as the land of the free. Having justified a bloody revolution on grounds of a national belief in human freedom, Americans call their history a freedom story. In the national imagination, expressed in the words of John F. Kennedy, the country is traditionally willing to "pay any price, bear any burden, meet any hardship, support any friend, oppose any foe to assure the survival and the success of liberty."[1] For a nation steeped in this self-image, it is embarrassing, guilt-producing, and disillusioning to consider the role that race and slavery played in shaping the national narrative. Any attempt to integrate these aspects of the national past into the American memory risks provoking defensiveness, anger, and confrontation. As Americans attempted racial conversations in private and public settings it became quite clear just how much history matters. It provides our national and our personal identity. It structures our relationships, and it defines the terms of our debates. Our tendency is to turn away from history that is unflattering and uncomfortable, but we cannot afford to ignore the past, even the most upsetting parts of it. We can and must learn from it, even if doing so is painful.

In calling for an expanded racial dialogue, President Clinton reiterated what national demographics have made clear. America is rapidly becoming a society of racial and cultural minorities. History education, aimed at cross-cultural understanding, will become an ever more significant route to social stability and coexistence. Yet, as experience makes clear, classrooms alone cannot be relied on to teach the lessons that must be learned by the vast number of Americans whose collective future may be at stake. History must be taught not only in the academy but in the variety of nonacademic settings where Americans go to learn. Here is where the role of the public historian, in charge of telling the complex and contradictory national story in public spaces, becomes crucial.

The history of slavery and its role in the formation of the American experience is one of the most sensitive and difficult subjects to present in a public setting. At historic plantation sites and historic houses, in museum exhibitions, in film productions, and in historic parks, public historians and historical interpreters are called upon to deal with this unsettling but critical topic, often under less than ideal teaching conditions. Moreover, they are asked to educate a public generally unprepared and reluctant to deal with a history that, at times, can seem very personal. The recent historical scholarship and new interpretations have refocused attention on slavery and its significance for understanding the role of race in American history. As we debate the possibility of broad public discussions about race in contemporary America, historians can play a central role in providing historical context for this conversation. Obviously this is not easy, but it is essential. John Hope Franklin said it directly: "We should never forget slavery. We should talk about it every morning and every day of the year to remind this country that there's an enormous gap between its practices and its professions."[2] As historians set about this task, it is useful to explore the efforts already under way, the impact of these efforts on interpreters as well as on the visitors, and the contemporary political and social climate that makes these efforts problematic.

Public historians giving presentations on the history and impact of slavery on America and Americans immediately confront a daunting problem: the vast majority of Americans react strongly to the topic, but few know much about it. Generally, Americans believe that slavery was an exclusively southern phenomenon. They date it from the decades immediately preceding the Civil War, and think of it as a relatively minor part of the American story. One striking illustration of this was revealed during a conference held in Boston that focused on slavery and the slave trade in New England. During a conference break a number of participants wandered through Boston's Old Granary Burial Ground, which contains the graves of such Revolutionary-era notables as Paul Revere, Samuel Adams, John Hancock, and Crispus Attucks, the African American hero of the Boston Massacre. A Boston tourist spying the conference program, with its titles printed in bold letters, was clearly shocked. "Was there slavery in New England?" he asked. He was at first disbelieving, then fascinated, and finally disappointed and saddened. "I thought we were better than that," he said as he walked away, obviously affected by the brief encounter.[3]

As this chance conversation between two strangers makes clear, confronting the contradiction between the American ideal and the reality of American history can be disturbing. The first task for the public historian is to attempt to address popular ignorance of slavery's diversity, longevity, complexity, and centrality. By the time of the Revolution, slavery in British North America was already 150 years old. It had become a significant economic and social institution in every one of the thirteen colonies and remained so in every region of the new nation well into the nineteenth century. In the tobacco plantations of the Chesapeake or the rice fields of Carolina, as cargo in slave ships fitted out in New England or as trade items financed by the merchants of New York and Pennsylvania, African slaves were integral to the American economy. Politically and philosophically, slavery was the major contradiction to the national purpose and a critical source of irritation at the core of the American conscience. It defined American freedom and simultaneously called into question America's commitment to natural human rights.[4]

As concern about the loss of independence spread through the colonies during the 1760s and beyond, white Americans worried aloud about Americans' loss of liberty. Ironically, they used the rhetoric of antislavery to express their greatest fears, defining themselves as slaves. In his 1768 publication *Letters from a Farmer in Pennsylvania to the Inhabitants of the British Colonies,* John Dickinson, Philadelphia's largest slaveholder at the time, exclaimed, "Those who are taxed without their own consent, expressed by themselves or their representatives, are slaves."[5] Boston's Josiah Quincy agreed, "I speak it with shame—I speak it with indignation—WE ARE SLAVES."[6]

This was the justification offered for resisting British-imposed taxes, for refusing to submit to British trade restrictions on American shipping, and finally for taking up arms to remove America from the British Empire. In July 1776, after Americans had issued their Declaration of Independence, British forces occupied Staten Island in New York Harbor. Upon hearing the news, George Washington, a Virginia planter who would lead the Revolutionary War effort, warned his countrymen of the hour of judgment. "The Time is now near at hand," he wrote, "which must probably determine whether Americans are to be, Freemen, or Slaves."[7] Throughout the Revolution, Americans saw themselves as engaged in a struggle against slavery, a bondage imposed on them by the British Crown.

When historians present this information to visitors at public sites, they are often confronted with the charge of presentism. We cannot use twenty-first-century morality to judge actions of the past, they are often told. Yet twenty-first-century Americans cannot excuse those of the eighteenth and nineteenth centuries with the argument that they were simply conforming to the accepted norms of their era, for many in the Revolutionary era understood the contradiction clearly and said so. Massachusetts patriot and lawyer James Otis believed that liberty was a God-given right of every human being, regardless of race. "The colonists are by the law of nature freeborn, as indeed all men are, white or black." He called slavery a "most shocking violation of the law of nature," and labeled slave dealers tyrants. Further, Americans' tolerance of slavery foretold grave consequences for the liberty of all Americans. "It is a clear truth," he wrote, "that those who every day barter away other men's liberty will soon care little for their own."[8] Some slaveholders also recognized the hypocrisy. "I will not fight for liberty and leave a slave at home," declared one Connecticut soldier who freed his slaves before he marched off to war.[9]

American Quakers, some of whom had opposed slavery since the late seventeenth century, continued to urge their members to manumit their slaves as a moral imperative. By the late 1770s, some Quaker meetings were voting to disown members who continued to hold slaves. In Virginia and North Carolina, Quakers encouraged manumissions among their members. As the Revolutionary era began, however, the new state of North Carolina made such manumissions illegal. Meanwhile, in Britain, Quakers joined with other abolitionists such as Granville Sharp and Thomas Clarkson in 1787 to form the Society for Effecting the Abolition of the Slave Trade.[10] As the twenty-first-century Boston tourist saw the obvious contradiction of slaveholders in the role of freedom fighters, so did many British and American observers at the time, but this is not an easy or popular point to make at historical sites where visitors come expecting a story of celebration.

Considerations of American slavery remained complex and uncomfortable as the nation matured into independence. During the first half of the nineteenth century slavery evolved into the institution that most Americans now picture. It became more associated with the production of cotton and more peculiarly southern. It also became increasingly controversial, even as it gained in economic and political power. As the nation expanded, Americans considered the spread of slavery, and the debate grew more heated as the century wore on. Thomas Jefferson, an elder statesman by 1820, feared the growing quarrel between the slave and free states. The dispute sounded an alarm throughout the land "like a fire-bell in the night," he wrote, as a harbinger of a national disaster to come. He warned that the nation his generation had brought into being might well be "thrown away by the unwise and unworthy passions of their sons."[11] On the eve of the Civil War, the political stands on slavery defined the battle lines of secession. Even after war brought the abolition of slavery, the racial assumptions that had rationalized slavery continued to circumscribe the lives and racial associations of Americans. For the next century and beyond, slavery provided the political, social, economic, and philosophical context for American race relations.

This is an important part of the history that Americans must understand if they are to have meaningful conversations on race in the twenty-first century. But most don't know enough about the history of slavery to intelligently participate in any national discussion on the subject, some would rather not know, and until recently there have been few opportunities for them to learn. Traditionally, textbooks scarcely mentioned slavery, and northern public schools taught almost nothing about its existence. Although black schools in the segregated South generally included some information, southern white schools stood mute on the subject. What meager treatment of slavery did exist generally posed it as a problem that surfaced during the sectional struggle of the 1850s and 1860s. Consequently, many assumed that the institution was born on the eve of the Civil War. Many public school curricula accepted the proslavery propaganda, influential beyond the nineteenth century, that pictured slavery as a benevolent system, well suited to the intellectual and social limitations of black people. Popular novels and films portrayed slavery in romantic and sentimental terms, casting slaves as childlike creatures who often exasperated lovingly benign white masters. Generally, textbooks reinforced this view. One influential and respected nineteenth-century historian explained to his readers that blacks were "in natural propensities and mental abilities . . . indolent, playful, sensual, imitative, subservient, good-natured, versatile, unsteady in the purpose, devoted, and affectionate."[12]

This historical interpretation, encouraged and reinforced by the emerging scientific racism of the period, proved resilient and was used to rationalize twentieth-century racial segregation. Students attending public school during the post–World War II period learned much the same racial interpretation. In 1979, Frances FitzGerald documented slavery's stereotypical treatment in some American history textbooks and its total absence from others. In the late 1940s and early 1950s, students were told that the abolition of slavery may not have been the best thing for blacks because "slaves had snug cabins to live in, plenty of food to eat and work that was not too hard for them to do." Then, as if to reaffirm the expected student conclusions, the text added, "Most of the slaves seemed happy and contented." [13] When, in 1950, noted historians Samuel Eliot Morrison and Henry Steele Commager discussed the antislavery movement in their text, one of the most popular of the period, they suggested that white abolitionists may have been more upset about slavery than were the slaves themselves. "As for Sambo, whose wrongs moved the abolitionists to wrath and tears," they argued, "there is reason to believe that he suffered less than any other class in the South from the 'peculiar institution.' " [14]

Public education prepared children to think about slavery and race in ways consistent with the assumption of white supremacy built into twentieth-century American law and custom. Depictions in the popular culture confirmed these notions for adults. Harriet Beecher Stowe's nineteenth-century antislavery novel, *Uncle Tom's Cabin,* and Margaret Mitchell's twentieth-century southern romantic novel, *Gone with the Wind,* and its film adaptation furnished the contradictory views upon which most American beliefs about slavery are based. Although Stowe condemned the institution, her depiction of slaves generally confirmed Mitchell's vision of the lovable but limited servant, an image paralleling that pictured in many twentieth-century textbooks. To one degree or another, this is the picture of slavery that most Americans growing to maturity before the mid-1960s carry with them. They formed their racial opinions in light of this socialization, and consciously or subconsciously, most expect to have these notions confirmed when they visit public history sites or museums.

Many college textbooks and a few used in the public secondary schools have changed in the last two generations, influenced by some of the more recent scholarship. Slavery and the role of race more generally have become part of the best accounts of American history, although sometimes in abbreviated form. Yet much of the best and latest scholarship never reaches high school students, in part because it almost never reaches high school teachers. A United States Department of Education study of public school history teaching in the mid-1990s shed light on this alarming situation. It found that most high school history courses were taught by teachers with inadequate training in history. In Louisiana 88 percent of the students who took history in high school were taught by teachers who had not even a college minor in history. In Minnesota the proportion was 83 percent, in West Virginia 82 percent, in Oklahoma 81 percent, in Pennsylvania 73 percent, and in Kansas 72 percent.[15] In New York State, where the percentage of students who were taught history by inadequately trained teachers was relatively low (32 percent), those who taught history (or social studies, as most history-based courses were called) were not required to have taken a single history course.[16] As one scholar has reminded us, in many public schools history teacher is spelled *C-o-a-c-h.*[17] No wonder that graduates of high school are likely to know little about the national past. This situation is even worse in many public schools, where history courses have been abbreviated or removed from curricula entirely.

History education at the college level is generally better, but in 82 percent of the nation's colleges U.S. history courses are not required, even for liberal arts majors. A recent survey of college students illustrates a possible consequence of this situation. A majority of college students could not identify such names as Abraham Lincoln, Thomas Jefferson, and Andrew Jackson, and many believed that George Washington was the president during the War of 1812. This lack of basic history knowledge speaks volumes about the quality of education at the college level, and the report that many college students in the South believe that Jefferson Davis was president of the United States during the Civil War is not encouraging. Even among the nation's most educated, knowledge of American history is frequently limited, and ideas about slavery are often stereotypical or nonexistent.

The federal government has been concerned about the quality of education in public schools for more than a decade, and in 2001 President Clinton signed into law an appropriations bill (H.R. 4577) providing $50 million to improve public school teaching. The next year this bill was augmented by Senator Robert Byrd's amendment, bringing the funding to $100 million through the Teaching American History grant program.

Other government-sponsored grant programs through such agencies as the National Endowment for the Humanities have added further resources, and several private efforts have proved significant over the last decade.

In the mid-1990s, a New York City group, the Gilder Lehrman Institute of American History, started funding summer seminars for public school teachers and provided significant assistance in the creation of History High Schools, public schools with a special focus on American history. The first of their teacher history seminars was conducted by Pulitzer Prize–winning Yale University historian David Brion Davis and University of Houston historian Steven Mintz at Yale on the history of slavery. The response from the teachers who attended the seminar was overwhelmingly positive. Over the past decade these seminars have multiplied and are now being taught at a dozen or more institutions across the country by some of the nation's most prominent scholars to hundreds of teachers. The history of slavery is starting to make its way into public schools because of these important public and private programs that are educating our public school teachers.

As more public schools teach students a broader, more comprehensive American history that includes issues of slavery and race, they better prepare them to function in the multiracial and multicultural society that characterizes our modern nation. This is a very important step forward, but this education must not remain on campus. Recent studies show that field trips outside the classroom are a particularly effective means of education. Apparently a visit to a historic site can stimulate interest in history and thereby generate learning.[18] As Roy Rosenzweig and David Thelen explain in their study of the popular uses of history, most Americans care about and are actively engaged in some activity that allows them to feel connected to the past. Moreover, like the students who learn best on field trips, most Americans feel most connected to history when visiting historical places. Apparently, Americans believe they are more likely to discover "real" or "true" history at museums and historic sites than in classrooms. While just over half of those surveyed in the Rosenzweig and Thelen study said that they trusted college professors to tell the truth about history and just over one-third trusted high school teachers, almost 80 percent had faith in museums. Public historians, then, have a significant opportunity to augment all levels of education, although they may find themselves teaching at the grammar school level even when their visitors are adults.[19]

Difficult as this task is, many in positions to affect public education on the question of slavery's historical importance have made notable attempts to do so. During the mid-1990s Roger Kennedy, then director of the National Park Service, embarked on a campaign to modernize the historical interpretations at National Park Service sites. Civil War historic sites were among those in need of consideration, especially on the subject of slavery. Indeed, in the mid-1990s the permanent exhibition at Gettysburg National Battlefield, for example, mentioned neither slavery nor slaves with regard to the war. Significantly, at that time Gettysburg was attracting almost two million visitors yearly. The pattern of ignoring slavery was widespread within the national parks. Most battlefield or other Civil War sites did not treat slavery as a significant cause of the war and were under pressure from Civil War heritage interest groups not to. Highly organized and strongly committed to maintaining an interpretation of the Civil War that emphasizes the issue of states' rights as justification of southern secession, these groups are ever watchful for what they pejoratively refer to as revisionist interpretations of the war.

Such groups as the United Sons of Confederate Veterans, the United Daughters of the Confederacy, and the Southern Heritage Coalition are dedicated to the preservation of a romanticized memory of the pre–Civil War South that, if it includes slavery at all, does so in the most benign manner. Many of these groups were highly critical of the 1990 Ken Burns PBS series on the Civil War because they believed that it had too much material on slavery. When John Latschar, the superintendent at Gettysburg, suggested in a lecture that the war may have been fought over slavery, the Southern Heritage Coalition condemned his words and flooded the Office of the Secretary of the Interior with 1,100 preprinted postcards calling for his immediate removal.[20]

Facing this kind of organized opposition, it was no easy decision to encourage a major reinterpretation at National Park Service sites that would tell the story of American slavery where it should logically be told. Yet Director Kennedy and NPS Chief Historian Dwight Pitcaithley, supporting the efforts of park superintendents, determined to do just that. In 1994 they negotiated an agreement with the Organization of American

Historians, the nation's oldest and largest scholarly association of professional historians focusing on American history, to bring noted scholars to park sites to assist in reviewing exhibits, site films, and presentations. In conjunction with these largely academic scholars the NPS began reassessing and redesigning many of its historical interpretations.[21]

This initiative was endorsed by a congressional directive calling upon the Secretary of the Interior to encourage the National Park Service managers of Civil War battle sites "to recognize and include in all of their public displays and multimedia educational presentations, the unique role that the institution of slavery played in causing the Civil War and its role, if any, at the individual battle sites." In support of this action Congressman Jesse L. Jackson Jr. noted the special role that the National Park Service plays in the education of the eleven million people who visit National Park Service Civil War sites each year. This education, he believed, was one essential means by which modern-day American society can "build the progressive [interracial] coalition we need to build a more perfect union."[22]

Although Jackson's hope may be realized in the long run, as an immediate consequence of this focus on slavery at Civil War historic sites, southern heritage groups protested loudly. During the mid- and late 1990s heated debates over the historical and cultural interpretation of American society reached from the local community level to the halls of Congress.[23] The South was a particularly explosive arena for issues of race and the interpretation of slavery. In 1998, Virginia governor James S. Gilmore's traditional declaration of April as Confederate History Month illustrated this point.

The month of April is significant for southern Civil War commemorations. In that month in 1861 Confederate forces fired on Fort Sumter, prompting the beginning of the war. In April 1865 Robert E. Lee surrendered at Appomattox, Virginia, bringing four years of fighting to an end. Gilmore's declaration echoed similar proclamations by governors in Louisiana, Tennessee, Georgia, and Alabama for their states. In 1998, however, for the first time, Virginia broke with tradition when Gilmore included a brief mention of slavery in his message:

> WHEREAS, our recognition of Confederate history also recognizes that slavery was one of the causes of the war;

WHEREAS, slavery was a practice that deprived African-Americans of their God-given inalienable rights, which degraded the human spirit, is abhorred and condemned by Virginians, and ended by this war . . . [24]

At first glance, the inclusion of a condemnation of slavery and its basic denial of human rights would not seem controversial at the end of the twentieth century. This was, after all, a relatively mild statement of the historically obvious. But there are few noncontroversial means of addressing the issue of slavery in a public setting and no comfortable way to deal with this question at the core of American identity and conscience. Reaction was swift and direct. R. Wayne Byrd, president of Virginia's Heritage Preservation Association, labeled Governor Gilmore's reference to slavery as an insult to the state and as bowing to what Byrd termed the political pressure of "racist hate groups such as the NAACP." He took issue with Gilmore's negative description of slavery, painting instead a picture of the plantation worthy of mid-nineteenth-century proslavery apologists. It is alarming that at the end of the twentieth century, in a public statement, Byrd could call the slave plantation of the old South a place "where master and slave loved and cared for each other and had genuine family concern." [25]

Byrd was not alone in his assessment of Gilmore's remarks. Centered in the South, but spread throughout the country, there are networks of Civil War reenactors, mostly men, who dress in period costume and meet on weekends to re-create their "authentic" versions of the Civil War. Members in these groups range from those who see this as an opportunity for outdoor recreation to "hardcores," serious history buffs who attempt to capture the look and feel of life in the Civil War military. Many of these groups are linked by the Internet, and almost immediately after Gilmore's proclamation their lines were buzzing with reaction. Larry Beane, past commander of the J.E.B. Stuart Camp #1506 of the Sons of Confederate Veterans in Philadelphia, Pennsylvania, attacked Gilmore's reference to slavery as "a slap in the faces of the Confederate soldiers, their grandchildren, and the State of Virginia as a whole." [26] Other Internet correspondents expressed similar sentiments. Probably most white Americans would not argue this case so blatantly. Still, most white Virginians accepted state recognition of Confederate History Month without question, as did other white southerners.

Gilmore may have hoped that the condemnation of slavery in his proclamation would defuse opposition to Confederate History Month, but some white Virginians, and most blacks in the state, were not happy with what they saw as a hollow racial gesture. Tommy J. Baer, president of B'nai B'rith International, questioned Gilmore's attempt to include a condemnation of slavery with a celebration of the Confederacy. "It's like Germany having a World War II—I would even call it Nazi—history month but [saying] We're going to include the suffering of the Jews," he argued. "It doesn't pass the common-sense test." Salim Khalfani of the NAACP Virginia State Conference acknowledged Gilmore's inclusion "respecting the horrors of African enslavement" but added, "We're not pleased that April once again will commemorate Confederate history and heritage month."[27] Civil rights groups generally view the celebration of the Confederacy, like efforts to maintain the Confederate flag, as part of a general attempt to preserve southern racist traditions. Many white southerners, on the other hand, continue to deny the racial connotations of these reminders of the pre–Civil War South. Frances Chapman, of Todd County, Kentucky, who supported the use of two Confederate flags as symbols of her county high school, claimed that they were neither racist nor a defense of slavery. Besides, she argued, "slavery was not all that bad. A lot of people were quite happy to be living on large plantations." Then, in what seems a contradiction, she added, "Blacks just need to get over slavery. You can't live in the past."[28]

The Confederate flags waved by fans at University of Mississippi football games, placed on special license plates in Maryland, or flown over South Carolina's state capitol continue to be controversial. The playing of "Dixie" at official state functions throughout the South, Virginia's recently retired state song, "Carry Me Back to Old Virginia" (with its references to "darkey" and "old Massa"), and the recent surge in Confederate reenactments are all relevant to the discussion about slavery and race that Americans seem unable to have.[29] Given the volatility of the topic, calls by thirteen members of Congress in the late 1990s that President Clinton issue a public apology to African Americans for slavery and the president's challenge to all Americans to join in a national conversation on race were bold and understandably controversial steps. Many whites refused to believe that an apology for slavery was needed or that a conversation on race would be fruitful. Some blacks feared that an apology at this late date would trivialize their history, resurrect the horror and pain of slavery, and divert attention from pressing contemporary racial problems. Conversations on race, many believed, would not be honest and would add little of value to the debates over welfare and economic disparity, affirmative action, and the lingering impact of racism in American society. For different reasons, Americans, both blacks and whites, are reluctant to bring a painful historical context to bear on contemporary race relations.

Thus, the discussions about race and history that often take place inside the academy are atypical. There, the state of historical scholarship has made it all but impossible for any serious study of American history, especially one focused on the nineteenth century or before, to ignore slavery. But, of course, few Americans have access to those conversations. Public historians confronted with uncomfortable, historically uneducated, and resistant visitors often find the subject difficult or unapproachable.

At historical plantation sites, where the subject of slavery is difficult to avoid, Park Service interpreters struggle to present the subject in the least offensive manner. Interpreters at Arlington House, a National Park Service historic site and pre–Civil War home of the Custis-Lee family outside of Washington, D.C., address the subject of slavery and Robert E. Lee as a slaveholder with extreme delicacy, if at all. White visitors often bristle at the mention of Lee as the owner of slaves and have difficulty accepting the fact that he and his compatriots took up arms against the United States in order to preserve a society based on slave labor and white supremacy. Stephanie Batiste-Bentham, an African American interpreter who worked for a number of months at Arlington House, explained that visitors sometimes took her aside to ask in hushed tones, "Were there really slaves here?" She also observed that some white interpreters at the site used the less emotionally charged term *servants* instead of *slaves* to describe the plantation laborers. In the last few years, historians at Arlington House have tried to include slavery in the plantation story and have opened the restored slave quarters at the rear of the main house. Batiste-Bentham found that visitor expectations made it easier to interpret slavery in the slave quarters than in the main house. Visitors were ready to ask questions and engage in discussion about slavery while in the slave quarters but expected the focus of the main house to be exclusively on the Custis-Lee family. When Batiste-Bentham suggested the extensive slave presence in Arlington House proper and slaves' role in its construction, for example, visitors were often surprised. She was careful to point out the kitchen and other workplaces in the house as almost exclusively slave work and social space. She explained the difficulty house slaves had navigating the steep, narrow, and dark back staircase carrying large trays or other awkward and heavy objects. Apparently visitors reacted positively to observations that suggested the reality of everyday slave life but were less willing to focus on the less pleasant aspects of slave/master relationships.

Most visitors thought of slavery and slaveholding in very simple terms. White visitors confronted with Robert E. Lee as a slave master were anxious that he be pictured as a "good master," although most had only the vaguest idea of what that might mean. On the other hand, black visitors anticipated being told about the atrocities of slavery and expected an African American interpreter to elaborate on them in the most horrendous detail. Both black visitors and white visitors seemed to expect an African American interpreter to deal with racial issues, including slavery, but were less likely to expect a white interpreter to do so. Regardless of their expectation, visitors generally were uncomfortable talking about slavery, especially in interracial groups. One memorable incident at Arlington House makes this point clearly. Batiste-Bentham was conducting a tour of the second floor of the house when from the floor below, ascending the back staircase, a black female visitor approached playfully chanting the refrain, "I's in the master's house, I's in the master's house." This visitor was not aware of the tour group and they could not see her, but her improvised refrain created a long, embarrassed silence, especially among the white visitors. Interestingly, Batiste-Bentham found that she had a somewhat easier time discussing slavery with white visitors than with black visitors, a fact she attributed to the pain that many black visitors report from talking about the subject.[30]

The discomfort many blacks associate with the public discussion of slavery was evident in interviews with interpreters at Colonial Williamsburg in Virginia. In this restored capital of colonial Virginia, costumed interpreters portray historical figures in "living history" vignettes designed to educate and entertain visitors. Costumed interpreters portray the colonial governor and his wife, eighteenth-century artisans, merchants, and various village workmen. In 1979, slavery was interpreted for the first time when Williamsburg employed six African American interpreters to present first-person portrayals of slaves, who accounted for roughly half of the town's population in the eighteenth century.

Immediately it became evident that interpreting slavery was not simply a matter of adding a few blacks to the presentation. Bringing visitors and the interpretive staff of Williamsburg face-to-face with the most blatant and extreme form of American racism was, for some, a wrenching experience. African American interpreters found that they had to make significant adjustments in their presentation. Originally, interpreters were instructed not to "break character," to act and respond in a manner appropriate to an eighteenth-century resident no matter what question was asked by twentieth-century visitors. Although most visitors quickly understood the period characterization, especially when white interpreters were involved, black interpreters found that sometimes visitors took their performance seriously. A few visitors became upset seeing a black person seemingly in bondage. One white visitor, outraged at the thought of slaves being kept in contemporary Williamsburg, actually wrote a letter of complaint to the local newspaper.[31]

Public anxiety about confronting the history of slavery mushroomed in the fall of 1994 when Colonial Williamsburg's African American Department announced that it would re-create a slave auction. The re-creation was part of a three-day program built around the annual commemoration of King George's ascension to the English throne. The sale of personal property, including slaves, was originally part of the celebration that went on in the eighteenth century, and the staff at the African American Department proposed the auction as a way to "teach the history of our mothers and grandmothers so that every one of you will never forget what happened to them."[32] The statement and the re-creation of the auction drew strong reaction. At the end of the extremely moving reenactment of a family being broken apart through the sale, the crowd of visitors grew silent and many wept. Clearly emotions were mixed. A black visitor and a white visitor jointly displayed a sign that read, "Say no to racist shows." The Richmond chapter of the NAACP and the Southern Christian Leadership Conference attempted to interrupt the event, accusing the reenactment of "glorifying the horrors and humiliation of the evil of slavery" and calling it a "trivialization of [our] African American heritage."[33]

One of the main concerns voiced by opponents of the reenactment was that it might be misinterpreted by visitors as entertainment instead of the educational dramatization that Williamsburg interpreters intended. Sensitive to this concern, Christy Coleman, then director of Colonial Williamsburg's African American Department, went to great lengths to prepare her staff. "We are eminently qualified to do this presentation," she explained, as they had extensively researched the general history of Williamsburg during the period and the history of the specific auction that was re-created. "Our programs have proved a success in the past because we do them in a dignified manner," she said. Still, many blacks were not convinced. Salim Khalfani, NAACP field coordinator, worried that "whenever entertainment is used to teach history there is the possibility for error or insensitivity and historical inaccuracy."[34] Yet for some, such as the political director of the Virginia branch of the NAACP, Jack Gravely, who had initially expressed opposition, the reenactment was a transforming experience. "Pain had a face," he said, "indignity had a body, suffering had tears."[35]

Academic historians were generally in favor of the auction re-creation, but they urged that great care be taken so that it not become entertainment. In the end, most seemed satisfied that Williamsburg's presentation was indeed educational. Princeton historian Nell Painter observed, "The whole point of slavery was [that] you made people into economic units, you dehumanize them and if you are an economic unit, you have the ability to be bought and sold. Slave sales were the bedrock of slavery."[36]

Painter was right, of course. Sale or the possibility of sale was a part of a slave's daily life, and it may be impossible to understand slavery, even in the most cursory manner, without facing the implications of slave sale and the inhumanity of the auctions that were public events in American slaveholding society. Even more disturbing for today's conversation about race and history is the realization that many people attended auctions not to buy but for their entertainment value. This point was apparently not raised in the debate over the Williamsburg reenactment, but it is the sobering truth of the impact of slavery on America's understanding of humanity.

Apparently, the experience of first-person interpretation at historic sites such as Williamsburg can be more difficult for blacks than for

whites. Wearing eighteenth-century costumes and presenting history before an interested public audience can be, as one said, a "thrilling experience." There is prestige attached to the role of a Williamsburg interpreter.
Although some blacks share this feeling, for most the feelings are more
complex. For them there is also the somber realization that their workday
centers on "playing slaves" for a public audience that is often unsympa-
thetic. As one wrote, "I had a job that very few would envy, especially if
[they were] black." This interpreter explained that many of his friends
and members of his family would not talk to him about his job once they
understood what he did, and few came to see his interpretation at
Williamsburg.[37] A number of Williamsburg's African American interpreters find it uncomfortable to leave the colonial area in costume. While
white interpreters might take a lunch break, going to the local fast-food
restaurant in costume, black interpreters almost never do. One woman
explained that she felt self-conscious eating at a restaurant dressed as a
slave. Some recalled incidents in which whites made racist remarks or
screamed racist insults from passing cars on seeing black interpreters in
costume. Public historians contemplating developing living history at
their sites should be aware of the potential problems involved in such a
venture.[38]

These complex feelings can affect the entire operation of the site or
museum when blacks and whites are working together. One African
American interpreter who participated in the slave auction reenactment
explained that even though it was a re-creation and not a real auction, he
felt strong emotions—anger and extreme sadness, as well as pride at
being part of this bold historical statement. Another found that all of his
vast research on the subject did not fully prepare him to stand on an auction block and contemplate the sale of his ancestors in such a public venue.
Frequent and honest discussions of feelings among interpreters encouraged blacks and whites to deal with the variety of feelings that arose after
a long day of interpreting. Interracial interaction under such circumstances required trust and tolerance.[39]

One chilling moment occurred when Williamsburg interpreters were
invited to attend the opening of a gallery of Colonial Williamsburg prod-
ucts in a shopping mall in Cleveland, Ohio. Interpreters dressed in their
colonial costumes were to parade through the mall to the gallery through
a large crowd of shoppers and invited guests. The center aisle of one of the

major stores was arranged with seats on either side, where special guests dressed in formal attire sat to review the procession. Local bands and a Cleveland ballet troupe were to lead the way, followed by local dignitaries. Toward the end of the procession came the Williamsburg interpreters, with black interpreters dressed as slaves at the rear. African American interpreters had intended to be part of the procession, but at the last minute some refused. Rex Ellis had not fully realized what it would be like until he was actually there, dressed as a slave, parading through a shopping mall. This was not interpreting slavery, he thought; this was playing a slave for a white elite audience. The context was wrong and too emotionally painful. Some of the white interpreters from Williamsburg had a difficult time understanding his explanation, but Ellis was adamant in his decision not to "be a slave in that context." Ellis's point is significant and underscores the major theme of this essay very well. Slavery is a sobering subject, too difficult to interpret in the atmosphere of a shopping mall or any place in which education is not the obvious intent. Central to these experiences is the realization that the contemporary racial atmosphere complicates any history involving race. It is hardly possible for historians to remain detached even in the most scholarly public setting. The public world can be an emotionally threatening place for such interpretation. Clearly, presenting this kind of history is no easy task, and there is much left to be done and understood, but Colonial Williamsburg has come a great distance in its willingness and ability to deal with slavery. In the last decade it has become a model for other sites in the region.[40]

Given the importance and the difficulty of their task, and the still largely uncharted waters of such presentations, there is a pressing need for public historians and historical interpreters to engage in serious discussions about techniques and strategies for addressing race in general and slavery in particular. Academic scholars can be of great assistance in this critical venture, helping to develop the historical context for public presentation as a step toward a broad public discussion about slavery and race in American history and in contemporary America as well. By now most realize that this is not easy and, at the same time, that it is very important to do. There are a few tentative models but no proven strategy. Perhaps each setting will require its own special approach.

As one who believes in the power of education, I argue from the premise that knowledge will facilitate understanding and tolerance. Although this cannot be taken for granted, evidence suggests a logic to this assumption. As recent changes at several historic sites and museums illustrate, scholarly research and interpretations of race in America have begun to reshape the public presentations of history. Especially since the late 1960s, some of the popular media have presented a more realistic view of the impact of race on the experiences of Americans. There is a distance yet to cover, but some Americans have become more sensitive to and aware of difficult subjects such as race and even slavery, and many have a more realistic picture of these topics than did their parents or grandparents. There is reason to believe that this awareness is associated with the greater racial tolerance revealed by recent sociological surveys. One study reported that "a massive and widening liberalization of racial attitudes has swept America over the last forty years."[41] One need not go that far to agree that America at the beginning of the twenty-first century is a more racially tolerant place than it was a half century ago.[42]

There may soon be more public opportunities to learn a more inclusive history of our nation. In late 2004, Congress authorized a $3.9 million appropriation to study, design, and staff the National Museum of African American History and Culture as part of the Smithsonian Institution. The new museum will be located on or near the National Mall in Washington, D.C. Although it is not clear at this point what the institution will look like or what it will exhibit, several distinguished scholars and museum professionals, including Professor John Hope Franklin, have been recruited to advise the project. Even so, if past experience is an indication, attempts at inclusive historical presentation will be difficult. As they are fully aware, the history of race in America, and especially of slavery, is a painful, contentious, anxiety-producing topic for Americans to confront, especially in a public setting. Yet the institution of slavery formed our understanding of race and has shaped the historical relationships between races in America. Even for recent immigrants, the history of slavery has relevance. It established a hierarchy of color into which people of varying shades are fitted. And it has defined the social, political, and economic meaning of skin color within the American setting. The things Americans take for granted about race, those assumptions for which no explanation is required, those feelings of which they are barely conscious, are the products of a culture that slavery and efforts to justify it have shaped. It is not practical to believe that we can realistically address our society's most vital contemporary concerns about race while ignoring the institution that has been so central to American race relations. If we are to have meaningful conversations on race in contemporary society, we must do so within the context of history. As we seek to confront our national history and its relevance to our present and future, the history of slavery matters a great deal. Difficult as it is, the discussion must start immediately, and historical scholars in the academy, in museums, and in historic parks and houses, wherever they do their work, are critical to the process. Theirs is the public historian's most difficult assignment.

In this photograph, taken about 1895, a mounted white overseer keeps a watchful eye on African American field hands at work in a cotton field. This picture became the center of the controversy over the "Back of the Big House" exhibit that the Library of Congress ultimately refused to display. COURTESY OF THE LIBRARY OF CONGRESS

4

The Last Great Taboo Subject: Exhibiting Slavery at the Library of Congress

John Michael Vlach

The difficulty and awkwardness that most Americans experience when discussing the history of racial slavery in the United States can be traced, suggests James W. Loewen, to the inadequate textbooks that they are compelled to read while in high school. He observes that the authors of these volumes generally recount the dramatic events of America's formation in such bland diction that these books become the printed equivalents of "mumbling lectures." Further, by being so committed to positive and uplifting portrayals, these writers unwaveringly follow a "progress as usual" story line and thus treat our long history of slavery as merely a temporary aberration that had no lasting consequences.[1] Such an approach not only marginalizes slavery and its attendant racist ideology but also marks the topic as one requiring no further discussion. When students are fitted with such intellectual blinders, they are likely to become citizens incapable of understanding why we remain a divided nation. The opportunity to engage this thorny aspect of American history is no more promising even at the very sites where slavery occurred. The hundreds of surviving antebellum plantations visited every year by thousands of tourists offer their visitors explanations that avoid almost any discussion of the former black workforces who performed all the essential tasks required to operate these impressive estates. A survey of 122 plantation sites in four southern states revealed that, except for four institutions, accounts of the lives of slaves were shaped by the interpretive ploys of deflection, trivialization, or erasure.[2] These tours only reinforce the flawed ideal of the conflict-free history that is presented in so many of our classrooms.

CREATING CONTROVERSY AT
THE LIBRARY OF CONGRESS

Understanding that slavery is a topic that most Americans are not prepared to face with any degree of enthusiasm or comprehension, one can readily assume that a museum exhibition devoted to the plantation experience would be met with considerable skepticism and suspicion. Any attempt to present a tension-producing topic is likely to encounter some degree of resistance because the public is trained to shy away, at first blush, from an uncomfortable topic. But slavery has proved to be among the most difficult topics that one can present in a public venue. Moreover, it can prove especially troubling for black audiences, who know all too well that the racism that grew out of the slave system continues to deny them their full measure of the American promise, particularly in the economic sphere. Many African Americans find that the best way to deal with their anger and disappointment is just not to talk about it in public. Lonnie Bunch, former president of the Chicago Historical Society, director of the coming National Museum of African American History and Culture, and an African American, once mentioned to me in conversation, "Slavery remains for most black people the last great taboo subject."

Unhappily, Bunch's assessment proved to be exactly on target when I created an exhibition on plantation slavery entitled "Back of the Big House: The Cultural Landscape of the Plantation." Within minutes of its opening at the Library of Congress there were cries of protest by a number of the library's African American employees, and by midday the exhibition's materials had been dismantled and locked away in storage. The event was seen by the library's administration as a terrible fiasco. The wider public that never got to see the images in "Back of the Big House" was both dismayed and confused. They witnessed a leading intellectual institution that was unable to display its own collections in its own galleries.

This failed exhibition at the Library of Congress was mounted in

Washington, D.C., in 1995, but the research on which it was based was initiated much earlier. I began a survey of the architecture of slavery in 1988, and in 1993 I completed a book entitled *Back of the Big House: The Architecture of Plantation Slavery,* a volume that drew heavily on two collections housed in the Library of Congress—the Historic American Buildings Survey and the Slave Narrative Collection of the Federal Writers' Project. Both of these vast bodies of data were amassed during the 1930s and 1940s; the building survey included measured drawings and photographs of about twenty-three thousand properties (about seven thousand from the southern United States), and the slave narrative collection contained interviews with former slaves, enough to fill forty thousand pages of typescript. While the narrative materials were well known to historians, there were images in the Historic American Buildings Survey that had never been seen by the public. I found more than six hundred photographs and scale drawings that presented the slave's side of the plantation: slave quarters, barns, stables, kitchens, workshops, and other outbuildings. By joining these images with the first-person commentaries found in the slave narratives, I was able to reconstruct a detailed portrait of the social landscape of slavery. Further, I was able to present the plantation environment as it was experienced by those who "knew the sting of the lash," those who claimed to have "worn the shoe." It was my position that the plantation was not merely a place of captivity but a culturally contested site, a social arena in which enslaved blacks began to piece back together their shattered lives.

> While ownership of a plantation clearly divided whites into distinct have and have-not classes, blacks generally found themselves drawn together in numbers large enough to constitute coherent social groups. Comforted by the fellowship of the quarters, they were able to confront the injustice of their captivity in ways both subtle and obvious; among their various strategies of accommodation and resistance was the creation of their own version of the plantation. Recognizing that they could define a space for themselves, they took back the quarters, fields, gardens, barns, and outbuildings, claiming them as parts of a black landscape. Empowered by this territorial gesture, they were able to forge an even stronger sense of community, which few planters would ever recognize or acknowledge.[3]

My book enjoyed an enthusiastic reception from academic specialists and general readers alike, a reaction that soon caught the attention of the exhibitions office of the Library of Congress. In the spring of 1994, I was approached by a member of the library's Interpretive Programs staff and invited to transform *Back of the Big House* into an exhibition suitable for libraries, historical societies, and college campuses. Given that the book drew so heavily on the library's own collections, it seemed to all concerned like an altogether fitting project. Because the exhibition was also to be entitled "Back of the Big House," the already extant book was seen as fulfilling the role of an explanatory catalogue. This is always seen as a bonus when presenting museum exhibitions, since the visitor will be offered both visual and verbal streams of information.

But the exhibition also contained images not used in the book. These were principally photographs of the former slaves whose testimonies I had quoted so extensively. The Interpretive Programs staff told me that they did not want to see an exhibition merely of architectural sites; they wanted me to provide some "faces" to go with the buildings, and I complied. The opening images in the exhibition presented a panoramic vista of a Virginia tobacco plantation as seen from the fields (the slave's point of view) accompanied by a portrait of former slave William Henry Towns. Next to the image of Towns was a lengthy quote from his testimony, in which he described the plantation where he was held:

> The Big House was a two-story house, white like most houses during that time. On the north side of the Big House set a great big barn, where all the stock and stuff that was raised was kept. Off to the southwest of the barn, west of the Big House, set about five or six log houses. These was built facing a space of ground in the center of a square what the houses make. Anybody could stand in his front door and see in at the front of the other houses.[4]

A fusion of buildings, people, and relevant first-person testimony was used throughout the exhibition. Viewers were offered a tour of the key elements of the plantation landscape, moving from the planter's Big House further and further into the areas dominated by slaves.[5] First, the major architectural components were presented, including kitchens, dairies, smokehouses, barns, and stables. In the next section slave quarters, the primary slave territory, were illustrated in some detail along with evidence of slave skills. These abilities had proved useful both to plantation owners and to the slaves alike. Anthony Dawson, a former slave from North Carolina, recalled, "Down in the quarters we had the spinning house, where the old women card the wool and run the loom. They made double weave for the winter time and the white folks and slave had good clothes."[6] Presented along with craft skills were talents for music and storytelling, creative abilities meant to be shared primarily within the black community. Perhaps the most important of the cultural institutions that slaves created for themselves was their distinctive set of religious practices. The hymns they sang and the sermons they preached were imbued with a liberationist ethic that transformed images of reward in an afterlife into a call for perseverance in the present. Booker T. Washington, who had been a slave in Virginia, testified that over time slaves "threw off the mask and were not afraid to let it be known that the 'freedom' in their songs meant freedom of this body in this world."[7] The final image in the exhibition was one of abandoned slave quarters, a view that former slaves might have seen when looking back over their shoulders as they left their old plantation homes in 1865. The last words in the exhibition came from former slave Houston Holloway: "I felt like a bird out of a cage. Amen. Amen. Amen. I could hardly ask to feel any better than I did on that day."[8]

The fabrication of the exhibition's components was completed near the end of 1994, and the exhibition was installed in February 1995 at Magnolia Mound, a historic plantation (now operated as a house museum) in Baton Rouge, Louisiana. The exhibition then proceeded on its itinerary of ten planned venues, making three more stops before arriving in Washington, D.C., where it was scheduled to be placed on view at the Library of Congress for six weeks in December 1995 and January 1996. The exhibit was set up on the morning of December 18, just in time for its opening the next day. The opening never happened, however. A number of the library's African American employees—somewhere between twelve and twenty—immediately protested that the exhibition was offensive. Within a few hours, all the elements of the exhibition were returned to their three large traveling crates.

RESPONSES TO CONTROVERSY:
THE LIBRARY OF CONGRESS

Because the exhibition's protesters were all African Americans, library officials paid special heed to their charges. The atmosphere for black employees at the library was already tense, it was later explained, because a long-awaited decision in a protracted civil rights case against the library, *Cook v. Billington,* had recently been announced, and $8.5 million in claims was to be awarded to more than two thousand black workers.[9] Given the palpable feelings of apprehension that existed between the library and its African American staff at this time, library administrators were more than willing to acquiesce to complaints made about my exhibition. One of the few critics of "Back of the Big House" willing to go on the record was a black man who was clearly disenchanted with his job; upon seeing a photograph of an overseer directing a gang of cotton pickers, he became so infuriated that he said he could not bring himself to look at the rest of the exhibition. He later admitted, "It reminded me of the white overseers here at the Library of Congress looking down over us to make sure we're in the fields doing our work." So intense was his dismay with his own work conditions, he further imagined that the white man in the photograph was aiming a gun at the workers, perhaps in the manner of a contemporary southern prison guard. In fact, there was no weapon of any kind in the picture. A similar projection of resentment tied to work-related complaints was expressed by another employee who upon seeing the portrait of William Henry Towns thought that he seemed to be crouching in a submissive posture when all that one could actually see was his face. A third library employee, who had assumed that any exhibition must glorify its topic, protested that slavery was nothing to celebrate. Thus she missed the key point that the exhibition aimed not to honor slavery but to identify the heroic responses of the enslaved.[10] To judge from these few recorded criticisms, the anger directed at "Back of the Big House" was more a protest against working conditions at the library than an attack on the exhibition. Black employees at the Library of Congress had previously demonstrated their reluctance to accept images of slavery at two other events: a screening of the historic 1915 film *Birth of a Nation* and an exhibition entitled "The African-American Mosaic," which provided a sampler of the library's collections relevant to black history. Apparently, the seething anger over long-standing grievances made *any* image that recalled the abusive dimensions of the African American past unacceptable. For some of the library's black employees the parallels between acts of victimization in the past and present circumstances were just too close. To this group "Back of the Big House" registered as one more of the library's racist insults.

That officials at the library would accede to the wishes of a small block of protesters proved to be perplexing both to other black employees and to the larger African American community of Washington, D.C. Brynda White, an African American woman working in the library's Development Office, responded to the uproar over the exhibition in *The Gazette,* an in-house newsletter for library employees:

> I saw the exhibit being put up and looked forward to viewing it for myself. The few pictures I managed to see piqued my interest. I felt that a strong message of our past was being recreated through historical documents. I know that the history of African Americans was extremely painful but it is a history that I do not want to ignore or forget. I want to understand and feel the pain that my people had to endure. I am proud of our heritage, and extremely proud of the sacrifice that blacks made to create a distinct culture in America. . . . I felt more saddened that some felt that the present racial discord engulfing the Library (and all America) should be enlarged by burying past injustices. Will we ever make gains or do we continue to point fingers? We blacks and whites are doomed if we do not gather the courage to face the worst aspect of our history together and gather the courage to create a real dialogue.[11]

W. Jerome McGee, a local architect, shared with me a letter he wrote to Librarian James Billington in which he took a stance similar to White's. Describing himself as "an African American of the plantation era" (he was more than eighty years old), he asked that the exhibition be reinstalled because the protest was, in his view, "reprehensible and obnoxious," and he added that those who opposed the display wanted nothing less than a repudiation of the African American past. Just one week after the closing of the exhibition, the *Washington Post* editorial page ran an opinion by David Nicholson, a black cultural critic. Arguing for the virtues of a frank discussion of the history of the slave experience, he suggested: "To deny slavery is to deny the suffering of those men and women who were powerless to prevent their bondage. Worse, we deny their strengths and their achievement in persevering despite hardships that are inconceivable to us today. They left us a heritage, customs, dignity and values that have enabled black America not only to survive, but to prosper." Further, he accused the protesters at the Library of Congress of "using their ancestors' suffering to extort concessions from a majority white institution." This, wrote Nicholson, was nothing more than "cultural blackmail." [12] While Billington tried to deflect attention from the event, calling it a "non-story," the inadequacy of his response soon degenerated into public name-calling. Byron Rushing, then a member of the state legislature of Massachusetts and former director of the African American Museums Association, said in a published interview that Billington's reaction was racist and that he had behaved like "a silly white man." [13]

While various supporters of my exhibition fumed about its removal, both print and broadcast media offered various accounts of the demise of "Back of the Big House." The *Washington Post,* the first paper to present the story of the exhibition's abrupt closing, treated the library's decision as an event of national significance. Placing its account on the front page of the December 20, 1995, edition, the *Post* underscored its dismay at a month's worth of administrative missteps by the library. While these other matters had given the newspaper cause to raise questions about the library's managerial decisions, shutting down an exhibition before the public had been given any opportunity to see it was an act that in its judgment merited a rigorous investigation. Here was a so-called bastion of free speech—the Library of Congress, what some like to call the keeper of the American memory—that had denied the American citizenry access to its own collections. The *Post* offered two consecutive days of coverage, accompanied by a follow-up story that went out on the Associated Press wire. Major dailies in New York, Boston, Baltimore, Chicago, and San Francisco followed the lead of the *Post.* Over the next two weeks, more than two hundred American newspapers carried stories on the fate of the exhibition, and segments of an interview with me were aired repeatedly on CNN as part of its year-end summary of national events. Further, editorials questioning the actions of the library appeared in the London *Times* and Paris's *Le Monde,* and my radio interviews were broadcast to both Germany and South Africa. There was a growing sense in Washington that "the whole world was watching." Pressure on the Library of Congress increased daily; its censorious response to my exhibition had placed it, in the words of a *Washington Post* editorial, "in a strange position to act as guardian of the nation's intellectual patrimony."[14]

RESPONSES TO CONTROVERSY:
THE D.C. PUBLIC LIBRARY

Early in January 1996 a decision was made to reinstall "Back of the Big House" under a new name—"The Cultural Landscape of the Plantation," a phrase that previously had served as a subtitle. However, even after it was relabeled, the exhibit still was considered too controversial to be displayed within the walls of the Library of Congress. To have presented it in any form would have been a clear admission of error. Thus, to honor its obligation to the taxpaying public, as well as to save face, the library offered the exhibition to the Martin Luther King Jr. Library, the main branch of the public library system of Washington, D.C.

Despite the atmosphere of anger and suspicion that was swirling around "Back of the Big House," and which had been well publicized for weeks, the D.C. Public Library enthusiastically welcomed the exhibition. Its director, Dr. Hardy Franklin, took the position that nothing was too controversial for a library to present, not even slavery. If there was any argument over my interpretation of this thorny topic, he and members of his staff suggested that it was a library's duty to help community members face the matter and to help them understand this strife-ridden aspect of American history. This positive stance was quickly sensed by the overflow crowd on opening night. The very same exhibition that had been declared to be so offensive to black people just two weeks earlier and a mere eight blocks away was now embraced by a largely black audience. My introductory remarks that evening at the King Library were followed by an hour of earnest questions and comments revealing deep interest in the topic. I will always remember the thankful words of the first respondent, Rohulamin Quander—a member of a local black family that proudly traces its roots deep into seventeenth-century Virginia—who declared that he was delighted that the exhibition had been "rescued." Indeed, that so many people came that evening was something of a tribute to the exhibition, since the city was at that moment under the assault of the largest snowfall in its recorded history.

For the next four weeks visitation was very high. Library officials reported that the exhibition had "generated more interest than any other exhibit we've had." And in a brilliant move, they transformed the exhibition into an interactive experience by soliciting written responses from viewers that were then printed as poster-sized statements and hung on the walls of the gallery. Day by day these comment signs became a growing conversational element as visitors not only reacted to the images but to these statements and thus to one another. Their public dialogue extended the impact of the exhibit out into the community; it gave them a stake in the exhibit's message. This tactic ultimately allowed the people of Washington, D.C., to take ownership of the exhibition. Unlike the employees at the Library of Congress who claimed that they could not bring themselves even to look at the pictures, at the D.C. Public Library visitors found themselves looking very carefully, and thus they found, much to the surprise of many, that they were presented with the opportunity to heal deep social wounds. Consider some of their comments:

> Thanks for letting me decide on the merit of this exhibit. History for most blacks is a painful and emotional study, but it is what happened. It serves me as a reminder of the strong people that are my past and [I] resolve that I too must endure.

> I thought the exhibit was thought provoking. I feel that that's a step of healing. I can't express enough gratitude for not letting this exhibit die.

> The exhibit moved me to tears. It was important to see how my ancestors lived, survived, and overcame. I'm bringing my husband and [children] back to see it.

> The plantation exhibit is full of images I needed to see and know, images which will stay in my mind . . . I'm so proud of the DC Public Library . . . Bravo!

> After [I] finished looking at the exhibit, I shed tears for the people who shed their blood so that we may have a chance to live. I like the exhibition.

It gives me a sense of who I am and where I am from and the values of my culture. We should learn to forgive but never forget.

The reactions of white visitors were equally compelling. One who signed himself or herself simply a "Library of Congress Employee" wrote:

> I saw in this exhibit buildings constructed by my ancestors to house those they believed they "owned." If anyone should want this exhibit to be hidden away because of embarrassment it should be me. But the exhibit compels the viewer to come to an understanding of those living in squalid quarters, their contributions to the plantation and American culture. The experience of the emotional impact of this exhibit should never have been censored. The irony of a higher body trying to control what others see should be noted. Thanks to the Martin Luther King Library for providing the opportunity.

Those who had negative things to say did not attack the core premises of the exhibition; rather, they expressed their desire for a larger display containing more images, or they wondered why only photographs were shown and not objects. Clearly they had been drawn into the topic and wanted to know more; they had become participants in the exhibition's call to face the history of slavery and to learn more about it from the slaves' perspective. Newspaper reports caught the spirit of growing public acceptance with headlines such as "Controversy Fades as Exhibit Is Big Hit," "The Fertile Ground of 'Plantation': Slavery Show Shut Down at Library of Congress Seen with New Eyes," and "Slavery Show Abolished by Feds, Rises Again."[15]

By the time the exhibition moved on to its next venue, public reaction was considerably more favorable. The exhibit still retained a hint of sensationalism, and thus many viewers came because they were curious to see for themselves what all the fuss had been about, but finally "Back of the Big House" had proved itself a useful introduction to a difficult topic. The sort of notoriety that accompanies censure by an institution as prestigious as the Library of Congress proved to be beneficial in an unexpected way, for it inspired more institutions to book the exhibition. The planned tour for the exhibition went forward without further complaint and was extended to an additional eight sites.

RESPONSES TO CONTROVERSY:
THE HISTORICAL SOCIETY OF WASHINGTON

While the D.C. Public Library was presenting "The Cultural Landscape of the Plantation," the nearby Historical Society of Washington (HSW) opened a small exhibition entitled "Plantations in the District of Columbia." This display contained only a few images that I had chosen from the collections of the Library of Congress. Intended originally to be a supplement for the "Back of the Big House" exhibition, this so-called sidebar display was another victim of the library's censorious actions. Barbara Franco, then director of the HSW, upon learning that I had assembled these items, quickly offered to put them on view. When challenged by a Library of Congress official about why she was interested in showing these images, she pointed out that such a display was well within the charter of the HSW—"to collect, preserve, and teach the history of the nation's capital."[16] She added further that photographs of D.C. plantation houses and old slave quarters were the sort of image that needed to be shown to the public. She finished the conversation by pointing out that *Washington History,* the society's magazine, had recently presented some of these same images.[17]

In "Plantations in the District of Columbia" I aimed at recovering a sense of the physical landscape of Washington during the late eighteenth century, just before the city was invented. Most accounts of the capital city give only passing notice of its settler period and move quickly to the moment in 1790 when the United States Congress voted to relocate to the banks of the Potomac River.[18] Explanations of the city's origins tend to focus mainly on the bold actions of surveyors, builders, and land speculators as a fresh, new city was carved out of a seeming wilderness. Consequently, Washington is presented as an instant city, a place that was always a capital, always an inspiration for high national purpose.

In the light of such perceptions, Washington is generally presumed to be set apart from the social experience of its physical region. The moral dilemmas associated with slavery were not thought to touch the District of Columbia. This smug conceit is exposed, however, when one realizes

the American capital was once a site occupied by twenty-two slaveholding farms and plantations. The White House, the monuments that sur-
round the Mall, even the Capitol building—all of them structures meant
to signal high national purpose and to inspire patriotic feelings—stand on
ground once worked by captive African Americans.

Most signs of Washington's slave past are today largely eradicated;
very few buildings where slaves were quartered still stand. The contemporary scene, a landscape created largely during the early years of the
twentieth century, presents a collection of neoclassical temples surrounded by bland office buildings. In order to illustrate something of
Washington's plantation era I was compelled to turn to old maps, drawings, and photographs. Particularly useful was an 1874 map entitled
"Sketch of Washington in Embryo" that presented the property lines of
the various rural holdings that existed prior to 1791, when L'Enfant first
presented his plan for a grand city of "pleasant prospects."[19] This map
showed quite clearly that the Capitol building stands within the boundaries of an 1,100-acre estate once owned by Daniel Carroll. Similarly, the
site of the White House was built on a parcel of land that once was part of
David Burnes's tobacco farm. Notley Young, the city's largest slaveholder
(he owned 265 slaves in 1790), built his house on the shores of the Potomac
River at a place that is very close to the site of the Jefferson Memorial.[20]
That the monumental core of Washington stands on slave ground proved
to be a revolutionary claim for many, even though the data had been in
hand for nearly two centuries.

The most thoroughly documented site that I presented was Daniel
Carroll's Duddington, a house that was located just five blocks south of
the Capitol grounds. Because of a controversy that flared up between Carroll and L'Enfant, this property was carefully mapped.[21] A plan of the
house site from 1796 shows, in detail, the layout of his mansion and its
grounds, providing indications of barns, stables, and other outbuildings.
One recognizes immediately the pattern of a southern plantation, with a
gated entry leading to a large house with its dependencies spreading out
behind it. Since the mansion stood until 1886, it was photographed several
times. These images show an impressive brick house decorated with classic revival details. While census data from 1798 make it very clear that the
Carroll family owned twenty-two slaves (enough to qualify their holding
as a plantation rather than a farm), the most compelling proof that they

were slaveholders was found in a photograph taken in 1862. This image shows the family sitting in front of the house under the shelter of its portico as a black man dressed in livery—doubtless the enslaved butler—serves them.

Accompanying my selection of graphic images were various artifacts from the collection of the Historical Society that illustrated the city's participation in slavery and the slave trade: a poster announcing a reward for a runaway slave named Sophia Gordon, a pass issued by the mayor of Washington in 1843 granting a black woman named Jane Taverns permission to live in the city for one year, an abolitionist's broadside declaring the national capital to be the "Slave Market of America" and the "Home of the Oppressed." These pieces of memorabilia, when joined with old maps, documentary photographs, and a surviving mantelpiece from David Burnes's old plantation house, revealed that Washington, contrary to the usual intonations that linked the city to high-minded national principles, was deeply implicated in the history of slavery. In accompanying text panels I explained that even though farmland soon gave way to urban development, the city became a significant slave market that supplied roughly 20 percent of the captive labor used on the cotton plantations in the deep South states. Gangs of black men and women chained together while being marched down to the river, where they were put on steamboats leaving for New Orleans, were a common sight in the District of Columbia. While the numbers of slaves held in the capital city declined decade by decade, at the beginning of the Civil War in 1861 some 1,774 African Americans were still held in bondage in Washington. In character, Washington had much in common with the South.[22]

The public response to this modest display—most of the items fit into two glass cases, with the remainder hung on the wall above them—was gratifyingly enthusiastic. It opened at about the same time as the King Library's showing of "Back of the Big House," and attendance was boosted significantly by a story appearing in the *Washington Post* on March 5, 1996. Reporter Mary Ann French, a distinguished African American journalist with deep family ties to the city, called the exhibit "small but powerful." French examined "Plantations in the District" in lavish detail, producing an account running some sixty column inches that was accompanied by five photographs. She not only studied the exhibit but also went out to see for herself the various places included in the display. Visiting the service wing at the Decatur House, just across the street from the White House, and the Maples, an old plantation house a mere six blocks from the Capitol, she asked questions of the current occupants and reflected on what they told her as well as on what they left unsaid. She finally decided that my small exhibit

> casts light on the city that allows you to look past its monumental features and into its very Southern soul. It shows the kinds of dwellings . . . that were built to house slaves. It examines the tactics—architectural and otherwise—that owners used to control them. And it leaves you wondering why we romanticize the life of the antebellum southern gentry so.[23]

French's assessment restated the position taken by the great abolitionist hero Frederick Douglass, who in an 1877 oration declared that Washington, though the national capital, was "southern in all its sympathies."[24]

"Plantations in the District of Columbia" was on view for four months. Many African Americans came to see the exhibition because of French's article; for most of them, it was their first visit to the Historical Society. Seizing the opportunity to open a dialogue on the legacy of slavery in the nation's capital, the HSW staged two public discussions. Both of these events were attended by overflowing audiences eager for guidance about how they might approach the thorny subjects of slavery and racism. That so many came and that they were so interested suggested that "Plantations in the District of Columbia" had achieved its intended effect. Eyes were opened to the significance of local history, even if it was a history consisting of shameful events.

CONCLUSION

The experience of exhibiting aspects of slave life in Washington, D.C., reveals the deep concern that many African Americans have for their history. By and large, they manifest what I would call a "hunger for memory." Frequently denied access to the means for achieving the so-called American dream, black Americans have come to see themselves as a virtuous people who have been continually wronged, and they believe that they deserve better. However, some will temper their bitterness with a measure of optimism and look into their enslaved past to find answers that will help to explain their prolonged victimization. The response at the Library of Congress, where a group of black people withdrew from the exhibition, proved to be an aberrant reaction to "Back of the Big House." The responses at the Martin Luther King Jr. Library and the Historical Society of Washington were much more representative. Collectively, most black respondents from Washington, D.C., voiced an interest in learning more about the onerous and taboo aspects of their history. Armed with credible visual images and direct verbal testimony about the awful days of slavery, most of them manifested a desire to learn and to endure. This was the most representative reaction of audiences at eighteen different sites from Boston to Baton Rouge.

A controversial topic such as the history of slavery cannot be expected to move serenely through the public; as the stuff of difficult history, it is guaranteed to provoke a strong reaction. But if the passions that are stirred can be harnessed to a useful social project, such as preparation for a sustained struggle for social reform, then difficult history can fulfill the promise at which all scholars aim. Historian Peter Wood provocatively suggests that when discussing slavery we should replace the pleasant word *plantation* with the more brutal term *slave labor camp* or even *gulag*. On the history of slavery, he observes that most Americans live in denial, "unwilling or unable to grasp the full depth of the huge collective wound that predated the country's founding and that haunted its infant and adolescent years." He goes on to propose an uncompromising therapeutic regimen:

> Would a tougher reexamination of enslavement resonate with those members of our dysfunctional national family who currently refuse to acknowledge that slavery has any enduring significance? . . . If America were able to review slavery in a prolonged and sustained manner, such a renewed effort might well stem from and then help to alleviate the deep racial malaise of the United States. . . . For societies, as for individuals, the act of remembering, acknowledging, and reliving the pain of terrible experiences can lead to awareness and empathy. Only then can grieving, reconciliation, and rebirth follow.[25]

Wood's musings parallel the strategy that I employed while creating "Back of Big House" in both book and exhibition form. By allowing

Americans the chance to encounter directly "those who wore the shoe" of slavery, they were given an opportunity to have a direct, face-to-face encounter with the hidden history of their nation. Further, they were provided with the means that might allow them to understand how they have become the people that they are. This is a circumstance full of promise; we dare not hope for more.

Constructed in England and hung in the spring of 1754 in the house of the Pennsylvania Assembly—now Philadelphia's Independence Hall—this flawed 2,080-pound bell cracked almost immediately. Still, it tolled in protest of British tax policy during the decade before the Revolution. Tradition has it that patriots rang the bell during the reading of the Declaration of Independence on July 8, 1776. PHOTOGRAPH BY ROBIN MILLER, COURTESY OF INDEPENDENCE NATIONAL HISTORICAL PARK

5

For Whom

Will the Liberty Bell Toll?

From Controversy to Cooperation

Gary B. Nash

I n early 2002, controversy erupted in the City of Brotherly Love over the interpretive exhibits planned for the venerable Liberty Bell, which would soon occupy a shimmering new glass-and-steel home. For many years after its arrival from France in 1752, the bell had hung in the bell tower of the Pennsylvania State House (later to be named Independence Hall); since 1976, it had made its home in an undistinguished building on Market Street between Fifth and Sixth Streets. The controversy hinged on matters of great importance to the National Park Service and the nation at large: how to present the history and meaning of the Liberty Bell to the several hundred thousand visitors, both Americans and people from overseas, who troop by the cracked bell each year. To be sure, the Liberty Bell is only a sliver of American history. But only a few slivers have had such resonance. Until the mid-nineteenth century, when abolitionists first named it the "Liberty Bell," it was an unremarkable two-thousand-pound piece of unstable mixed metals that could not even ring properly.[1] Since then, the Liberty Bell has captured American affections. With its inscription "Proclaim liberty throughout the land and to all the inhabitants thereof" (Leviticus 25:10), it has become a stand-in for America's vaunted qualities: independence, freedom, unalienable rights, and equality—virtually a touchstone of American identity. For years, people have gazed at the bell, reached out to touch it, dabbed their eyes, and departed, perhaps without quite knowing why the bell grips them so emotionally. Put on the road a century ago for national and international exhibitions, and held up as a symbol of the best America stands for, the Liberty Bell has achieved global reach as a symbol of freedom and human rights. It has become what one former Park Service staffer calls "the greatest relic of America's heroic age." [2]

Planning for new Liberty Bell exhibits began in the early 1990s, when Independence National Historical Park (INHP) planners decided to build a new Liberty Bell Center and move the bell to what had been 190 High Street in the eighteenth century, the site of one of the city's stateliest mansions. Much was at stake here, and nobody knew better than the superintendent and staff at Philadelphia's INHP that they were the custodians of one of the premier sites of our revolutionary heritage. The Liberty Bell and Independence Hall are beacons, attracting people sensing or searching for links between the past and the present and trying to refresh their memories of what many nostalgically think of as a golden age. Now, with some $13 million for a new pavilion to be erected at the southeast corner of Sixth and Market Streets, right across the street from the new Independence Visitor Center, INHP had a chance to rethink what the Liberty Bell meant at different points in its history and what it means today. INHP shouldered a weighty responsibility; it also enjoyed a rare opportunity.

INHP planners had to reckon with how American history had unfolded in the last generation and how the National Park Service had been changing, particularly since its 1997 General Management Plan, which called for "a new *VISION* for the park in the twenty-first century." [3] Had the opportunity to build a sparkling new home for the Liberty Bell arisen in the 1950s, the task would have been simpler—tell the story as the National Park Service rangers in their nifty World War I–style hats had told the story for a long time: how the founding fathers engineered independence and constructed the world's most durable constitution and how liberty was proclaimed throughout the land and seized by all the good people. This was a story drained of ambiguity, complexity, paradox, and irony. It was an account that thrilled most visitors, to be sure, yet it was a simplistic tale that catered to a barely historically literate public rather than offering nuanced interpretation, contradictory meanings of the Liberty Bell, new ideas, and fresh information for visitors to chew on as they looked over their shoulders after they left the Liberty Bell Center. To do this, INHP leaders would have to take account of how the civil rights movement, the Vietnam War, the women's rights movement, the American Indian movement, and the countercultural revolution of the 1960s fractured the historical consensus interpretation popular in the post–World War II period and ushered in a wholesale questioning of how the American democracy had produced a decidedly undemocratic, elitist interpretation of its past.

The special challenge for the INHP leaders was how to treat African American history, particularly slavery, in its new interpretative exhibits at the Liberty Bell Center. How should the Park Service, which conducts one of the largest outdoor history classrooms in the world, address how the new nation, fresh from wresting its independence from England, built a freedom-loving republic based on slavery? This would require going beyond the institutional history of the Liberty Bell and the plain-vanilla story of the nation's founding. How, asks one former staffer, would INHP "deal with a national sin older than the nation itself" in "a park and a city long accustomed to a glorious role in American history?"[4] Would the symbolic power of the bell be compromised if visitors learned that if the bell tolls for the independent and free, this freedom and independence was built on the backs of the enslaved one-fifth of the American colonial population? Might the public accept a proposition argued thirty years before by Edmund Morgan that "to a large degree it may be said that Americans bought their independence with slave labor" and that this "paradox is American, and it behooves Americans to understand it if they would understand themselves"?[5] Would this draw charges of being antipatriotic? Or did the Park Service have a civic responsibility to encourage visitors to become more reflective and engaged citizens in a dangerous and complex world?[6] As the INHP leaders planned the exhibits for the new Liberty Bell Center, they were acutely aware that Americans were fresh from a series of smoking debates over whose history we learn, or should learn, at public history sites, who gets to tell the stories, and who, in the end, owns the property of history.[7]

Adding to the drama in presenting the Liberty Bell anew was the chunk of real estate upon which the new glass-and-steel pavilion was to be erected. The site is where the widow of William Masters, mighty merchant and Philadelphia mayor in the 1750s, erected a fine mansion in about 1767–68. As it happens, Masters was probably Philadelphia's largest slave owner. In 1761, after his death, his probated estate listed the names of thirty-four slaves. Some may have helped build the house. In 1772, Masters's widow gifted the mansion to her daughter Polly, who had married Richard Penn, grandson of William Penn. Polly and Richard Penn were also slave owners, but on a small scale. The mansion's next occupant, shortly after the Revolution erupted, was Sir William Howe, the British general whose army occupied Philadelphia from September 1777 to June 1778. After Howe's recall, Sir Henry Clinton moved in and, like Howe, his enslaved Africans toiled on this site. After the British decamped, a new occupant arrived: Benedict Arnold, who ruled the city under martial law. Two enslaved Africans were among his household retinue of seven. Then came John Holker, French consul to the new United States, who was residing in the mansion when it suffered great damage from a fire on January 2, 1780. A year later, Robert Morris, financier of the American Revolution in its closing years, purchased the house and began to reconstruct it, probably with the labor of his several slaves.[8] Thus, for the late colonial and entire Revolutionary period, the lives of the free and unfree mingled intimately on this piece of Philadelphia ground.

Morris's rebuilding of the Masters-Penn house made it suitable quarters for George and Martha Washington after the nation's capital moved from New York to Philadelphia in 1790. But some alterations were needed, especially for sheltering a household staff of about thirty—a mixed lot of waged employees, white indentured servants, and enslaved African Americans. Through the work of Edward Lawler Jr., an urban archaeologist and architectural historian who for several years has been researching meticulously the history of the Morris mansion and its use by Washington, we know that each day the thousands of visitors at the Liberty Bell Pavilion will be walking directly over the "servants hall," as it was called, as well as near the smokehouse, the octagonal icehouse, and the stables.[9] After the Washingtons decamped for Mount Vernon in 1797, John and Abigail Adams became the new tenants at what Philadelphians were coming to call the President's House.

For nearly seven years, George Washington and the First Lady occupied the President's House; the indentured servants and slaves prepared the meals, cleaned the mansion, groomed the horses, drove the coaches, tended the fireplaces, hauled the ashes, and performed countless other tasks indispensable to running the executive office efficiently and graciously. Like their well-to-do owners, these men and women had emotions, ideas, spiritual yearnings, hopes, and fears; they also had family commitments, agendas to pursue, and thoughts of improving their condition. They speak to us as much as Martha and George Washington about what it meant to live in Philadelphia at the center of the new American republic, though history had dictated that they carry out their lives in severely circumscribed stations. They speak to us, however, only if we give them voice.

Site and symbol, freedom and slavery, black and white, upstairs and downstairs—how should the INHP explain the Liberty Bell and its new site to the swarming visitors who would come to venerate the bell? In December 2001 I had an inkling that the Liberty Bell story line, as it had been devised by INHP, would be simplistic and vainglorious and that this piece of history-soaked land where the new pavilion would soon rise would be ignored. Philadelphia's National Public Radio station, WHYY, had interviewed me on December 5, 2001, by hookup from Los Angeles, and having read Edward Lawler's account of the slaves from Mount Vernon who had served the First Family at this site for nearly seven years (to be published in the *Pennsylvania Magazine of History and Biography* a month later), I mentioned that it would be a misfortune to perpetuate the historical amnesia about the founding fathers and slavery at the Liberty Bell venue. But the alarm bell I tried to ring had no effect whatever. I had not read the exhibit script written by several INHP staffers, nor did I know that they were moving ahead at flank speed to get bids to construct the new exhibits. That became apparent when I went to Philadelphia on March 12, 2002, to give a talk on my book, *First City: Philadelphia and the Forging of Historical Memory,* published by the University of Pennsylvania Press a few months before. I had e-mailed Philip Lapsansky, curator of the Afro-Americana Collection at the Library Company, before going east to see if my December attempt had borne fruit. He told me that "INHP regards the whole thing as a nuisance in the way of paving over everything for the Liberty Bell plaza" and opined that "this might be one of the most significant black history sites in town, clearly and physically factoring in African American slavery to the founding and early governance of the nation." Lapsansky promised to try "to build a black constituency . . . at the least insisting on some major and very public interpretation at the site." But the story of the president's mansion and its many slaves would never surface if the Independence Hall leadership had its way. "How naive of me," e-mailed Lapsansky, "to have thought your WHYY bit in December, which was very powerful, would actually be heard by many folks much less acted upon." At this point, on March 7, I e-mailed Dwight Pitcaithley, chief historian of the National Park Service, to alert him to the situation and asked what he knew of what promised to be a disturbing burial of poignant history at one of NPS's most visited and revered sites.[10]

After reaching Philadelphia on March 12 and talking more with Lapsansky, I called Chris Schillizzi, the chief of interpretation and visitors' services at INHP, to ask what visitors would learn about the history of the President's House, its many illustrious tenants, and their slaves and servants. Not much, he replied. His staff had done research for several years in devising the interpretative plan, he had solicited scholarly and public input, and he had made the decision to keep the focus squarely on the Liberty Bell and its venerable history. Drawing attention to the President's House and the deep historical significance of the site on which the new pavilion was being built, he explained, would confuse the public and divert attention from the venerable bell. I objected that the Liberty Bell meant many things to many people, among them slaves for whom the biblical inscription on the bell—"Proclaim liberty throughout the land and to all the inhabitants thereof"—surely had a hollow ring. Were not liberty and unfreedom locked in deadly embrace? Wasn't the liberty of some built on the enslavement of others? Whether this was true or not, Schillizzi replied, they were out of time and out of money. "The train has left the station," he claimed, using a metaphor not designed to continue the conversation and easy to recognize as a rationale for stifling dissenting views. Would the public hear not a word about how they were walking over the sleeping quarters of indentured servants and slaves, no less the human property of the first president, as they approached the entrance of the Liberty Bell Pavilion? Would they learn nothing about how they were stepping in the footprints of Richard Penn, Benedict Arnold, Sir William Howe, Robert Morris, John and Abigail Adams, and a host of others? The most I could garner from Schillizzi was a half-promise to consider a curbside plasticized panel on Market Street that would note that this was the site of the President's House, the executive mansion of our first two presidents.

Muttering to myself as I walked to the old Friends Meetinghouse at Fourth and Arch to give a talk on *First City,* a book about the contest for public memory that had agitated Philadelphia for generations, I pondered whether my concluding chapter, titled "Restoring Memory," was too optimistic. I mused about how the property in history has been redistributed as Philadelphia's collecting institutions have widened their vision about what is collectible and as the production of stories about the past has increased. I recalled how the Republican National Committee had sanctioned a thirty-foot-high mural portraying the Underground Railroad and its radical abolitionist leaders in Philadelphia and unveiled it as the convention of July 2000 met to nominate George W. Bush.[11] And I remembered the letter INHP Superintendent Martha Aikens showed me from Tony Johnston of Williamstown, New Jersey. Johnston had written how his children wanted to see Independence Hall when he and his family were visiting Philadelphia on July 4, 1995. "I did not want to go," he explained. "I am an African American and spent most of my life in the west. I did not think this place had anything to do with me." But their tour guide, Frances Delmar, changed his mind. "She made me understand that even if I am not blood related to those men in Independence Hall, I am idea and dream related," he wrote. "She told her story just like my mother used to do her quilts. She put the pieces together and when she was done I saw the pattern and where I fit in the pattern." Ranger Delmar, Johnston concluded, "saw I was uneasy being African American in that place. She faced the race thing head on with charm and truth. Thank you for giving us tour guides like her. Bless you." [12]

At the Quaker meetinghouse, I spoke of these things and concluded with what I had just heard from INHP's chief of interpretation. To my surprise, the audience was more interested in the disremembering of history at the Liberty Bell Pavilion than in my new book. One after another, those attending deplored INHP's inattention to the Liberty Bell's historically rich site. Then Randall Miller, former editor of the *Pennsylvania Magazine of History and Biography* and a prolific author who teaches in the Department of History at St. Joseph's University, suggested that I write an op-ed piece for the *Philadelphia Inquirer* to bring the issue before the public. Not quite ready to have him paint a bull's-eye on the back of someone who had made useful target practice for the ultrapatriotic attack on the National History Standards in 1994–96, I agreed only if Miller would coauthor the piece. When he agreed, we were off to the races. The next day, Marty Moss-Coane, host of WHYY's *Radio Times,* interviewed me about my book, and she followed my suggestion that she segue into a discussion of the planned Liberty Bell exhibits. This gave me a chance to be provocative. "Our memory of the past is often managed and manipulated," I said. "Here it is being downright murdered." The switchboard lit up as people called in from all compass points. Overwhelmingly, they supported my plea for presenting the history of the Liberty Bell site, along with the bell itself, in ways that mingled stories of freedom and unfreedom, black and white, mighty and humble, giving the public food for thought rather than leaving them simply with a warm, cozy glow about the old cracked bell.

Fifteen minutes of on-air discussion about the Liberty Bell on *Radio Times* proved a crucial turning point. The public was getting aroused. Equally important, Stephan Salisbury at the *Inquirer* decided to cover the story.[13] Writing with Inga Saffron, he splashed the story on the front page on Sunday, March 24, with a headline reading "Echoes of Slavery at Liberty Bell Site." Thousands of *Inquirer* readers were learning about a chapter of forgotten history—"the presence of slaves at the heart of one of the nation's most potent symbols of freedom." Salisbury and Saffron included a defensive statement from INHP that "the Liberty Bell is its own story, and Washington's slaves are a different one better told elsewhere." Philadelphia's African American mayor, John Street, was quoted as being disturbed by this and calling for "a very earnest dialogue . . . about how to address the issue of Washington and his slaves." The *Inquirer* quoted Randall Miller at length. The Park Service, he charged, was missing an opportunity "to tell the real story of the American Revolution and the meaning of freedom. Americans, through Washington, were working out the definition of freedom in a new republic. And Washington had slaves. Meanwhile, the slaves were defining freedom for themselves by running away. There are endless contradictions embedded in this site." I was quoted as saying, "Maybe the National Park Service feels it would besmirch the Liberty Bell to discuss [the slavery issue] and that the Liberty

Bell should be pure. But that's not history [in the whole that] people deserve to know."[14]

Two days later, the *Inquirer* devoted a full page to the issue, with a clever headline—"Site Unseen"—and an article about how Mayor Street was dialoguing with Park Service officials, who now seemed willing to rethink their exhibits a bit, especially if the mayor agreed that work on the new pavilion would not be delayed. Meanwhile, Miller and I began organizing a committee of Philadelphia-area historians and institutional leaders to hold the feet of Park Service officials to the fire, while offering to work with them to rethink their plans for the Liberty Bell pavilion and the site on which it would rise.[15] Among them were Charlene Mires, an American historian at Villanova University and author of a soon-to-be-published history of Independence Hall. Mires told the press about how Independence Hall, as well as the President's House, was deeply involved with slavery—in fact, was the place where fugitive slaves were tried as late as 1854. "These issues of slavery and freedom run throughout Independence Mall," Mires said to the *Inquirer*. "It doesn't diminish the story to address them."[16] Nancy Gilboy, president of the Independence Hall Association, a volunteer group, argued for making the footprint of the President's House visible to visitors.

The *Inquirer*'s March 27 lead editorial, titled "Freedom and Slavery: Just as They Coexisted in the 1700s, Both Must Be Part of Liberty Bell's Story," turned up the heat. The *Inquirer* wagged its finger at INHP, reminded them that "the old cracked bell will be situated on ground that enhances it as a cherished symbol of the struggle for liberty, especially to African Americans," and expressed confidence that "the Liberty Bell in its new home will not bury an ugly part of the country's history."[17]

Then on Easter Sunday, March 31, the *Inquirer* published an op-ed piece that Randall Miller and I had written, along with an essay by Charlene Mires.[18] A eye-catching image dominated the op-ed page: a slave's ankle shackles superimposed on a replica of the Declaration of Independence. The next day, the Associated Press put a story on the wire, to be picked up around the country, titled "Historians Decry Liberty Bell Site." The history of slavery on Independence Mall was now becoming a hot issue. Letters were pouring in to the *Inquirer,* mostly favoring our position.

In our op-ed essay, Miller and I argued that the Park Service should enlist historians to help bring out the rich stories showing how freedom and slavery commingled at the Liberty Bell site and elsewhere. "Washington was the living symbol of freedom and independence," we wrote, and "Washington's slaves were living symbols of the most paradoxical part of the nation's birth—freedom and unfreedom side by side, with the enslavement of some making possible the liberty of others. An exhibition of documents and artifacts should show slavery's and freedom's many meanings at the dawn of the new nation. Doing so will make the Liberty Bell's own story ring loud and true." "A free people," we concluded, "dare not bury evidence or silence long-forgotten African Americans, whose stories make the meaning of the Liberty Bell and the Revolution real and palpable, here and abroad."[19] We also pled for exhibits that would document the battery of servants and slaves who made the lives of the President and the First Lady comfortable, how they "prepared the meals for incessant banquets for congressmen and dignitaries, drove the founding father and his family around the city in their carriages, washed their clothes, groomed their hair, tended their horses, cleaned the house, chopped the wood, and much more." " The Park Service," we concluded, "must deliver on its promise that these stories will not be buried."

In the Easter Sunday issue, the *Inquirer* also ran an article by Inga Saffron about how the Park Service was marginalizing the President's House and its thought-provoking history. Chiding the Park Service for its announced plan to have a "wayside panel" that would point out where the executive mansion stood during the presidencies of Washington and Adams, Saffron asked bitingly: "Would the Park Service make do with a sign on the site where the Declaration of Independence was signed and the Constitution written? Where the battle of Yorktown was fought?" Struggling to defend the interpretive plan for the new Liberty Bell exhibits, Superintendent Martha Aikens argued that NPS rangers often spoke of slaveholding in Philadelphia (especially at the infrequently visited Morris-Deschler House in Germantown, eight miles from the city center) but conceded only that "public interest" convinced her that INHP could mark the sidewalk along Market Street to indicate that the President's House had stood there and that "people in the household, including Washington's slaves," toiled at this location.[20]

From this point forward, the key was to move from publicity to concrete results that would go far beyond what Aikens promised. To this end,

Randall Miller convened the Ad Hoc Historians on April 8, 2002, for a brown bag lunch at the Library Company of Philadelphia, where the group agreed to reach out directly to Aikens to meet and discuss what we regarded as a flawed plan. "The planned interpretation of the Liberty Bell's new site, as we understand it," we wrote in a letter to her a week later,

> will focus on the Liberty Bell, its history, and its significance as a national icon symbolizing the commitment to freedom in America. But the Liberty Bell story so envisioned speaks mostly to the achievement of American independence and the devotion to the ideal of freedom thereafter. This does not address the braided historical relationship between freedom and slavery, how interdependent they were, and how the freedom of some was built upon the unfreedom of others. Moreover this singular focus on liberty as the achievement of white Americans leaves African Americans out of the story, except as objects of others' benevolence and concern. The issue of how white freedom lived cheek by jowl with slavery, and how this played itself out on the now sacred ground of the Independence Hall area (including the presidential house in the 1790s), is what has occasioned so much public interest and comment.[21]

We ended our letter with a request for the interpretive plan, which we had not been able to pry from her office.

Protracted negotiations with the Park Service leaders now ensued. Three stages evolved. First, INIIP's leaders, under a barrage of negative press commentary (intensified by a long *New York Times* article on April 20), continued its finger-in-the-dike approach.[22] On April 20, Aikens released a brief description of the ten exhibit zones designed to interpret the Liberty Bell inside the pavilion, our group's first glimpse of the interpretive plan. Two days later, she invited five of our ad hoc group to talk about Zone 6, which included a brief mention of slavery and the antebellum abolitionists' use of the bell (calling it "the Liberty Bell" for the first time). The superintendent remained silent on giving us access to the script, would not agree to discuss the exhibit in its entirety, and warned that the Park Service would not contemplate any major changes inside the pavilion because "the plans and specifications for the Liberty Bell Center were completed on March 22, 2002." However, she invited us to discuss possible interpretations of the President's House site, where people would line up to enter the Liberty Bell Pavilion.[23] Drafting a second letter for the ad hoc group, Miller and I asked again for the interpretive plan, noted that we did not believe it had ever received non-NPS scholarly review, suggested that the bidding process for constructing the exhibits should be suspended while the plan was being fully reviewed and revised, and resisted the implication that all interpretations of the site of the pavilion should be relegated to curbside or wayside panels rather than in the Liberty Bell Center itself. Delivered on April 25, this letter urged that at the meeting the slavery issue should be addressed as it related to the entire exhibition rather than to a single exhibit panel on slavery inside the pavilion.

Second, the intervention of the NPS's chief historian, Dwight Pitcaithley, became crucially important. When he first saw the interpretative plan, Pitcaithley was dismayed to find a chest-thumping, celebratory script, "an exhibit to make people feel good but not to think," an exhibition that "would be an embarrassment if it went up," and one that "works exactly against NPS's new thinking." With these indictments, Pitcaithley urged Aikens to rethink the exhibits along lines advocated by the Ad Hoc Historians. "The potential for interpreting Washington's residence and slavery on the site," he counseled, "presents the National Park Service with several exciting opportunities." The President's House, he prodded, should be explained and interpreted, and "the juxtaposition of slave quarters (George Washington's slave quarters, no less) and the Liberty Bell" provided "some stirring interpretive possibilities."

> The contradiction in the founding of the country between freedom and slavery becomes palpable when one actually crosses through a slave quarters site when entering a shrine to a major symbol of the abolition movement. . . . How better to establish the proper historical context for understanding the Liberty Bell than by talking about the institution of slavery? And not the institution as generalized phenomenon, but as lived by George Washington's own slaves. The fact that Washington's slaves Hercules and Oney Judge sought and gained freedom from this very spot gives us interpretive opportunities other historic sites can only long for. This juxtaposition is an interpretive gift that can make the Liberty Bell "experience" much more meaningful to the visiting public. We will have missed a real educational opportunity if we do not act on this possibility.[24]

Shuttling between Washington and Philadelphia, Pitcaithley's meetings with the INHP staff and its NPS eastern regional supervisors began
to bear fruit.[25] In a summary of his criticisms of the exhibition text, he explained that "if the exhibit only celebrates the Bell, the visitor will learn
nothing about the meaning of liberty as it played out in this country over
the last one hundred and fifty years or so." Pitcaithley cautioned,

> The text assumes that the inspirational message of the Bell has resulted in
> a steady progression of the expansion of liberty throughout the United
> States and the world. . . . It assumes there is only one interpretation of the
> message. . . . How much more interesting (and useful) the exhibit would
> be if it acknowledged that the "liberty road" has been filled with potholes
> and obstacles and while the United States has a more expansive definition
> of freedom and liberty than it did one hundred or even fifty years ago, the
> struggle is not over. There is a long tradition of assumed freedoms sliding
> backward on occasion.[26]

Providing many detailed examples, Pitcaithley concluded:

> The complexity found in the history of liberty in this country is not to be
> found in this exhibit. . . . The exhibit should make people *think* about the
> concept of liberty, not just *feel good* about it. Quality interpretation pro-
> vides revelation, offers provocation, and demonstrates relationships. . . .
> There is much work to be done on this exhibit before it is ready for public
> display.[27]

Pitcaithley left the meeting encouraged that his advice to reconsider the
plan and collaborate with the historians who had intervened in the matter
would bring results.

This brought us to the third stage of the process: many months of par-
leying and jockeying. At 9 A.M. on May 13, 2002, a group of twenty met at
the Independence Visitor Center, a stone's throw from where the Liberty
Bell pavilion would shortly begin to rise. The Park Service enlisted Tom
Tankersley, an interpretive planner for the Harpers Ferry National Historic Park Design Center, as facilitator; Dwight Pitcaithley, who came up
again from Washington; Russell Smith, chief of interpretation for the
NPS northeast region; key staff members of INHP; and David Hollen-

berg, associate northeast regional director, representing director Marie Rust.[28] Five of our group—Rosalind Remer, Randall Miller, Ed Lawler, Charlene Mires, and Stephanie Wolf—filed into the room. Showing that the furor over the Liberty Bell exhibits had become a potent political issue, Congressman Robert Brady had sent three representatives, including Charles Blockson, an African American historian at Temple University.

With the air fairly crackling with electricity, an INHP staffer gave a PowerPoint walk through the much-guarded interpretive plan. As facilitator, Tankersley then tried to lay down narrowly defined ground rules so as to limit the discussion to only a small part of the exhibition. But this circle-the-wagons approach fell apart. Blockson opened by questioning the accuracy of the present interpretive materials on slavery being sold at the Visitor Center. Karen Warrington, representing Congressman Brady, challenged the governing philosophy of the exhibit. Russell Smith argued for a discussion of *all* issues rather than confining comments to a single panel on slavery, and urged an integrated discussion on slavery and the President's House rather than having them sit as separate issues. Remer spoke at length about why a segregated, isolated slavery panel would ghettoize the subject and miss the opportunity to raise more compelling interpretive issues of freedom and unfreedom. After a coffee break—really a chance for Pitcaithley to play the role of Metternich by huddling with recalcitrant INHP staffers—the dynamics of the meeting changed. The door, which previously had been open just a crack, was now flung wide open. In what Randall Miller characterized as an "honest and intelligent discussion," the INHP leadership agreed that (1) the meaning of freedom in a democracy built on slave foundations would be a central theme in the exhibit; (2) that the treatment of the President's House outside the pavilion would be interpreted with attention to the slaves and servants who toiled there; and (3) that the Park Service people would mull over all ideas brought forward in order to modify and improve the script, which would then be sent out for review by noted scholars of the African American experience and the history of liberty in America. David Hollenberg pledged that "we are looking at the bell as a symbol of an ongoing continuous struggle for liberty rather than [a symbol] of liberty attained."[29]

Within days INHP leaders contacted a group of highly respected historians to review the revised exhibit script as soon as it was available—precisely the kind of collaboration with scholars that the Ad Hoc Historians had urged.[30] Stephan Salisbury, of the *Philadelphia Inquirer,* optimistically wrote on May 14 that the daylong meeting "effectively ended the controversy over the depiction of slavery at Independence National Historical Park," as park officials agreed that the "story of the Liberty Bell will acknowledge the nation's complex and contradictory roots in freedom and slavery"—a "major departure from the current bell story told by park rangers, which focuses almost exclusively on the bell's presence during the Revolutionary War era." *Inquirer* columnist Acel Moore was less sanguine, opining that the controversy was far from over and that "the battle for a more accurate account at the park concerning African American history and the role of the bell in the abolitionist movement . . . may just be beginning." Letters continued to fill the op-ed pages of the *Inquirer,* reinforced by another Salisbury article, which floated rumors of an African American protest at the site of the new Liberty Bell Center on July 4, 2002.[31]

INHP called another summit meeting for May 29–30 to digest and refine the frantic work of their internal group to shore up their exhibition. Rosalind Remer represented the Ad Hoc Historians (which was allowed only one representative), but now the working group included two key figures who had not helped plan the exhibits. The NPS insider was Martin Blatt, former head of the NPS historic site at the textile mill village at Lowell, Massachusetts, and now chief of cultural resources for Boston National Historical Park. The outsider was Edward Linenthal, veteran of many contests over historical memory and commemoration at NPS sites, author of several books on the subject, and coeditor of *History Wars: The* Enola Gay *and Other Battles for the American Past.* Pitcaithley, Russell Smith, and a full array of INHP staffers were present, including the African American supervisory ranger, Joseph Becton, who had never been consulted in the development of the interpretive plan.

Pinned up on the walls of the meeting room were blown-up images with large-print captions as well as the text that would guide visitors through the ten zones or panel displays. The task at hand was to rewrite the script in order to implement the reconceptualization agreed to at the May 13 meeting. The comments of Blatt, Linenthal, and Columbia University historian Eric Foner, who had been asked to review the original

script, were read to the group. Inasmuch as their comments aligned with
Pitcaithley's criticisms, it was now agreed that the breathless and uncom-
plicated prose relating the history of freedom that the bell symbolized
should be toned down, while the issue of freedom intertwined with slavery was given a central place in the interpretation. Now the group split
into teams of two in order to tackle the subheads, new images, fresh text,
and captions for each zone. In sum, INHP abandoned the attempt to re-
strict changes to one panel and work only around the edges of the original
script. Working at breakneck speed, the group overhauled five of the ten
zones in two days on May 29–30, rewriting the text, modifying captions,
and dropping some images while adding others. For example, INHP
agreed to adopt my suggestion to use a slave's head harness with a bell that
would ring if the slave took flight—what might be called an "unfreedom
bell" intended to thwart those seeking freedom. In many other cases,
mindful of the need to use as many images already contracted for as possible, INHP agreed to new text designed to give visitors varying interpretive readings of an artifact rather than simply an informational caption.

Here is one example. In the initially planned exhibition, in a section on
how the Liberty Bell traveled around the country in the late nineteenth
and early twentieth centuries, the INHP interpretive team had captioned
four photographs of visitors at San Francisco's 1915 Panama-Pacific Expo
with these words: "1915 scenes: men holding children up to the Bell; top-
hatted men lining up for a picture at the Bell; Native American; Thomas
Edison." The new text reads: "As the Liberty Bell increased in popularity
as a symbol of freedom and liberty for white Americans during the last
quarter of the nineteenth century, it reminded African Americans, Native Americans, other ethnic groups, and women of unrealized ideals.
While the Bell traveled the nation as a symbol of liberty, intermittent race
riots, lynchings, and Indian wars presented an alternative picture of freedom denied." Under the photo of Chief Little Bear, the caption now
reads: "Forced to choose between segregation and assimilation that insisted upon the suppression of their unique cultural practices, Native
Americans may not have seen the hope of fair treatment and equal rights
embodied in the Bell."[32]

Remer reported back to the Ad Hoc Historians that the two exhausting days were "extremely productive" and that she believed the result
would be "an amazingly thoughtful, provocative exhibit that will ask vis-

itors to confront the complex relationship of freedom and unfreedom as part of their consideration of Liberty Bell–as–icon. The ongoing struggle for equality is central to all of the panels. The celebratory tone is gone, replaced by subtle discussion of symbols and popular uses of the past. . . . The complicated story of Reconstruction and racism is at the heart of the exhibit—in some ways, I think, a pivotal section that makes clear that all of the appropriations of the Liberty Bell image are not the same—nor do they stem from the same impulses. . . . Images that were before seen simply as celebratory odes to the bell can now be interpreted in various ways." Remer commended the "responsiveness and openness" of the INHP staff and credited Pitcaithley's intercession for much of this. The major reconceptualization and rewriting left the INHP staff "a little nervous," reported Remer, "but also strengthened . . . because they very clearly seemed to see that this is now an exhibit to be proud of, rather than one to hide from scholarly scrutiny."[33]

A team of INHP staffers, including Doris Fanelli, Coxey Toogood, and Becton, none of whom had seen the original script, produced a much-revised script in several weeks. It went out to scholars on June 14. Replies from Eric Foner, James Oliver Horton, Fath Davis Ruffins, and Spencer Crew brought further changes, and then the script went to the Ad Hoc Historians group for a final review. Betokening the new spirit of collaboration with non-NPS historians, INHP accepted most of the changes and wove them into the final text. The involvement of political, scholarly, and public groups that occurred in these action-packed months was, in effect, what the General Management Plan of 1997 had promised. The result after a half year of controversy was that "the paradox of slavery in a land of the free will be a major exhibition theme when the $12.6 million Liberty Bell Center . . . opens next spring," as the *Inquirer* reported on August 11. "The text of the exhibition . . . has been completely reworked over the last three months and is nearing completion, according to NPS officials."[34]

With general agreement on the Liberty Bell exhibits, the focus now shifted *outside*—to the site of the President's House and its interpretation. Giving special urgency to addressing how INHP might incorporate interpretation of the executive mansion and its inhabitants was the involvement of black Philadelphians, who constitute about half the city's population. On July 4, 2002, hundreds of African Americans demonstrated at the Liberty Bell site, while the Avenging the Ancestors Coalition, headed by lawyer Michael Coard, organized a letter-writing campaign and a petition with several thousand signatures that called for a monument to commemorate Washington's slaves. The African People's Solidarity Committee wanted more discussion of slavery inside the pavilion, much along the lines that the Ad Hoc Historians had recommended. In what would turn out to be a key move, Congressman Chaka Fattah introduced an amendment to the 2003 budget of the Department of the Interior requiring that the Park Service report to Congress about an appropriate commemoration of the President's House and the slaves who toiled there. The Appropriations Committee, which oversees the National Park Service, voted unanimously for the amendment. Shortly, the Multicultural Affairs Congress, a division of the Philadelphia Convention and Visitors Bureau, joined the call for a "prominent monument or memorial" fixing in the public memory the contributions of Washington's slaves to the early years of the new republic and making Philadelphia a premier destination for African American visitors. The City Council followed suit with a resolution endorsing this idea.[35]

The site of the President's House is where crowds were expected to stand while waiting to see the sacred bell, in effect a captive audience for ranger presentations. Dwight Pitcaithley had argued that this was a rare interpretive opportunity where rangers could show the outlines of the Morris house and relate stories of the First Families—the Washingtons and Adamses—who lived there, along with the slaves and servants. The power of the place was inarguable. What Park Service ranger would not want to stand on this history-drenched site and tell stories to knots of visitors waiting to enter the pavilion? I fantasized that I was starting a new career as an INHP ranger. "Come over here," I would say to a group of overseas visitors. "Here the first two presidents wrestled with how the infant United States would deal with the French Revolution, which divided Philadelphians, like the nation at large, into warring camps. On this spot he signed orders for a federal army to march west to suppress the Whiskey Rebellion in 1794." "Step right here," I would tell a group of schoolchildren. "Just over where you are standing, Nelly Custis, on the second floor of the executive mansion, helped her grandmother prepare for bed and kneeled in prayer with Martha Washington and sang her to sleep." "Now come a few yards this way," my fellow ranger would tell a group of African American visitors. "From this spot, George Washington watched white planters, who were fleeing the black revolution in Haiti in the early 1790s, come up Market Street after tumbling off ships a few blocks east of here with scores of slaves in tow. These French-speaking slaves would soon be free in Philadelphia, as the 1780 Act for the Gradual Abolition of Slavery required, and many would worship at the city's Catholic churches, giving St. Joseph's and Holy Trinity bilingual congregations and new cuisines." When another ranger spotted visitors from Oklahoma, he would say, "Please step right here, good people. You are standing just over the place where the young John Quincy Adams sat in the mansion's front hall with President Washington and seventeen visiting Chickasaw chiefs, passing a ceremonial peace pipe around the circle."

Most compelling of all, perhaps, are the stories rangers could tell of two prized slaves who lived in the executive mansion. Oney Judge, born of an enslaved Mount Vernon seamstress and sired by a white indentured servant from Leeds, England, had served Martha Washington since 1784, when the young mixed-race girl was about ten years of age. Martha Washington brought her to Philadelphia in 1790, when Oney was sixteen. Six years later, in 1796, her privileged position in the Washington household notwithstanding, she fled the president's mansion just before the Washingtons were ready to return to Mount Vernon for summer recess.[36] Her days of helping the First Lady powder up for levees and state functions, running errands for her, and accompanying her on visits to the wives of other political and diplomatic leaders were now at an end. Many years later she recalled to a journalist from the *Granite Freeman,* a New Hampshire abolitionist paper, "I had friends among the colored people of Philadelphia, had my things carried there [to a waiting ship] before hand, and left while [the Washingtons] were at dinner."[37]

The Washingtons railed at the ingratitude of Oney Judge fleeing slavery—"without the least provocation," as Washington wrote. Oney's "thirst for compleat freedom," as she called it, did not register with the president. The Washingtons sent agents to track her down, cuff her, and bring her back. Hunted down, Oney sent word that if guaranteed freedom, she would return out of affection for the Washington family. The First Family refused, fearing that rewarding her flight from slavery with a grant of freedom would set a dangerous precedent among their several hundred slaves. At that, Oney Judge swore she "should rather suffer death than return to slavery." When Washington persisted, his agent in Portsmouth, New Hampshire, reported in September 1796 that "popular opinion here is in favor of universal freedom," which made it difficult for him to seize and shackle Oney. Two years later, the Washington family was still trying to snag Martha's ingrate chambermaid by sending George's nephew, Burwell Bassett, after her. The Washingtons conducted all their attempts to capture her surreptitiously because they wanted no public knowledge, in the middle of the new nation's fierce debates over the *liberté, egalité,* and *fraternité* of the French Revolution, about their attempts to quash Oney's quest for freedom. Not until Washington's death in 1799 could Oney feel some measure of safety. By now she was married to a man named Staines, had a baby, and had put roots down in New Hampshire, where she lived out her life, poor but free.[38]

Just as the site on which the new Liberty Bell Pavilion was rising had been a stage for a personal declaration of independence by a twenty-two-year-old enslaved woman, it became so again nine months after her escape, just as the Washingtons were leaving Philadelphia for good to take up life as private citizens on their beloved Mount Vernon plantation. To the Washingtons, their prize cook, Hercules, enjoyed a special status in the executive mansion, one that in their view should have made him immune to the fever for freedom. Celebrated for being "as highly accomplished and proficient in the culinary art as could be found in the United States," the handsome, well-appointed chef had prepared countless state dinners over the ten years he had been with them, as well as the daily family meals.[39] But Hercules, like Oney Judge, had mingled with numerous free black Philadelphians, who by this time had built two churches of their own, started schools and mutual aid societies, carved out niches in the urban economy, purchased homes, and begun mounting attacks on the fortress of slavery.[40]

Hercules slipped away from the President's House, melted into the countryside, reached New York, and outwitted all of Washington's attempts to capture him. When a visitor to Mount Vernon asked Hercules's six-year-old daughter whether she was brokenhearted at the prospect of never seeing her father again, she replied, "Oh sir! I am very glad because he is free now." All that Washington had feared since first arriving in Philadelphia was being realized. Writing his secretary Tobias Lear in 1791, he opined that he did not think his slaves "would be benefited" by achieving freedom, "yet the idea of freedom might be too great a temptation to resist," and breathing the free air of Philadelphia, where the pesky Quakers were helping enslaved Pennsylvanians break their shackles, might "make them insolent in a state of slavery." Near the end of his presidency, and still grating at Oney Judge's flight, he ordered his secretary to get his slaves out of Philadelphia and back to Mount Vernon. "I wish to have it accomplished under a pretext that may deceive both them and the public," he wrote. "I request that these sentiments and this advice may be known to none but yourself and Mrs. Washington."[41]

In the fall of 2002, while articles, op-ed essays, editorials, and letters to the editor continued to pepper Philadelphia newspapers,[42] INHP and Eastern regional staffers agreed that the executive mansion and the people who had lived and worked there deserved commemoration in the wide space over which visitors would walk to enter the new Liberty Bell Pavilion. Representing the Ad Hoc Historians, noted Philadelphia historian Stephanie Wolf presented three important themes that INHP had earlier dismissed as a diversion from the Liberty Bell focus and a potential source of confusion: treating the executive branch of government that has always been missing in the Independence Mall interpretations, since park rangers had no physical representation around which to work this story; interpreting the President's House as home and office of Washington and Adams—one a slave owner, the other a protoabolitionist—as a way of expressing the split that runs through the nation's history; and focusing on the diverse people who lived and worked at this site or in neighboring households. By late summer, INHP had commissioned two design firms—Olin Partnership of Philadelphia and Vincent Ciulla Design of Brooklyn—to work on a plan. On January 15, 2003, the Park Service unveiled plans for the outside exhibits. They included most of what the Ad Hoc Historians and other community organizations had asked for: passages condemning slavery that were stricken from drafts of the Declaration of Independence, to be inscribed on the front wall of the Visitor Center (which faces the Liberty Bell site); physical representations of the President's House, such as a partial footprint of it, perhaps in slate; side walls detailing the presidencies of Washington and Adams; a curved black marble wall winding through the spacious approach to the pavilion, with stories of the free, unfree, and partially free people who labored there; the history of slavery in Philadelphia and in the nation at large; material on the emergence of the free black community in Philadelphia and the struggle to dismantle the house of slavery, represented by a breach in the wall through which the enslaved figuratively escaped; and, finally, large sculptures of Oney Judge and Hercules, twelve to sixteen feet high and visible from both inside and outside the Liberty Bell Pavilion, with a contemplative garden space as well as a third sculpture interpreting enslavement and emancipation. The sculptures, if effected, would be the first federal monuments to individual slaves. The Ad Hoc Historians viewed the design as innovative, exciting, and responsive to what they had urged. Michael Coard from the Avenging the Ancestors Coalition applauded the designs, predicting that "our little Black boys and girls [will] beam with pride when they walk through Independence Mall and witness the true history of America and their brave ancestors."[43]

However, at a tumultuous public meeting on January 14, 2003, held at the city's African American Museum, long-simmering resentments about INHP policies and procedures, particularly harbored by African American activists, showed that the controversy over the Liberty Bell Center and the site it occupies was not over. Calls for a new design involving African American planners and architects was one issue. More fundamental was how to raise about $3 million (supplementing $1.5 million promised by the city's mayor) to transform the area outside the pavilion into a contemplative and commemorative set of exhibits. The text panels that would explain the history of the President's House, the administrations of Washington and Adams, and the lives of those who served their presidencies remained to be written once a final plan was in place. The images, such as a reproduction of the painting of Hercules that has been uncovered in a Spanish museum, still needed to be selected.[44]

The arrival of a new INHP superintendent, Mary Bomar, on February 10, 2003, helped clear the air as soon as it became evident that she backed the efforts to interpret fully the President's House site and was determined to work cooperatively with interested citizens and the professional groups that had formed over the past year.[45] Though absorbed with security issues after September 11, which played havoc with the flow of visitors along Independence Mall, Bomar opened her door to parties in this dispute and participated vigorously in meetings and roundtable discussions. This led to a meeting on November 18, 2003, where scholars pored over primary evidence about Washington's residency at the Morris mansion and attempted to determine precisely where slaves and indentured servants had been housed. After nearly four months of e-mail discussion, including the emotionally freighted matter of whether "servants hall" or "slave quarters" should be the operative term, INHP released a Consensus Document on these controverted issues.[46] Where each slave and servant put his or her head down at night is an issue about which architectural historians have passionate arguments, but far more important for rangers and historians was agreement that at various locations of the property—in the garret of the main house and in several outbuildings—scores of documented slaves and servants were part of the scene and therefore should be incorporated into the narratives told about the new nation's first White House.[47]

Almost a year later, on October 30, 2004, a high-spirited overflow crowd gathered at the Visitor Center to see what thirty-two months of contention, confrontation, and cooperation had accomplished. Supervisory ranger Joseph Becton opened the session with a PowerPoint presentation about the many lives of the house that had stood at 190 High Street. Six panelists, representing a spectrum of interested parties, then summarized the progress made and the issues still unresolved.[48] In a Philadelphia version of a New England town meeting, people from assorted backgrounds unburdened themselves of complaints, criticisms, and suggestions. Nobody present thought it was a tame affair. Some activists thought that INHP was still dragging its feet on the matter, but the Ad Hoc Historians believed that to have come so far was a clear victory for progressive public history. By the end of the day a firm if not quite stable consensus emerged, taking the form of a long-range and a short-range plan:

• Bomar would push ahead to obtain the $4.5 million needed to redesign and build the sculptures, walls, plaques, and other features outside the Liberty Bell Center and would urge the NPS regional director to give priority to this project. Choosing a new design firm would go forward.

• INHP agreed to mark the site, only a few feet from the door through which visitors will pass to enter the Liberty Bell Center, where Washington's stable hands (both white servants and black slaves) were housed. By marking the place where slaves worked and resided, visitors, remarked Michael Coard, would metaphorically "pass from the hell of slavery into the heaven of liberty."

• While awaiting the completion of the site, INHP would add two wayside panels providing temporary interpretation of the President's House site, produce a leaflet interpreting the site for visitors, schedule the PowerPoint presentation of the President's House for visitors inside the Liberty Bell Center, and offer first-person interpretations of Oney Judge Staines and Hercules.

This much agreed upon, the finish line was within view. In the prolonged Liberty Bell contretemps, two matters seem especially salient to the practice of public history as it pertains to race and slavery. First, the media—newspapers, radio, and television—were essential in bringing about a major overhaul of INHP's plans for the Liberty Bell Center. The *Philadelphia Inquirer* and other area newspapers ran nearly two hundred stories, editorials, op-ed essays, and letters to the editors, while WHYY, Philadelphia's National Public Radio station, interviewed many of the contestants in this battle. Overwhelmingly, the media supported the efforts of the Ad Hoc Historians, Avenging the Ancestors, the Independence Hall Association, and other groups in urging a drastic rethinking of the narrow and unflinchingly heroic rendering of the Liberty Bell story and the near-exclusion of the rich African American history intimately connected to the site. Once engaged by the media, the public strongly backed the view that not to treat the conjunction of freedom and slavery in the historic heart of old Philadelphia and the nation's capital in the 1790s, and not to bring forward the stories of African Americans, indentured servants, women, and others struggling to find their place under the canopy of freedom and equal rights, ignored the wishes of the city's large African American population, the views of professional historians and institutional leaders, and the Park Service's own self-defined civic responsibilities. Some public squabbles waste time and bring about no lasting good. But this controversy, acrid at first, moved from confrontation to edgy cooperation and produced results that promise to please most Philadelphians, most visitors to Independence National Historical Park, and most National Park Service people. The outcome of this controversy may provide an example of how academic historians, the public, and government custodians of iconic sites can work together for the benefit of all.

Second, the Liberty Bell controversy laid bare the struggles within the National Park Service to redefine its mission in the new millennium. Largely hidden from public view, the backdrop of the Liberty Bell controversy was a tension between local Park Service sites, whose leaders have plenty of muscle to protect their own turf, and broader attempts by Park Service leaders, who operate at the regional and national levels, to shepherd the NPS toward a terrain where they practice history in a more inclusive and mature way in the twenty-first century. In a step emblematic of its leaders' broader vision, the Park Service signed a cooperative agreement in 1995 with the Organization of American Historians whereby individual sites could draw on professional historians to deepen and gain new insights on their planned interpretations. Specifically, the Park Service pledged itself to address previously neglected and controversial topics including the history of slavery and Native American history.[49] Then in late 1999, the northeast region of NPS, to which INHP reports, became a founding member of the International Coalition of Historic Sites of Conscience. Further bulwarking this commitment was a report of the National Park System Advisory Board in 2001, which asserted that "in many ways the National Park Service is our nation's Department of Heritage" and that its several hundred sites "should be not just recreational destinations, but springboards for personal journeys, of intellectual and cultural enrichment," which could be nurtured only by ensuring "that the American story is told faithfully, completely, and accurately."[50] In December 2001, only a month before the Liberty Bell controversy erupted, northeast regional director Marie Rust launched the Civic Engagement Initiative. From a meeting in New York City came a report that quoted the advisory committee's advice that "in a democratic society such as ours, it is important to understand the journey of liberty and justice, together with the economic, social, religious, and other forces that barred or opened the ways for our ancestors, and the distances yet to be covered."[51]

That was the picture at the national and regional level. But at the local level, the INHP leadership team largely ignored collaborative interpretive planning with scholars and the public (as well as with some of its own historical researchers and park rangers). We may never know exactly why, but it can be surmised that the INHP leadership team regarded the new thinking of the Park Service, particularly the Civic Engagement Initiative, as a migraine in the making. As former INHP staffer Jill Ogline puts it, "creating dissonance for visitors is the park's greatest fear"—a dissonance that the superintendent believed would be the result of introducing freedom's complex and symbiotic embrace of slavery at the Liberty Bell site, both inside and outside the center. "Not only acknowledging the Liberty Bell's proximity to a site upon which enslaved people toiled, but actually integrating that story of enslavement into the bell's narrative of freedom might possibly be the greatest dissonance ever to be interpreted at a national historic site," writes Ogline.[52] Yet dissonance is not synonymous with dissatisfaction, alienation, or anger. At the national and regional levels, "an intellectually unsettled visitor" was what civic engagement proponents hoped for, a sign of a citizen in a mature democracy who would not hate the Park Service but thank its rangers for telling hidden stories, uncovering buried ironies and paradoxes, and provoking thought.[53] At the local level, bringing the train back to the station for overhaul seemed nightmarish. Surely, it seemed, this would delay the opening of the Liberty Bell Center and invite further controversy. But because of the way the train was freighted, controversy was all but certain.

With the near-consensus on the Liberty Bell exhibits, everyone involved in public history can take satisfaction in a matter of great importance: that it is not unhealthy in a democracy that a tension between the commemorative voice and the historical voice should manifest itself in public history sites and that the National Park Service can serve American democracy best if its sites become forums, as Edward Linenthal has said, where "diverse interpretations of complex historical events can be aired or taken home to contemplate."[54] What started out as a nasty fight turned into a cooperative effort to revamp and extend a narrow interpretive plan. The struggle was not between historians and the National Park Service but between a local Park Service leadership team and a combination of historians, community activists, journalists, and the Park Service's chief historian. After months of resisting, the plan's originators came to understand that they were much in the minority and that it was best to move ahead with what David Hollenberg now describes as a "radically transformed" plan. It probably helped that the historians' group tried not to personalize the argument or ascribe dark motives to anyone involved. Rather, the Ad Hoc Historians argued that the Park Service staffers had underestimated the public's capacity for grasping complex issues and— most of all—did not follow the Park Service's own dictates in the form of the General Management Plan, which calls for close collaboration with historians and other scholars, as well as the public, in arriving at a final exhibition plan.

In the heat of the National History Standards controversy in 1995, historian Kenneth Moynihan asked whether the scholars' history can be the public's history. He hoped that Americans were weaning themselves from a "just-get-the-facts-straight history" and reaching an understanding that history is "an ongoing conversation that yields not final truths but an endless succession of discoveries that change our understanding not only of the past but of ourselves and of the times we live in." Ten years later, this appears to be the case in this local situation. The Liberty Bell Center opened on September 12, 2003, and an appropriation of $3.7 million has been dedicated to exhibition outside the Liberty Bell Pavilion. When the statues to Oney Judge and Hercules are unveiled on July 4, 2007, the old cracked bell will toll symbolically for all the people, and the scholars' history will become the public's history.

UNITED STATES SLAVE TRADE.
1830.

The international slave trade was a major aspect of Rhode Island's economy, as the internal slave trade was for Kentucky. This 1830 abolitionist image with the U.S. Capitol in the background was entitled "United States Slave Trade," and emphasized the contradiction between America's commitment to freedom and the role of the slave trade in the nation's formation. COURTESY OF THE HISTORICAL SOCIETY OF PENNSYLVANIA

6

Recovering (from) Slavery:

Four Struggles to Tell the Truth

Joanne Melish

An old white woman recalled exactly
How Nat crept down the steps, axe in his hand,
After murdering a woman and child in bed,
"Right in this here house at the head of these stairs"
(In a house built long after Nat was dead).

> —From Sterling A. Brown,
> "Remembering Nat Turner"

In 1970, Vincent Harding wrote that the emphasis of black history must be on "exposure, disclosure, and reinterpretation of the entire American past."[1] At the beginning of a new century, many historic sites still do not offer fully integrated histories. This is especially true where the missing part of the story concerns slavery, although other intersections of the histories of people of color with those of whites are also left out or oddly marginalized in many cases. But integrating the story is a complicated problem. Persuading administrative, curatorial and educational staffs to recast their interpretations to incorporate the lives of slaves and free people of color is one issue; getting trustees, members, subscribers, and especially donors to buy into new interpretations that not only challenge the celebratory narratives of "their" founders and patriots but also move the objects and documents many of them have donated off center stage is another. A third challenge is retraining so-called front-line staff—docents—to tell a new story that is less celebratory (of whites), introduces more "negative" aspects of the people and events at the center of the site's history (involvement in slave trading, use of enslaved labor), and squarely faces that most uncomfortable of American subjects, race.[2]

But the issue is more complicated even than this. Resistance takes many forms and sometimes emerges from unanticipated directions. The problem is not merely to uncover hidden events and perspectives or fill in the silences—like nature, history too abhors a vacuum. In the absence of balanced accounts in which the voices of all actors can be heard, the marginalized often devise counternarratives to explain the disjunction between their lives and celebratory official accounts. Fashioned by political logic out of partial information and deep, well-founded suspicion, these counternarratives can be as difficult to dislodge as the celebratory versions they seek to undermine. Thus it is that efforts to revise an interpretation in the interests of achieving a more textured and balanced account can be denounced simultaneously for desecrating hallowed traditions and for covering up "the real truth."

Then too, because effacing the history of bondage was not always a tidy process of blotting out a single story, restoring it is not always about recovering one story, either. Sometimes the obliteration of the history of slavery has entailed masking some elements and highlighting others in successive historical moments to conform to changing ideologies and interests, in language expressive of those ideologies and interests, until finally the whole of the original story has become obscured. Excavating such history involves uncovering these successive layers of language and meaning, sometimes in bits and pieces over a long period of time. Interpreting the history of a particular place or event involving groups with different social identities can be tricky when the groups are invested in the language and meaning of the site as reflected in two different layers of interpretation. In such cases, acknowledging the past presents the problem of reconciling dissonant but fully developed interpretations.

The emergence of an aggressive reparations movement has complicated the picture still further. On one hand, making a full acknowledgment of the significance of slavery and the degree to which nearly every region settled before 1865 was committed to it and benefited from it—simply putting slavery into the story—*is* a form of reparations. Many African Americans argue that acknowledgment is indeed the single most important reparative gesture the U.S. government and other institutions can make. But many institutions as well as individuals whose histories connect them with slave trading and slaveholding fear that to acknowledge involvement is to court litigation. Hence at this juncture we encounter a paradox: the reparations movement has both stimulated public interest in slavery and sealed off historical resources that would flesh out the story.

Exposure and disclosure of matters associated with slavery seem especially contentious in two regions. In New England, many public history sites struggle to reconcile the region's fame as the birthplace of immediate abolitionism and its leadership role in the successful Civil War assault on the southern slave power with two centuries of their own involvement with slavery and especially the slave trade. The split personalities of the so-called border states—slave states that remained formally loyal to the Union—makes the acknowledgment of the role of slaves and slaveholding a difficult issue for many public history sites there as well.

I would like to examine the very recent efforts of four institutions to reconnect the histories they celebrate with those of people of color, slavery, and the slave trade in their public scripts. Two are house museums, one in New England and one in Kentucky; one is an elite private New England university with historical connections to the slave trade; and one is a commemorative park, also in New England. In three of these contexts I have been directly involved in one way or another in the process of revising the official story. I became aware of the ongoing struggle over meaning and representation with regard to the fourth site through my involvement in other related public history projects. Each of these cases illuminates a different set of unintended consequences of ignoring, suppressing, or attempting to contain the narratives of slavery and the complex negotiations required to reconstruct these narratives and decipher their tangled legacies of racial meaning.

HEROES AND VILLAINS
AT THE JOHN BROWN HOUSE

The John Brown House on the historic East Side of Providence, Rhode Island, was built in 1786 by merchant, patriot, and slave trader John

Brown and has been owned and operated as a house museum by the Rhode Island Historical Society since 1941. The Browns were prominent merchants and manufacturers in Providence beginning in the 1720s.

The Browns also were involved in the slave trade. Family members invested in two slaving voyages in 1736 and 1759, and John Brown and his three brothers, as Nicholas Brown and Company, attempted a third in 1764–65. After that, the company dissolved, and only John remained in the trade, investing in several additional voyages. John Brown was the first Rhode Islander tried for violating the 1794 federal Slave Trade Act, which made outfitting slavers in American ports illegal; he had been brought to trial by the Providence Society for Promoting the Abolition of Slavery, organized by his brother Moses, a Quaker. John Brown was one of only five members of the U.S. House of Representatives who voted against expanding the 1794 statute, and in 1801 he strongly supported the creation of a separate customs district for Bristol, Rhode Island, home port of Rhode Island's most notorious slave trader, Brown's friend James D'Wolf. After the slave trade closed, Brown continued to trade with the West Indies, Suriname, Virginia, the Carolinas, and Europe, became more widely involved in banking and insurance, began manufacturing rum and gin, and entered the China trade. The house he built on the aptly named Power Street in 1786 is promoted by the Rhode Island Historical Society with a quote from John Quincy Adams pronouncing it "the most magnificent and elegant private mansion that I have seen on this continent."[3]

Since 1941, the Rhode Island Historical Society has maintained the house as a decorative arts museum, reflecting the aesthetic approach to objects with historical significance and the passion for high-style furnishings pioneered by well-known collectors such as Marsden Perry, who owned the house and used it as a showcase for his collections in the early twentieth century. Objects have remained the focus of the tours today; docents explain where the furnishings came from, what they cost, and how they were used. They also talk about the restoration of the house. The ten-minute video shown at the outset of each tour has a different orientation, placing John Brown in historical context and describing his career as a merchant, banker, and patriot (he was among the group who sank the British revenue cutter *Gaspee* in 1772). Brown's involvement in the slave trade is discussed briefly in the video, but the standard tour never mentioned either the slave trade or Brown's personal ownership of slaves until the issue was raised by a coalition of community leaders.

The shot across the bow on behalf of full disclosure with respect to John Brown and slavery was an October 9, 2001, letter to the acting director and board of the Rhode Island Historical Society from Carolyn Fleur-Lobban, professor of anthropology at Rhode Island College, and eight other educators and community and church leaders, including Joaquina Bela Teixeira, executive director of the Rhode Island Black Heritage Society. They complained that "the telling of the full, complex story of the Brown family, as well as other Rhode Island families, regarding slavery is inadequate at the present moment." In the tour of the museum and its promotional brochure, they argued, "the fact of the Brown family's significant involvement in slaving, his owning and operating of slave ships throughout his merchant years, and that he personally owned slaves five of whom worked in this house is omitted," while the promotional brochure for the house museum refers to his "long career as an entrepreneur, patriot, privateer, and China Trade merchant" without reference to "the Brown family's significant involvement in slaving." The letter concluded by noting, "At a time when the issue of slavery and reparations is before us as a nation, it is the responsibility of Museums and Historical Societies to help the public to know the truth and the full story of America." As "custodians of this historical record," the Historical Society was asked "to take appropriate action to begin to remedy this situation by consulting with knowledgeable local scholars and educators." In response, the Historical Society agreed to convene a committee, awkwardly named the Committee to Review All Aspects of the Content and Presentation of the John Brown House Tour, to develop a plan to incorporate John Brown's role as a slave trader into the interpretation of the house.

Professor Fleur-Lobban invited the signatories to the original letter and other educators, local African American community leaders, and students to be members of the committee. Michael Gerhardt, acting director of the Historical Society, appointed a matching contingent, including the executive director of the Rhode Island Historical Preservation and Heritage Commission (a Historical Society board member), several members of the staff, and two historians, of whom I was one. The acting director asked the board chair, Ray Rickman, to chair the committee. This placed Rickman, a very-high-profile African American who had previously served as a state representative, assistant secretary of state, executive director of the Providence Human Relations Commission, and president of the local chapter of the ACLU, and who was also a respected authority on local black history, in a delicate position as the only African American in the contingent appointed by the Historical Society and, as board chair, in some sense its defender.

The potential for contentious debate was heightened by the fact that two of the academics on opposing sides of the invitation process had a long history of sparring over the importance of slavery in Rhode Island history. One, a signatory to the original letter of complaint, was Richard Lobban, also a Rhode Island College anthropologist and Fleur-Lobban's husband, who was vice president of the board of the Rhode Island Black Heritage Society. Lobban had become well known in recent years as an outspoken advocate for public recognition of the significance of the slave trade and slavery in Rhode Island history, and especially John Brown's role in it, in a variety of public venues. The other was J. Stanley Lemons, a Rhode Island College historian and member of the Historical Society board who also lectured and published on Rhode Island slavery. His work placed the slave trade and slavery within the wider commercial and manufacturing interests of Rhode Island and emphasized the widespread acceptability of both slave trading and slavery in their own historical moment, as well as Rhode Island's pioneering role in ending both the trade and slavery itself. Lobban saw Lemons as an apologist for slavery; Lemons saw Lobban as an ahistorical and factually inaccurate zealot. As a historian who also lectured in public venues about the significance of slavery, I was seen as, and indeed was, a sort of centrist in this debate—that is, very supportive of the need to expand the Historical Society's interpretative attention to slavery without necessarily being in agreement with the emphasis of Lobban's arguments.

The first meeting of the newly formed committee in November 2001 was devoted to statements of interests and positions by all parties present. Carolyn Fleur-Lobban reiterated her group's complaint that slave trading was not discussed by docents conducting tours of the John Brown House and received only passing reference in the video on Brown's life that begins each tour. The museum staff explained the steps already taken to educate docents about John Brown's role in the slave trade, efforts that included docent training sessions conducted by Stan Lemons. Discussion became heated at times. Richard Lobban repeatedly insisted that the Historical Society needed to acknowledge slave trading and slaveholding as central features of John Brown's life, and thus integral to the interpretation of the house, while Lemons continued to insist that slave trading was a relatively minor aspect of John Brown's life, contributed little to his fortune compared to his other manufacturing and commercial interests, and thus could not be represented as central to the house interpretation.

The discussion also revealed other difficulties in embedding the subject of slavery in the house tour regardless of the consensus reached on its actual significance to John Brown and his house. The interpretation of the John Brown House takes a decorative arts approach, focusing on the assemblage of objects displayed in the house and their connections to the Brown family; in the absence of artifacts of slavery and the slave trade, the staff felt there was no point in the tour at which docents were provided with a logical prompt for a discussion of these matters. The curator insisted that the museum could not display items not authentically connected specifically to John Brown and his family or include in its tours general information not directly associated with the house itself and the items displayed in it within the present interpretive focus of the museum. But recommending a major shift in emphasis toward the house as the locus of a comprehensive exploration of John Brown's world was obviously beyond the scope of the committee. It also became clear that the docents—all volunteers, mostly older and retired women—were uncomfortable with the topics of slavery and slave trading under any circumstances. More training on the specific history of John Brown's connections to slavery and the slave trade would not necessarily enable docents to bring them up any more easily "out of the blue."

The first meeting yielded sixteen overlapping recommendations. These included placing documents and artifacts connected to the slave trade in the house and training the docents to use them as focal points for talking about slavery and the slave trade on the tours; creating a free-standing brochure focused specifically on John Brown and slavery; and setting a definite date for the placement of a bronze plaque on the house, describing John Brown's involvement in the slave trade and identifying the house as an African American historic site. The plaque already existed, one of a series cast several years before as part of a Black History Trail project undertaken by the Rhode Island Black Heritage Society. It was agreed that the committee would draft the brochure, while the Historical Society staff would revise the script and organize an event to celebrate the marker placement.

Beginning in December 2001, the committee worked steadily on the text for the brochure throughout the spring and early summer of 2002. The academics produced alternative drafts and generally dominated the discussions, and meetings were often rancorous. The deceptively simple source of dispute was this: was John Brown a man of a time and place in which slave trading and slaveholding, while horrific in present-day terms, were commonplace and accepted—that is, was he an exemplar of a culpable society? Or was he individually and uniquely culpable, a stubbornly persistent participant in and advocate for an activity his larger society was coming to know as morally reprehensible? To some extent, the argument may have been shaped by the national reparations debate, with its focus on identifiable institutions and individuals with demonstrable legal liability, although the issue of reparations was never mentioned in any of the actual discussions. It also seemed to break down along disciplinary lines: the two anthropologists saw John Brown's immediate environment—his brother's Quaker convictions and persistent efforts through the Abolition Society to thwart John's slave-trading activities—as an important justification for indicting Brown's actions. The two historians saw the Abolition Society and Quaker activism in Rhode Island in the Revolutionary period as admirable but still relatively unusual and found Brown's wider involvement in manufacturing items used in the slave trade (spermacetti candles, rope, iron), as well as his extensive trade in tobacco, rum, and Dutch bills of exchange with Suriname and other slave-based economies, to be at least as important in linking him to slaving as his personal investment in six slaving voyages and his personal ownership of slaves. To the historians, such activities made Brown typical of a period in which the involvement of the society as a whole in slaving and slaveholding was the important story to be told at the John Brown House.

In other words, the debate at the John Brown House was over the degree to which a virtual silence about slave trading should be replaced with a new interpretation that made slave trading its focal point and Brown himself a major slave trader. Adding fuel to this fire, in February 2002, shortly after the committee began its work, the *Providence Journal,* as part of its annual observance of Black History Month, published an article headed "Slavery in R.I.: Shameful Origin, Heroic Opposition" that pointed to "the Bristol DeWolfs and the Providence Browns" as having "made their fortunes from the slave trade."[4] The claim was undeniable with respect to the D'Wolfs, but it considerably overstated the role of the slave trade in the Browns' amassing of wealth.

Meanwhile, the Historical Society formally installed the bronze plaque describing John Brown as a slave trader, cast so many years before by the Rhode Island Black Heritage Society, on the wall outside the John Brown House. The plaque was unveiled on August 1, 2002, at a moving ceremony that included West African traditional libations and drumming and the recitation of Rhode Island slave names. The ceremony had been scheduled to coincide with the anniversary of emancipation in the British West Indies on August 1, 1834. The plaque reads, "John Brown House: The home of John Brown, reflecting his wealth and position gained from his lucrative career as a slave trader, privateer, China trade merchant and patriot." The text substitutes "slave trader" for "entrepreneur" in a phrase otherwise identical to the one used in earlier Historical Society literature about the John Brown House.

The plaque was installed just as the committee, after much word-by-word rewriting and sporadic wrangling, came to a final agreement on the draft text of the brochure. But newspaper coverage of the installation ceremony sparked new controversy between Lobban and Lemons. In an article the day of the event, the *Providence Journal* noted that "historian Richard Lobban and other members of the Rhode Island Black Heritage Society do not mince words in describing it. 'This is the house that slavery built . . . that's our mantra.' "[5] In response, Lemons wrote an editorial column published eleven days later entitled "John Brown House Is *Not* 'House That Slavery Built.' " He noted, "I wish the *Journal* had talked to a real historian before it ran the article," and argued that "the comments by my colleague at Rhode Island College, anthropology Prof. Richard Lobban, on the role of the slave trade in building Brown's wealth were mostly wrong." He went on to describe the special committee convened "to consider how the RIHS might recast its interpretation," and noted that "Professor Lobban and I were both members of that committee, which has since drafted a pamphlet that fairly presents both Rhode Island's place in the slave trade and John Brown's part in it."[6] Norman Fiering, director and librarian of the John Carter Brown Library at Brown University, specializing in materials associated with the exploration and settlement of the Americas before 1825, also responded to Lobban's editorial, "Acknowledgement of 'House That Slavery Built,'" and the earlier Scott MacKay article, "Shameful Origin, Heroic Opposition." In a letter to the editor headed "Sloppy Versions of History on Brown, Slavery," Fiering insisted that the Browns were "bit players, at worst, and in fact better than most, in the huge international (and universally accepted) crime and tragedy of the African slave trade over three centuries." Fiering called John Brown's ardent defense of the trade in 1786 a "disgracefully retrograde, but hardly exceptional, attitude for the time." Lobban, angered by Lemons's "snide comment" implying that Lobban was not a "real historian," responded in turn in *The Anchor*, the Rhode Island College student newspaper, in an article entitled "The Struggle for the Truth About Rhode Island, John Brown, and the Slave Trade":

> Truth [about slavery in Rhode Island] goes through various stages. First it is denied; secondly it is ridiculed or declared as irrelevant, thirdly it is violently opposed and the "messenger is killed" and fourthly it is accepted as being self-evident. Most Rhode Islanders, myself, and the standard historians of this topic including William G. MacLaughlin [*sic*], Robert J. Cottrol, Barbara Mills, Edgar J. McManus, Martin J. Blatt and David Roediger, Leon Litwack, and Jay Coughtry have long ago shown the very important role of Rhode Island in the maritime slave trade. For all of them and myself included we are already at stage four. But two Rhode Islanders, Professor Norman Fiering at Brown University and Professor Stanley Lemons at Rhode Island College, are still struggling to break out of stage one while resisting the move to stage two.[7]

Lobban went on to explain the factors that contributed to his understanding that the John Brown House should be considered to have been "built by slavery." He noted that "John Brown came from a prominent slave trading family from which he got his family wealth in the first place." Literally, that would suggest that the family had been involved "prominently" in slave trading before John himself became involved, whereas only one of the Brown family's slaving voyages—and that a modestly successful one—predated John's involvement, along with various family members. Probably Lobban meant something else, suggested in the paragraphs that followed his initial assertion: that it was the participation of the Browns in banking, manufacturing, shipping, sugar production, and other forms of commerce and industry inextricably bound up with the slave trade that made John Brown's house the "house that slavery built." Lobban concluded that "it is these two individuals themselves who are truly guilty of 'sloppy' history. Indeed they have committed worse by resting on their positions and prestige to falsify history to serve their own bizarre interests of defending the notorious slave trader, law breaker, and official pirate, John Brown."[8]

Lemons, Fiering, and Lobban all saw Brown's personal involvement in slave trading and his persistent defense of it as reprehensible; all three understood how Brown's other income-generating activities were also embedded in a transatlantic commercial world inseparable from—indeed, dependent on—the slave trade and slavery. But for Lobban, participation in these other activities had an aggregative effect, deepening Brown's personal moral accountability; for Lemons and Fiering, it reduced it by making him a man of his time.

A year after the installation of the plaque, the Rhode Island Historical Society published the beautifully illustrated and printed brochure. Its title—*Rhode Island and the African Slave Trade: John Brown and the Colonial Economy of Slavery*—mirrors the careful placement in the text itself of Brown within the larger context of a slaveholding and trading economy, but it also clearly suggests Brown's complicity. The unveiling of the brochure, like the unveiling of the plaque, was a ceremonial event that was hosted by the Historical Society, the Rhode Island Black Heritage Society, and the Providence Human Relations Commission and was scheduled to commemorate the fortieth anniversary of the 1963 civil rights march on Washington.

A final factor to be taken into account in considering the expanded role for slavery in the public narrative of John Brown and his house, a result achieved with so much controversy, is the mythology about those connections that had grown up in the absence of full disclosure at the John Brown House and other public venues. In Providence's several communities of color, "everybody knows" that there were tunnels under the hill rising from the wharfs on the waterfront in the commercial center of the city to the residential East Side of Providence near John Brown's house, and "everybody knows" that John Brown was the biggest slave trader and slaveholder in Providence, a man who had iron rings embedded in the basement walls of his house at 52 Power Street, where he held slaves captive for sale. In fact, a man named Cyprian Sterry actually sent out the largest number of slaving voyages of any Providence slave trader, while James and John D'Wolf of Bristol were the largest traders in Rhode Island. Many Providence residents held more slaves than John Brown.[9] And while there are indeed tunnels connecting the old wharf area of Canal Street with the East Side, there is no evidence that these had anything to do with slaving, a legal enterprise—slaves could be marched openly through the streets. Finally, there is no evidence, and no reason, that John Brown ever had slave manacles in the basement of his 1786 house.

In the absence of readily available public information on the actual role of slave trading and slaveholding in Rhode Island, however, this mythology developed a death grip on the public imagination. In February 2004, during the question-and-answer period following one public reading of a play entitled *Plantation Complex* about Rhode Island slave trading and slavery, an elderly black man in the audience objected to the amount of attention that James D'Wolf had received as a slave trader in the script.[10] He got up and walked out, loudly insisting, "John Brown was the biggest slave trader and slave holder in Rhode Island. Yes he was! He was! You can't say no different!"

CONTAINING THE STORY OF SLAVERY: MY OLD KENTUCKY HOME

While the controversy at the John Brown House resulted in an effort to integrate information about his slave trading into the tours widely, cued by objects and documents strategically placed throughout the house, elsewhere the histories of slaves and free blacks often seem to get confined to narrowly defined "appropriate" spaces. Even at the John Brown House, the publication of a separate brochure on Brown's connections with the slave trade could have been interpreted in this way if it were not part of a larger, clearly integrative effort to restructure the tours.[11]

The containment strategy seems closely linked to the mechanics of denial. While New England would seem to be the quintessential "not here" region, a close second is the four border states that remained in the Union but continued to hold slaves. Of these, Kentucky seems the most New England–like in its peculiar relationship to its history of slavery. Kentucky was a Union state in which nearly 20 percent of the population— almost a quarter of a million people—were enslaved on the eve of the Civil War. Its border location and extensive trade with Ohio and other free states led Kentucky to lay claim to a myth of mild treatment, or "presumption of benignity," as Barbara Fields called it in her 1985 study of slavery in Maryland, another border state.[12] But after the war, an overpowering sense of loss and the presence of such a large number of blacks no longer "controlled" by slavery led many Kentuckians to adopt an ex post facto Confederate identity.

Present-day Kentucky, in other words, may be said to claim two incompatible histories, and this split personality seems to be manifested in an either/or choice for its historic sites. Some have pressed forward to give slavery a center-stage role. An example is Waveland, the estate developed by Daniel Boone Bryan (nephew of the frontiersman) and his son, the Web site of which promises guests that they will tour the "slave quarters" and "learn about slave life in Kentucky."[13] At other sites, a carefully contained and circumscribed story is just now breaching slavery's long-standing unmentionability.

My Old Kentucky Home is a mansion built in 1818 at Federal Hill, the 285-acre estate of judge and U.S. senator John Rowan, in Bardstown, Kentucky, and maintained as part of a state park. It is in a sense the official state symbol, depicted on the Kentucky quarter minted in 2001 and the inspiration for the state song written by Stephen Foster, a distant Rowan cousin. The last resident Rowan descendant sold the estate to the State of Kentucky in 1922, requesting that the property be maintained as a memorial to Stephen Foster.[14] The Web site that promotes the site touts its "large visitor center, family cemetery, garden, picnic area, and a replica of Judge Rowan's Law Office," "year-round 18-hole regulation golf course" with "pro shop and rentals," and "39-site campground."[15] Also present but unaccounted for is a slave cemetery with a monument that reads, "This memorial is dedicated to the faithful retainers of Judge John Rowan; immortalized in the songs of Stephen Collins Foster. Erected July 4, 1945 by the Honorable Order of Kentucky Colonels. 'Well done, good and faithful servant'—St. Matthew: 25:21." The cemetery contains the remains of an undetermined number of slaves—some or all of the thirty-three slaves who labored on the estate for John Rowan Sr. in 1830 (making him the second largest slave owner in Nelson County).[16]

Tours of the house have never mentioned slavery. Work done by "servants" might be mentioned once or twice, without further elaboration, but the presence of "Old Black Joe" on a souvenir postcard (local musician Lem Reed in costume, playing for the tourists in the 1950s) or the "darkies" in the original version of the song "My Old Kentucky Home" were never explained. But in the fall of 1999, a young docent, Eric Browning, who was also a student at that time at Elizabethtown Community College, became interested in the "hidden" history of Federal Hill when one of the instructors, Terri Stewart, began taking her African American studies classes to tour Federal Hill as an object lesson in the invisibility of slavery. She and another instructor, Beth Cahaney, told Eric he must stop calling the workers "servants" on his tours, because undoubtedly they had been slaves.

In the fall of 2002, Eric, who was by then a student at the University of Kentucky, began to research the history of slavery at Federal Hill and prepared an alternative tour script that would, in his words, "incorporate the experiences of slaves into the fabric of the tour and give them their rightful place in the story."[17] By the beginning of November 2002, he had located considerable documentation for the slaves enumerated above and incorporated it into a new tour script that made slaves and their labor an integral part of the story of Federal Hill.

The script introduced the subject of slaves in the first room on the tour, the parlor, calling them "the backbone of this and many antebellum homes in Kentucky. . . . They made all the bricks cut and hewed all the trees used in framing, and did all the labor." In the dining room, visitors were informed that "the slaves prepared all the meals"; in one bedroom, "the furniture was dusted and kept clean by the slaves"; in the other, "the slaves were the ones to cut, haul, and season the wood, and carry it up two flights of steps to the bedrooms . . . just to keep the fires burning"; in the nursery "children were kept on the third floor with a slave woman to care for them and serve as a wet-nurse"; in the children's room, for the "hip bath . . . the slaves pumped water from the well, heated it in the kitchen, carried it up two flights of stairs, and poured it in the bottom" and later would "drain the water."

Eric presented this script to Alice Willett Heaton, the park superintendent. She objected to one section Eric had written that would have had docents saying, "No matter how much we want to believe that a slave in one house, plantation, or state was treated better than those owned by neighbors, the chattel slavery system of the United States was a dehumanizing institution in which people of color were bought, sold, gambled, and bequeathed with no concern for those affected." She thought it was too negative, but she commended Eric's efforts in general and agreed to send his script to Brooks Howard, the assistant director of historic sites for the Kentucky Department of Parks.

Eric received no response for three months. Suspecting that Howard might not actually have received the script, Eric mailed her a second copy, enclosing a letter from me attesting to its historical accuracy. A month after that, Howard notified him that a meeting of Howard, Heaton, and Howard's superior, Edward Henson, director of historic sites, to which Eric was also invited, would be held on April 9 to discuss the script. He offered to bring me along, but Howard politely declined his suggestion that I be invited "for a scholar's point of view," noting that "we would prefer to keep this between ourselves; sometimes things get interpret[ed] in the wrong way when people not connected to Parks are brought into the discussion." [18]

At the April 9 meeting, Howard alone met with Eric. As he reported the meeting, she told him that while she and Henson both agreed that slavery needed to be interpreted at the site, it should not be mentioned in the parlor or "sprinkled throughout the Home." Instead, it should be limited to the dining room or hall because slaves had a "better connection" to those rooms. She also suggested that "slave bits wouldn't have to be told in every tour" and suggested Eric and other docents should "read the group and get a feel for what they want to hear" before introducing the subject. Howard pointed out that plans already existed to place an interpretive sign in the garden that would describe the slave cemetery and the slave cabins that had stood there at one time, to serve as a springboard for interpreting the slave experience at Federal Hill. However, no money was available to commission and install such a sign, so information on slaves' activities would have to be provided in the dining room. Finally, Howard insisted that she wanted the script to say something "positive" about slavery; Eric told her "there was no positive" and that to suggest that there was would be to sugarcoat the experience of enslavement. Eric noted in an e-mail to me that "Howard wants us to mention life in the quarters, how slaves were 'free to a certain extent' there, and that 'in some places the master had to ask permission to come in to the quarters or had to pay a fine if he didn't.' " He said that she also wanted to use the word *servant* as "an overarching word for servitude of any kind," but that he had told her "our focus is not the overarching aspect but the specific institution of slavery." Finally he indicated that "[s]he wants more research before we do any more." Eric felt that enough research had already been done; in the spirit of weary compromise, one imagines, he finally agreed to condense what he had into one explanatory paragraph that could be delivered in one room.[19] Howard concurred with this plan, and Eric revised and re-submitted the script.

The final revision, dated January 2004, was approved in August 2004. It leads visitors through the dining room by first explaining the family portraits, then describing the coin-silver forks, pitchers, and julep cups and the Limoges dinnerware. Finally, it points to the door leading outside to the kitchen. There

> the slaves prepared the meals. Like any other large estate owners of the early nineteenth century, the Rowans owned slaves. The slaves were the ones who built and maintained the home and land and tended to the needs and desires of their white owners and children.

The paragraph concludes by listing the numbers of slaves at the Rowan estate in ten-year increments through the antebellum years. This single reference contains all the information on the actual involvement of slaves in the lives and work of the Rowan household that visitors potentially receive.

Confined to the dining room (but present even there only by reference to another unseen, offstage location), slaves were nonetheless poised on the brink of making a reappearance on the margins at Federal Hill in the new, approved script. But the new script has yet to be implemented. The task of providing for docent retraining on slavery has been left to Eric Browning, now only a part-time employee at Federal Hill as he nears completion of his undergraduate degree and prepares to enter an M.A.T. program.

Eric is working on material for the docents, and he reports cautious optimism on another possible revision of the tour. After visitors receive a tour of the house, "there is talk of going out back with them to discuss kitchen, smokehouse, and added carriage house along with the garden. This will also allow for an opportunity to point at the slave cemetery while standing at the back of the garden . . . you know me, I'll be sure to tell people about the slave cemetery plaque" (the one that reads, "To the Faithful Retainers of JUDGE JOHN ROWAN").[20]

NATURALIZING REPARATIONS

Brown University is a different kind of institution struggling with the complex problem of telling the truth about slavery, involving the same family of Rhode Island slavers and abolitionists who built the John Brown House. Here the catalyst was the publication of David Horowitz's paid ad, "Ten Reasons Why Reparations for Slavery Is a Bad Idea— and Racist Too," in the March 13, 2001, edition of Brown's student news-paper, the *Brown Daily Herald,* and the struggle by the Coalition of Con-cerned Brown Students to get the *Herald* to provide a free advertising page for a student-written rebuttal and to contribute the money it had received from the Horowitz ad ($580) to Brown's Third World Center or a minority-run community-based organization.[21] When the editors re-fused both demands, all 4,600 copies of the March 16 edition of the *Herald* disappeared from distribution points around campus. National media attention provoked hate mail and racist messages to the university's Third World Center and Afro American Studies Program (now the Africana Studies Department).[22] It also led to a faculty forum and passionate, campus-wide discussions weighing competing commitments to free speech, responsible speech, and nonracist speech on campus. The article describing the incident in the next issue of the *Brown Alumni Magazine* included a prominent two-column sidebar headed "History Lesson: Did Brown Profit from Slavery?"[23]

The March incident at Brown focused attention on various aspects of the reparations debate across the state of Rhode Island.[24] At the university, it also sparked renewed student interest in the specific historical connec-tions between Brown and slavery. In a sort of preemptive public relations move, the university hired Ricardo Howell, an African American gradu-ate of Brown who was employed in the Office of Public Affairs and University Relations, to research and write an essay released as a special report in July 2001 entitled "Slavery, the Brown Family of Providence and Brown University."[25] For this piece, Howell interviewed several local historians, looked at the relevant secondary sources, and produced an essay that rehearsed many of the connections between the Browns and the University, and between slavery and the Browns.[26] These included the role of sometime slave trader John Brown as signatory to the original college charter, longtime treasurer, and contributor; the use of some slave labor by Nicholas Brown and Company in the construction of the College Edifice (now University Hall) in 1770; the abolitionism of Moses Brown and Nicholas Brown Jr.; and the renaming of the college in 1804 in honor of Nicholas Junior, a 1786 alumnus, after he contributed $5,000 to endow a professorship. (Howell missed the fact that funds to establish the college, originally Baptist, were solicited from prominent Baptists in Georgia and South Carolina, many of them substantial slaveholders.)[27] The release of the special report occasioned little comment in a summer month when there were almost no students on campus.

In that same month, the university trustees appointed a new president—Ruth Simmons, great-great-grandchild of slaves and the first African American to head an Ivy League university. While the slavery issue remained somewhat dormant at Brown during her first two years as president, Simmons must have been aware of the controversy sparked by the Horowitz ad. Undoubtedly she also knew of the essay, entitled "Yale, Slavery and Abolition," published by three Yale graduate students the month after her appointment, that examined Yale's connections to slavery. That essay had prompted Yale to hold a major conference about a year later, cosponsored by its Gilder Lehrman Center for the Study of Slavery, Resistance, and Abolition and the Yale Law School, whose stated goal was "to examine, in moral, legal and religious terms, the contemporary implications of the history we in New Haven and at Yale have inherited, along with all other Americans."[28]

Perhaps Yale's initiative contributed to Simmons's thinking on this subject, perhaps not; nonetheless, in April 2003 Simmons appointed a faculty-student steering committee charged to "help the campus and the nation come to a better understanding of the complicated, controversial questions surrounding the issue of reparations for slavery." Simmons noted in her charge to the committee, "As you may know, Brown's history makes this an issue about which we have a special obligation and a special opportunity to provide thoughtful inquiry."[29]

The appointment of the University Steering Committee on Slavery and Justice, chaired by James T. Campbell, associate professor of Africana studies and history, was announced to the university community in a March 2004 letter from the Steering Committee.[30] The public learned of the committee's existence in a four-column article by Pam Belluck in the March 13 edition of the *New York Times* under the caption, "Brown U. to Examine Debt to Slave Trade." The university had decided to make the *Times* the exclusive source of information on the committee, as part of its effort to ensure that the project would be represented accurately as an intellectual project. To that end, President Simmons and committee chair Campbell gave extensive interviews to Belluck for the article.

But for Belluck, the significance of the project, or at least its newsworthiness, seemed to lie in the connection between the African American descent of its proponent and the prospect that it might result in some form of monetary compensation to others similarly descended. The article described the committee's work as "an unprecedented undertaking for a university: an exploration of reparations for slavery and specifically whether Brown should *pay reparations* or otherwise make amends for its past" (emphasis added). A midstory heading perfectly encapsulated what the *Times* thought was most significant about the university's initiative: "An African-American Initiates a Reparations Study."[31]

The article rehearsed the Horowitz controversy, gave a brief sketch of the history of Brown's founding and its most famous founders, and placed Brown's investigation in the broader context of the national reparations movement, emphasizing Simmons's personal stake in the subject. Belluck quoted her as saying, "What I'm trying to do, you see, in a country that wants to move on, I'm trying to understand as a descendant of slaves how to feel good about moving on." Asked if "her history will sway the inquiry's results," Simmons said, "I don't think there can be a person with a better background for dealing with this issue than me. If I have something to teach our students, if I have something to offer Brown, it's the fact that I am a descendant of slaves."

And Belluck represented both Simmons and Campbell as quite willing to discuss the committee's inquiry as more than a purely intellectual exercise. Paraphrasing Campbell, the article said that "if the committee did recommend that Brown make reparations, several remedies must be considered, for example providing scholarships or helping African students attend Brown." It concluded by noting that while Simmons would not reveal her opinion on reparations because she did not want to influence the committee, she was willing to say one thing: "If the committee comes back and says, 'Oh, it's been lovely and we've learned a lot,' but there's nothing in particular that they think Brown can do or should do, I will be very disappointed." [32]

It seems clear that what Simmons meant was that she was hoping to receive recommendations for new academic initiatives. Nonetheless, two days later, the *Providence Journal* reported the official announcement of the Slavery and Justice Committee's formation in an article headlined "Brown Begins 2-Year Scrutiny of Slavery and Reparations." [33] Local coverage actually had begun eight days before the *New York Times* piece was published, when Jennifer Jordan, a reporter for the *Providence Journal,* got wind of the committee's existence and broke the story in an article entitled "Should Brown Make Amends for Its Ties to the Slave Trade?" Brown officials, having granted interviews to the *Times* exclusively, had declined comment, and Jordan's piece merely noted that the committee had been created; the article referred for its facts to the *Brown Alumni Magazine* article published the summer before. [34] The second *Journal* article included more information and also announced the committee's first public event, a panel presentation entitled "Unearthing the Past: Brown University, the Brown Family and the Rhode Island Slave Trade" to be held on March 18. [35]

The *Times* article, bracketed by the two local stories, raised a storm of controversy. A day after the second article about the new initiative appeared in the *Journal,* but written in response to the earlier one, a letter to the editor from Conrad Leslie of Oxford, Ohio, noted that "two of my great-grandfathers were killed in the Civil War freeing Dr. Simmons's relatives. What kind of reparations are they allocating for me and each of the many members of our family?" [36] Ten days later, the *Journal* printed an editorial entitled "Simmons's Hypocritical Race Hustling," written by Thomas Sowell, a senior fellow at the Hoover Institution at Stanford University and a nationally syndicated conservative columnist who is an African American. His reading of the *Times* article, and especially Simmons's concluding comment, was that "this is to be no academic exercise of scholarly research. There is obviously supposed to be a pot of gold at the end of this rainbow." Sowell accused the current reparations movement of being "a fraud" for its "attempt to depict slavery as something uniquely done to blacks by whites," an attempt being made "for the same reason that Willie Sutton robbed banks: That's where the money is." He insisted that "only in America can guilt be turned into cash," but warned that "white guilt" is a "declining asset . . . Ruth Simmons may squeeze a few bucks out of Brown, but it is doubtful whether whatever good that does will balance the resentments and polarization it creates."[37]

But Simmons's initiative also received some strong support. In a *Journal* editorial entitled "Simmons Embraces Civic Responsibility," Frank Newman, a former president of the University of Rhode Island (then director of Brown's Future Project: Policy for Higher Education) argued that the "firestorm" raised by critics had "just plain missed the point." While they had assumed that the issue was whether Brown was "about to divert resources from its mission of education to the payment of reparations to the descendants of slaves," he asserted that the central question was really "Can American society discuss, in a thoughtful way, an issue as controversial as whether this university should acknowledge its connections to slavery, and what the implications of that acknowledgment should be?" He referred to "Simmons's careful effort to structure a useful discussion," and concluded, "I applaud President Simmons's multifaceted approach in leading Brown to not only academic greatness but civic responsibility."[38] John Tessitore, editor of *The Assault on Diversity: An Organized Challenge to Racial and Gender Justice,* called Sowell's editorial "a classic right-wing diatribe" and, while he found the issue of historical responsibility "admittedly debatable," said that that was the point, "debate being at the heart of the intellectual process that President Simmons clearly encourages."[39] William Atwater of Providence saw reparations in a similar way: "If reparations are to be made, they need to be made to change [racial] attitudes, to reclaim the conscience that America sold for slavery's profits."[40]

Simmons clarified her position in a letter to all members of the Brown community, including parents and alumni, about a month after the appearance of the *Times* article. In a substantial item headed "Committee on Slavery and Justice," Simmons explained, "Some of the national reports on this effort have been inaccurate, and I wanted to clarify the goals of this important venture." She stated emphatically, "The press surrounding the committee's work has often focused on the prospect of payments Brown might make for ties to slavery. This is not and never was the intention of this effort." She emphasized the work of the committee as a "study and educational program" and the committee's membership as including "scholars knowledgeable about various aspects of world history, with expertise in areas such as the Holocaust, civil rights, Japanese internment during World War II, apartheid in South Africa, and so on." She invited readers to "follow the progress of the committee's work as it invites speakers from around the world to cast light on this provocative subject," and she provided the committee's Web address.[41]

In the meantime, the Committee on Slavery and Justice put together just the kind of program of panel discussions, lectures, symposia, and other activities that Simmons envisioned.[42] Events planned through the spring of 2005 included examinations of various topics ranging from the issue of historical memory itself, to aspects of the local Rhode Island and New England histories of slavery and the slave trade, the movement for reconciliation in South Africa, and the Tulsa race riot of 1921. Other projects included involving students in research and curriculum development around these issues. In the fall of 2005, speakers and panels were slated to begin to historicize and then discuss the reparations issue itself from a variety of perspectives.

After the initial flurry, the "resentments and polarization" prophesied by Sowell failed to materialize in any substantial way. Some observers anticipated the possibility that alumni giving might plummet following Simmons's initiative, and a student calling on behalf of the Brown Annual Fund, the yearly alumni giving campaign, not long after the appearance of the *Times* article confided that several of the alums she had called had expressed initial reluctance to donate money to Brown that might simply be given away as a consequence of the initiative. However, Simmons's clarifying letter seems to have satisfied that concern; six months after the initiative was announced, the *Brown Daily Herald* reported that the 2003–04 Brown Annual Fund had received $22.9 million from a record 28,278 donors.[43] Audiences for the talks and panel discussions were sizable, and the tenor of the question-and-answer periods and the one "town meeting" session was remarkably civil and constructive. The chair of the committee hopes that Brown's inquiry into its own connections to slavery and the national problem of slavery, acknowledgment, justice, and reconciliation in comparative international context will serve as a model for other institutions of higher learning whose histories are similarly interwoven with slavery.[44]

Brown's experience may also serve as a cautionary tale for such institutions about the power of the language of litigation to complicate scholarly inquiry and limit the range of possible avenues in the quest for restorative justice. It also demonstrates the power of racialized assumptions to drive expectations in the face of all evidence to the contrary.

COLORING THE FIRST RHODE ISLAND REGIMENT

The power of racialized assumptions also became evident in a struggle over the cultural ownership of an important historical event commemorated at a site called Patriots' Park in Portsmouth, Rhode Island. Where Rhode Island Routes 24 and 114 on Aquidneck Island merge in Portsmouth, near Newport, the two roads form an island of land that sits in the heart of the site of one of the most famous battles of the American Revolution. There, on August 29, 1778, the first Continental regiment composed entirely of men of color, the First Rhode Island, repelled three waves of Hessian assault in what is called the Battle of Rhode Island.[45]

In 1974, when the National Historic Landmarks Program chose to focus on African American history as its theme study in preparation for the Bicentennial, it selected the battleground as a historic site and called it Patriots' Park.[46] Support for the park was mobilized by Fred Williamson, an African American who was then head of the Rhode Island Department of Community Affairs.[47] A small monument, a flagpole, and a boulder with a plaque commemorating the "Black Regiment" were placed in the park, and ceremonies commemorating the role of the Black Regiment in the Battle of Rhode Island are held every year at the site.[48] For the last ten years, however, Patriots' Park has been the site of a different battle, a struggle over identity and representation. Who exactly were the soldiers of the First Rhode Island? What does it mean to call this unit the "Black Regiment"?

In colonial Rhode Island, not only Africans were subject to enslavement. There and throughout southern New England, native peoples were enslaved or consigned to bound servitude for extended terms as a consequence of their defeats in the Pequot War and King Philip's War, and in bondage they lived, worked, and sometimes formed families with African slaves. Under these circumstances, by the 1770s, many slaves and indentured servants were of mixed Indian and African descent. Public officials still made some effort to distinguish people of different varieties of descent by employing the terms *African, Indian, mustee, mulatto, colored,* and *negro* selectively to individuals; as individuals, people of color themselves also manipulated these characterizations in their struggles to assert a measure of control over their lives. At the same time, by the beginning of the American Revolution, black, Indian, and mixed race slaves and servants as a group were often characterized as simply "black"— "blackened" by their common servitude—and this characterization was beginning to be applied by whites to people of color of all sorts whether or not they had been enslaved or indentured.

In addition, there were groups of Indian people living tribally— primarily Narragansett, but also Pequots, Nipmucs, and members of Pokanoket and other Wampanoag bands—in Rhode Island in the Revolutionary period. Narragansett oral tradition regards these people as having been tributary to the Narragansett and therefore Narragansett themselves, but other tribes and bands that have or are seeking federal recognition claim them as members of their own groups.[49] Other Narragansett had moved outside Rhode Island to other New England states and to New York but still identified themselves as Narragansett and were recognized as Narragansett by the tribe. By the 1770s, whites often referred to many of these people collectively as "black" or "coloured" as well.

In 1994, when the Federal Highway Administration made funding available for "enhancement projects" to improve or preserve historic sites associated with highways,[50] the Newport City Branch of the NAACP, serving as spokespersons for a less formally constituted Black Patriots Committee, together with the Rhode Island Black Heritage Society, spearheaded a proposal to improve the site.[51] In 1996, William F. Bundy, head of the Rhode Island Department of Transportation (RIDOT), an African American, and a former naval officer, selected the Patriots' Park Landscape Project as the state's first enhancement project under the transportation funding bill. Paul Gaines, an African American, chaired the Patriots' Park Improvement Project. Bradford Associates, the architectural firm of Derek Bradford, a white architect on the faculty of the Rhode Island School of Design, was selected to design a new monument to celebrate the "Black Regiment."

By 1999, Derek Bradford had submitted a site plan for the project to RIDOT and Gaines, who shared it with his committee and members of the Newport County NAACP and reported "a very favorable and supportive atmosphere, a lot of excitement about this project."[52] Subsequently Bradford completed the design for the new monument. The design was very simple: a platform with a wall that would have two doorways, and the names of soldiers in the First Rhode Island engraved on the wall. Initially, Bradford proposed engraving just the names of those directly involved in the battle at that site on the wall, but because there were no rolls available for the battle day, he agreed that the names of all known members of the regiment would be included. Louis Wilson, professor of Afro-American studies at Smith College, who had spent several years recovering the names of all men of color who served as soldiers in the American Revolution and documenting their service, provided these names to Bradford on a printout that included various categories of identification: city of birth, slave status, and various racial characterizations. One category identified individuals as "Black (people who are Black but not noted in record . . .)." Others identified individuals as "Mulatto (Indian/Black/European)," "Africa (West Africa/Guinea coast)," "Negro," "Indian," and "Mustee (Indian/Black)." Many of the names on the list were coded in the last two categories.[53]

Since every transportation enhancement project funded by the Federal Department of Transportation requires an Environmental Impact Assessment, in which groups with a direct interest and involvement in the history of the project site are given an opportunity to comment on the design, in late 1999 RIDOT invited twelve groups, including a variety of Indian tribes and bands, African American organizations, and representatives of assorted local institutions and government agencies, to participate as consulting parties. They included the Rhode Island Historic Preservation and Heritage Commission (RIHPHC), the Narragansett Indian Tribe, the Wampanoag Tribe of Aquinnah (Gay Head) on Martha's Vineyard, the Mashpee Wampanoag Tribe, the Pokanoket/Wampanoag Federation/Wampanoag Nation, and the Rhode Island Black Heritage

Society. The Newport branch of the NAACP, as project proponent through its Patriots' Park Enhancement Committee, was also, by definition, a party to the assessment.[54]

Paul Gaines of the NAACP Patriots' Park Enhancement Committee indicated that he wanted the monument to include more than a list of names of members of the regiment. He wanted it to tell the whole story of the raising of the regiment and its achievements, not only in the Battle of Rhode Island but throughout the Revolution. By February 2001, two narratives had been written, one by Louis Wilson explaining the creation of the regiment, to be installed on the front of the monument, and one describing the actual battle itself, to be engraved on the back panel, written by Carl Becker, a military historian. These narratives, together with a wall plan prepared by Bradford Associates, were forwarded to the various consulting parties.[55] While after one revision agreement was easily reached on the description of the battle, it took four years and eleven drafts to reach consensus on the description of the formation and membership of the regiment.[56] Serious issues were raised by the first paragraph, which stated that "the heroic events that brought this nation into being" had been "shared by a significant number of " 'blacks,' which at that time included Negroes, Mulattos, Mustees and Native Americans," and went on to refer to the men of color in the regiment as "slaves," "blacks," and "free blacks."[57]

The NAACP, through Paul Gaines and his committee, was delighted with the plan and the text.[58] The director of the Heritage Harbor Museum and former director of the Rhode Island Historical Society said, "The texts of Professor Louis Wilson and Carl Becker do a fine job in telling the story. Their scholarship is accurate and represents the best of what we know of the events surrounding this subject."[59] But John Brown of the Narragansett Indian Tribe Historic Preservation Office (NITHPO) wrote directly to the Advisory Council on Historic Preservation in Washington, D.C., to say that the text on the monument was "bad history," and in a letter to Paul Gaines he indicated his disagreement with its "false characterization and misinterpretations" of Indians as "blacks."[60] From the Narragansett perspective, while it was true that some Narragansett women had intermarried with African men in relationships associated with their forced labor as slaves and indentured servants, in matrilineal Narragansett society their children were considered to be Narragansett.

But Brown's problem with the text was not simply the inclusion of Indians as blacks. While he was willing to acknowledge that some men of Indian descent who fought in the First Rhode Island had been slaves, and some of these may have been of African as well as Indian descent, he insisted that most Indians fighting in the Battle of Rhode Island had been fighting *with,* not in, the Rhode Island First as representatives of the sovereign Narragansett nation—not so much to support the Americans as to defeat the British, under whose long and deceitful colonial rule they had suffered the loss of land and power. Thus he argued that Indians had "different reasons [for fighting] than those persons who were African or European," and requested that all textual references to Indians and the names of Indian enlistees be deleted from the wall.

In an effort to resolve both these issues, Richard Greenwood at RIHPHC drafted a second text. The first revision changed "a significant number of 'blacks,' which . . . included Negroes, Mulattos, Mustees and Native Americans" to "blacks and Indians fighting *alongside* the white soldiers in the various Rhode Island regiments and militia groups" (emphasis added). The description of the 1778 act opening enlistment to "every able-bodied Negro, mulatto, or Indian man slave in this State" in exchange for freedom was explained: "A significant number of Native Americans served in the regiment, but the majority of the soldiers in the First Rhode Island were of African descent, which has led to its being known as the Black Regiment." [61]

Brown revised Greenwood's text to read, "This monument is dedicated to these Rhode Islanders who devoted themselves to the cause of American liberty even though they labored under the burdens of racial discrimination and slavery, and to the soldiers of the Narragansett Indian Nation who fought alongside them." He characterized the act that opened enlistment "to every able-bodied Negro, mulatto, or Indian man slave in this State" as offering freedom to "Negro and mulatto slaves and indentured Indians" (sidestepping Indian enslavement). His version stated, "A significant number of Native Americans served in the regiment, but the majority of the soldiers in the First Rhode Island Regiment were of African descent, which has led to its being known as the Black Regiment. The Narragansett Indian Chief Sachem sent soldiers from the Narragansett Indian Nation to fight with these soldiers for America's independence." [62]

The lack of acknowledgment of other tribes' participation led RIHPHC, the Newport NAACP, the Pokanoket/Wampanoag Federation, and the Pokanoket Tribe/Wampanoag Nation all to reject the text.[63] But when Richard Greenwood prepared a new draft that removed Narragansett specificity and circulated it to consulting parties, NITHPO rejected it. According to Narragansett oral tradition, the other tribes and bands were tributary to the Narragansett in the Revolutionary period, and thus their members *were* Narragansett. To arguments that the recorded birthplaces of many soldiers designated "Indian" were outside Rhode Island, he countered that birthplace was unrelated to affiliation and that dispersed Narragansetts were called home by their sachem to participate in this battle.[64]

But the real problem remained a twofold one of the cultural identification of both the First Rhode Island Regiment and the Battle of Rhode Island. Could the regiment continue to be called "black" if there were Indians in it, and was the battle won by a Continental regiment made up principally of slaves, or was it to be understood as a joint enterprise of this regiment and a unit of Indians acting independently? An abortive meeting led to more versions, which oscillated back and forth on these two issues with no resolution.[65]

At this point, J. Michael Butler of the Federal Highway Administration, giving consulting parties thirty days to object, issued an opinion that, to resolve the deadlock, "the monument should be erected void of all names and affiliations."[66] RIHPHC and NAACP felt strongly that the commemorative value of the monument would be diminished by eliminating soldier's names, and Sanderson of RIHPHC also felt that the elimination of any reference to the Native American participation would reduce historical accuracy.[67] NITHPO appeared to agree with the Federal Highway Administration that names should be left off the monument: "By being left out of a sham, the Narragansett Indian Tribe is better off," John Brown said. In response to a counterproposal that the whole idea of a narrative be jettisoned in favor of simply listing soldiers' names, John Brown agreed—but only if the plaque bearing the words "Black Regiment" on the boulder erected in 1974 be removed. The NAACP was adamant that the original memorial remain intact.[68] Another version of the narrative was floated and rejected.

In April 2004, the RIHPHC made a final stab at the wording for the front panel of the monument. This time, when NITHPO proposed a few changes, the NAACP, the Narragansett Tribe, RIHPHC, and all other consulting parties but one pronounced the text acceptable. The Federal Highway Administration found the result to represent sufficient consensus and directed RIDOT to "please move this project forward to completion."[69] Derek Bradford, the architect, spent the summer of 2004 revising the plans, and the project finally went out to bid. On August 28, 2005, the first part of the new memorial, a stone marker that says "Patriots Park. August 29, 1778. Memorial to 1st Rhode Island Regiment" was unveiled. The granite wall was slated to be completed in October 2005.[70]

The final text, headed simply "The Rhode Island First Regiment," reads,

> One of the most noteworthy contributions [to the War for American Independence] was made by African-Americans, Indians, and by members of the sovereign Narragansett Indian Tribe who fought alongside them in their battle for independence. . . . From the beginning of the war, there were blacks and Indians fighting alongside the white soldiers . . . the rank and file were predominantly blacks and Indians, both free men and those recently freed. The majority of the soldiers in the First Rhode Island Regiment were believed to be of African descent, which has led to its being celebrated as the Black Regiment; regimental rosters reveal a significant number of the soldiers to be Indians.[71]

All the individual names of the soldiers of the First Rhode Island will appear on the front panel of the monument, above the explanatory text. According to the final plans, the boulder with the plaque engraved "The Black Regiment" will also remain on the site.

Keith Stokes, executive director of the Newport Chamber of Commerce, an African American of mixed descent who speaks and writes widely on the history of African Americans and Jews in the Newport area, shakes his head over the whole struggle. To him and most of the other African Americans interested in Patriots' Park, the "blackness" of the Black Regiment is historically accurate because it reflects the language and ideology of its own time. "The soldiers of the First Rhode Island were always referred to as 'black,' " he argues. "I'm Jewish, but look at me. Nobody calls me 'Jewish'—I'm black. It's the same thing."[72] To John Brown, it's not the same thing at all; he has no investment in an interpretive moment in which association with bondage, and an alien concept of patrilineal descent, "blackened" the social identities of people the Narragansett know to be wholly or partly of Indian descent and, today, can serve only to undermine acknowledgment of their persistent sovereignty.

Ironically, the resolution of the struggle over the Patriots' Park monument coincided with the release of the first children's book ever written about the First Rhode Island Regiment, published by Moon Mountain Publishing of North Kingstown, Rhode Island. Its author, Linda Crotta Brennan, acknowledges close collaboration with the Rhode Island Black Heritage Society and with a past historian of the Rhode Island NAACP in preparing the text. *The Black Regiment of the American Revolution,* written for children ages seven through eleven, includes this paragraph:

> Who were the "Blacks" in the Black Regiment? Although a few of them were free Blacks, like Richard Cozzens, most of them were slaves. Some, like Prince Jenks, were Africans who had been captured from their native countries and carried across the sea into slavery. Some, like Joseph Brown, were African-Americans whose parents or grandparents had been born in Africa. Some, like Harry Gideon, were Native American slaves. Many were people of mixed race, with African, Native American, and European blood.[73]

While Brennan is careful to include Indians in her explanation of the composition of the Black Regiment, the sense and emphasis of her book restores cultural "ownership" of the First Rhode Island primarily to slaves—slaves whose African descent is highlighted, reflecting Louis Wilson's research; it includes no free or sovereign people of unmixed Indian descent. As of this writing, there has been no official response to the publication on the part of the Narragansett Tribe.

HISTORY AS REPARATIONS

All four of the cases described here represent attempts to put Vincent Harding's dictum about "exposure, disclosure, and reinterpretation of the entire American past" into practice.[74] In other words, in some sense these were all efforts at reparations—that is, attempts to repair and restore the effaced or distorted histories of people of color in bondage and in freedom. These examples illustrate how difficult those efforts can be, and how the most intelligently conceived and well-meaning projects can run afoul of the misunderstanding, misinformation, false assumptions, and deep-rooted suspicion that are the legacies of the very silences and distortions the projects seek to correct.

These experiences suggest that while it is the histories of people of color that are missing or distorted and need to be acknowledged and restored to the historical record, in a very real sense it is American history as a whole that is ailing as a consequence of their absence and needs repair. One of the most important aspects of the notion of reparations, then, is its promise of restoring completeness to everyone's American history.

A PHILOSOPHIC COCK

The Philosophic Cock, an 1804 color drawing by James Akin, was part of a political attack on then-President Thomas Jefferson, charging him with having illicit sexual relations with his slave Sally Hemings, represented by the hen in the drawing. The cock was also symbolic of the French Revolution, which Jefferson favored to the displeasure of his political enemies. COURTESY OF THE AMERICAN ANTIQUARIAN SOCIETY

7

Avoiding History:

Thomas Jefferson,

Sally Hemings, and the

Uncomfortable Public Conversation

on Slavery

Lois E. Horton

T he fact that Thomas Jefferson, the nation's third president and author of the Declaration of Independence, was a major slaveholder is
well known. Nor was it unusual, since slaveholders occupied the White
House for the vast majority of the time before the American Civil War.
Thomas Jefferson penned the principles of liberty that underlay the Revolutionary War, a war that brought America independence and many
American slaves their freedom. In the South during the Revolution many
slaves fled their masters, seizing their own freedom or fighting for the
British on the promise of freedom. In the North many joined the American army to fight for both the nation's freedom and their own. After the
war, some individual slaveholders in both regions took the pronounce-
ments of freedom seriously and freed slaves. The Revolution also began
slavery's more general demise in the North, immediately in Vermont,
Massachusetts, and New Hampshire, and gradually in Rhode Island,
New York, Pennsylvania, and New Jersey.[1] Some of America's founders,

such as Benjamin Franklin, himself a slave owner, John Jay, and Alexander Hamilton, belonged to antislavery societies. Thomas Jefferson, on the other hand, inherited 150 slaves from his father and father-in-law and held more than 150 slaves when he wrote the Declaration of Independence in 1776. At times he owned more than 200 slaves and over his lifetime counted more than 600 people as his possessions.[2]

In Virginia, voluntary private manumissions became legal in 1782. The great increase in Virginia's free black population between 1790 and 1810, much greater than the increase in either the slave or the white population, indicates that many of Jefferson's fellow Virginians had freed their slaves. In 1782 there were about 2,000 free blacks in the state; in 1790 there were nearly 13,000; in 1800 over 20,000; and by 1810 there were well over 30,000. In 1785, for example, Joseph Mayo of Powhatan, Virginia, freed his more than 150 slaves, and in the 1790s Robert Carter not only freed his more than 500 slaves but gave them land and housing as well. Others freed slaves in their wills, as did founding father George Washington, who freed his 124 slaves and provided for the freedom at his wife's death of 153 people who belonged to her. A relative of Jefferson's, John Randolph of Roanoke, freed his hundreds of slaves in his will in 1833, also providing land for them. Thomas Jefferson, on the other hand, freed only 8 slaves, 3 during his lifetime and 5 in his will. Jefferson sold or gave away 161 slaves between 1784 and 1794 and left 130 people to be sold to settle his estate when he died in 1826.[3]

Slaveholding was common, especially in the South, but it was by no means universal. By 1790, about one-third of America's total population was enslaved, and, in the South, one-quarter of the white population were members of slaveholding families.[4] Although slaveholding was generally approved among Virginia's aristocracy, one aspect of Jefferson's slave ownership did occasion controversy, even in his own time. Accusations that he had a slave mistress first surfaced in 1802. Though he soundly denied them, rumors persisted that Jefferson had fathered children by his slave Sally Hemings. This story was passed down in the oral histories of the families of those children, some of whose descendants claimed the Jefferson lineage. Most historians discounted the stories, however, even though it was common for slaveholders to father children by their slaves. The best-respected Jefferson biographers were adamant, citing both Jefferson's morality and his expressed revulsion at the idea of "race-mixing."[5]

JEFFERSON AND THE HEMINGS FAMILY

During Jefferson's time, the numerous Hemings clan constituted an elite class of slaves at Monticello, many occupying the statuses of house slaves and artisans at the plantation. Historians have generally accepted the fact that Jefferson was related to the Hemings family by marriage. Elizabeth Hemings, called Betty, was the slave mistress of John Wayles, the father of Jefferson's wife, Martha. Betty's children included Sally, Robert, James, and Peter. Thus, Sally Hemings was the half-sister of Jefferson's wife. A few historians were convinced that circumstantial evidence indicated another link between the families and believed that the widowed Jefferson had fathered children by Sally Hemings. The only slaves Jefferson ever freed were members of the Hemings family. Sally Hemings's older brother Robert was allowed to buy his own freedom, using money advanced against years of service by the man to whom he had been hired out. Her brother James gained his freedom by agreeing to train another brother, Peter, in French cooking, a process that took three years. James signed this agreement with Jefferson when they were together in the free state of Pennsylvania. Both of these men could have pressed their own legal claims to freedom, since Robert had gone with Jefferson to the free state of Massachusetts, and James had lived with Jefferson in Paris and in the North. Two of Sally Hemings's children, her twenty-year-old daughter Harriet and twenty-four-year-old son Beverly, ran away together, and Jefferson did not pursue them. Jefferson then freed Harriet but not Beverly. In his will Jefferson freed two of Sally Hemings's nephews, Joseph Fossett and Burwell Hemings, and her brother John Hemings. Joseph Fossett's and Burwell Hemings's wives remained in slavery, and Fossett was separated from his wife when she was sold to help settle the debts of Jefferson's estate. Jefferson's will also provided for the manumission of Sally's sons Madison Hemings and Eston Hemings when each reached the age of twenty-one. Thus, all of Sally Hemings's surviving children were among those very few slaves freed or allowed to remain at large by Thomas Jefferson. Sally herself was never freed.[6]

In her book *Thomas Jefferson and Sally Hemings: An American Controversy,* published in 1997, legal scholar Annette Gordon-Reed provided other circumstantial evidence of Jefferson's fathering of Sally Hemings's children. As one piece of evidence to support her conclusions, conclusions passionately disputed by Jefferson historians, Reed computed the times each of Hemings's children was conceived and correlated them with Jefferson's presence at Monticello, noting that none of the children was conceived when Jefferson was not present. To such evidence she added the many claims of black oral histories asserting descent from Thomas Jefferson.[7]

INTERPRETING SLAVERY AT MONTICELLO

There have been significant changes in the way that slavery has been presented at Monticello over the last twenty years. Up to the mid-1980s guides only occasionally mentioned "servants" in the tour of the mansion, as the story centered on Jefferson and his activities. Indeed, Jefferson was the actor in these accounts: he "designed and built" the house, an elaborate clock, and many other inventions, and "experimented" with particular crops. Guides referred to things that were accomplished by slaves, on the other hand, in the passive voice. Meals "were served" and furniture "was built." By the 1990s, archival and archeological research supplemented the information about the slaveholding family at Monticello with a great deal more information on the black community of Mulberry Row, an area populated by slave artisans, many of them Hemingses. Additionally, Monticello established an advisory committee to bring more recent historical interpretations on the issues of race and slavery into the public interpretations. Rather than avoiding questions about slavery at Monticello, tours of Mulberry Row were designed to encourage discussions of the issue. Initial reactions to this tour were overwhelmingly positive, and some African American visitors were so overcome with emotion that they could not complete the tour. There were a few reports of uncomfortable incidents, as when one recently recruited black guide about to conduct his first tour was greeted by a white visitor who declared, "So you are our slave for today." Fewer than 10 percent of visitors took this specialized tour, which is separate from the house tour, but it marked a major advance in the interpretation of slavery at Monticello, and the reaction did encourage some guides to mention slavery on the house tour as well.

JEFFERSON AND THE DNA CONTROVERSY

In 1998, science stepped into the Jefferson-Hemings controversy via DNA testing of Jefferson and Hemings descendants. In carefully controlled laboratory studies scientists at three independent laboratories in the United States, the Netherlands, and Britain compared Y-chromosome DNA haplotypes (a combination of genetic markers) from the Jefferson line with those from Hemings's descendants. These haplotypes are so rare that they have never been observed outside of the Jefferson family. Most such chromosomes pass unchanged along the paternal lines of descent. Since Thomas Jefferson had no surviving (legitimate) sons, DNA testing was conducted on five male-line descendants of two sons of his paternal uncle, Field Johnson; five male-line descendants of Sally Hemings's first son, Thomas Woodson; and one male-line descendant of her last son, Eston Hemings Jefferson. (Sally had six children: three daughters, two of whom died in infancy, and three sons.) Descendants of the usual suspects, Jefferson's nephews Samuel and Peter Carr, were also tested and ruled out as progenitors of Sally Hemings's sons. Testing supported Jefferson's paternity for Eston Hemings Jefferson with a certainty of 99 percent, a particularly strong finding when combined with historical evidence. The study concluded that Jefferson probably was not the father of Sally Hemings's first son, Thomas Woodson—although, since the testing was indirect, he still could have been if there was illegitimacy in the paternal line of descent somewhere between Thomas Woodson and his tested descendants. The results of the testing were reported in the journal *Nature* in November 1998, setting off an enormous wave of media attention and requiring many historians to rethink their positions.[8]

STAFF AND VISITOR RESPONSE TO THE SCIENTIFIC FINDINGS

On May 22 and 23, 1999, James Oliver Horton and I supervised a research project in which four Ph.D. students in American studies at George Washington University conducted interviews with visitors at Monticello, Virginia, the home of Thomas Jefferson. Researchers conducted these interviews just after visitors had finished the tour of Jefferson's house. This was one week after a controversial meeting of the Monticello Association "family reunion" weekend to which descendants of Hemings were invited by one faction of the white Jefferson descendants. Just before that meeting a DNA Study Committee of the Thomas Jefferson Memorial Foundation had been unable to agree on the validity of the DNA findings. Members of the committee had issued both a majority report, acknowledging Jefferson's likely paternity of at least one of Sally Hemings's children, and a minority report, disputing that conclusion and clinging to the notion of Jefferson's nephew Peter Carr as the father of Eston Hemings.[9]

Interviews with six experienced staff interpreters, all of whom were white, gave an indication of the training they received, how they had experienced changes in interpretation at Monticello, their sense of the importance of talking about slavery on the tours, and their feelings about visitor reaction to their presentations. The greatest change in the presentation of slavery at Monticello, according to the guides, occurred with the introduction of the plantation tour in 1993. Although the main attraction is Thomas Jefferson's house, a relatively small number of visitors take the black-oriented Mulberry Row tour, a tour designed to tell the story of the slave artisans who lived and worked in a row of houses near the main mansion. In response to visitor interest, according to some guides' reports, the coverage of general information on slavery on this tour has increased since it was initiated. One staff member reported that when this tour began it was a very emotional experience for both interpreters and visitors, and many people expressed their gratitude that Monticello was addressing the issue of slavery. According to one interpreter's estimates, only about 6 percent of visitors to Monticello take this outdoor tour, which is not given in the winter. They generally agreed that Jefferson's slaves were mentioned on the house tour, and reported that they answer visitors' questions, but also noted that time is limited and they have a great deal to cover. Generally guides refer people with an interest in slavery to the Mulberry Row tour. Many school groups take only the house tour, according to one interpreter, because taking both tours takes too long—well over two hours.

Interpreters reported a wide variety of visitor responses to presentations on slavery. All reported feeling comfortable talking about the subject, one after some initial trepidation talking to African American groups. Some expressed pride in receiving compliments from black visitors. One emphasized an attempt to maintain a balance in the presentation between the "degradation" of slavery and the story of black contributions. Staff members perceive two different groups who take the plantation tour: those with a special interest in black history and those waiting their turn to enter the house. There has been some negative response. One man objected to stories about slavery, saying, "We're not going to fight the Civil War again, are we?" and left the tour. Reportedly, black interns who give the tour are asked very different questions from the white interpreters, often being questioned about their own feelings about slavery. The guides generally report stronger responses from visitors on the plantation tour. Older people, especially men, are most likely to be uncomfortable talking about both the DNA evidence and slavery in general, although one interpreter reported that a man from the South had taken the guide aside after the tour and confided that everyone in their group had "slave blood" but wouldn't admit it. Some visitors also try to argue that the position of the slave is analogous to that of the poor farmer today, or that a slave woman deemed worthless and auctioned off at age fifty-five was much like a person who is laid off at age fifty-five today. Others asserted that slavery wasn't so bad, since planters took care of their slaves. Whites, another interpreter observed, tended to romanticize slavery.

Generally the interpreters seemed well trained and comfortable talking about Jefferson and slavery. One reported finding it challenging talking about slavery, and reported having to learn a great deal about the subject before feeling comfortable discussing it. Interpreters perceived that when blacks are on the tour, the white visitors seem to be particularly hesitant to discuss racial issues for fear of offending the blacks. In this case, one guide made a special effort to broach the subject early in the tour. It is clear from the staff responses and from visitor responses that slaves are routinely mentioned on the house tour, though the coverage of slavery depends on the individual tour guide and on visitor interest. There seems to be some disagreement over whether guides are responsible for telling the whole story of how the people lived at Monticello or whether they should be mainly entertainers who must be careful that visitors are told a story that will not upset them.

Interview questions for visitors were designed to discover their reactions to the DNA testing, their opinions about Jefferson as a slaveholder and about his relationship with Sally Hemings, and their views on the importance of slavery for the presentation of history both at this site and in American history generally. The interviewers, one white man, two black women, and one white woman, interviewed seventy-nine visitors. The interviewees were thirty-three white men, thirty-eight white women, three black men, four black women, and one Asian man.[10] Fifty-six percent of those interviewed were women, and 10 percent were black. Approximately 35 percent were judged to be in their twenties and thirties, 47 percent in their forties and fifties, and 16 percent sixty years of age or older. Not all visitors answered every question.

MONTICELLO AND
THE PRESENTATION OF SLAVERY

When asked about the tour of Monticello generally, most visitors had a very conventional view, mentioning the architecture and Jefferson's inventions and gadgets as having made the greatest impression on them. It was most important, one commented, on the house tour to learn about the interior and the "amazing architecture." Others were impressed with the grounds, the guide, or individual rooms in the mansion. There has been an obvious change in the way that Jefferson's house and his life are presented by guides at Monticello. A generation ago, slaves were not mentioned—they were "servants" in any allusion to their work, and things done by slaves were generally reported in the passive voice. All except four visitors interviewed in this study said that they had heard about slavery on the tour, although fifteen said it was mentioned "not much," "a bit," or "very little." Their comments indicated that slavery was mentioned on the house tour primarily in places where slaves acted as servants, in the dining room, the kitchen, and the sewing room. About seven visitors indicated that slavery was mentioned "everywhere" or discussed "throughout" the house.

FACING HISTORY: SLAVERY AT MONTICELLO

Responses to the series of questions dealing with the importance of slavery reflected not only the public's awareness of slavery but their view of the impact of slavery on American history as well. They may also reflect the effects of thirty years of intense scholarship on the subject. The over-whelming majority of those interviewed said that slavery was important for understanding Monticello. The greatest number remarked that slav-ery was a part of history or the "way of life" in Jefferson's time and there-fore needed to be discussed. Three of the people who said it was part of the way of life, however, also said they didn't believe the presentation of slav-ery was important for understanding Monticello. The next largest group of answers referred to the fact that it was the slaves who built Monticello, many observing that the place "wouldn't have existed" without slavery. Surprisingly, eleven visitors were even more emphatic, believing that slav-ery was "very" important to the site or should "absolutely" or "definitely" be presented, whereas only seven said it was not important to understand-ing Monticello. Older people were less likely to think slavery should be a part of the historical interpretation; most of those who believed slavery was not important for the public presentations were sixty or over.

Only 47 of the interviewees responded to the question about slavery's importance for understanding Thomas Jefferson. The vast majority of those believed that knowing about slavery at Monticello was important to understanding Jefferson. Only seven did not think so, four of whom were in the forties–fifties age group, and two of these were African Americans. A measure of the progress made by social historians of recent generations may be found in people's view of slavery's importance to American his-tory generally, another question answered by just about half of the re-spondents. All recognized its importance as historical reality, but many believed it shouldn't be overemphasized. Of those who answered this question, no one denied its importance. Many people were ambivalent about discussing slavery in American history, seeing it as a historical fact but finding it "troubling" or "disappointing." A few believed that there was too much emphasis on slavery in American history, since it was "only a part" of the past. Another who didn't see a direct relationship between slavery and "what was created" at Monticello thought it wasn't appropri-ate to go "deep into the slavery question" there. Despite the general am-bivalence, a few of the visitors said they found the information about slavery interesting and wished they had learned more about the contribu-tions of slaves to America.

REWRITING HISTORY TO RECONCILE
JEFFERSON'S CONTRADICTIONS

The most emotional and reflective responses were evoked by questions about Thomas Jefferson as slaveholder and his relationship with Sally Hemings. With these questions, people often drew parallels to the place of race and morality in today's society. They were also likely to reflect on the contradictions that slavery posed for the nation. Although Jefferson's slaveholding was certainly a part of the written record, and presumably part of popular knowledge, the controversy over his relationship with Hemings seemed to focus greater attention on this aspect of his life. A number of people noted that thinking of Jefferson as a slaveholder brought him down off the pedestal upon which the history they learned had placed him: Jefferson the icon had "feet of clay." This more realistic sense of history, they thought, was better than having a "false sense of pride." The realization that he was not perfect, one said, keeps him from being "deified." A few believed the discrepancy between his philosophy and his life made him appear to be a hypocrite, but the overwhelming majority excused Jefferson the slaveholder with the observation that slaveholding was simply part of the culture at the time. One thought the contradiction made him "all the more fascinating." Ignoring the controversies over slaveholding in Jefferson's time and the post-Revolutionary demise of slavery in much of the North and undoubtedly unaware of the fact that even some of Jefferson's fellow Virginians freed their slaves on principle, visitors said Jefferson should not be judged by today's standards. Most people were convinced that Jefferson believed slavery to be wrong, since guides had mentioned his "abhorrence" of slavery, but they were sure that he could do nothing about it. "Wealthy people at the time all had slaves," one said.

AVOIDING HISTORY
BY RE-CREATING THE STORY

Narrative elaborations emerged with the question of understanding Jefferson as a slaveholder. In one view, Jefferson became the benevolent paternal slaveholder. He grew up with slavery, one visitor said, but had progressive ideas about it. Accordingly, this person thought, he freed those who were able to support themselves but didn't feel it was right to free those who would be left helpless. Another visitor reflected on Jefferson's commitment to the idea that all people were equal but was sure that he didn't know how to free his slaves, since he felt a parental responsibility toward them and "cared for them as people." Others felt sure that Jefferson was a compassionate slaveholder who was not abusive but treated his slaves well.

Another narrative created a Jefferson who was powerless to free his slaves. According to some this was because he was dependent on their labor to maintain the plantation and his way of life. In another version, he was simply a victim of his time and station. Or perhaps, one said, he had slaves because everyone of his status did, and he didn't want to draw attention to himself by not having slaves. Another perspective came from some visitors who had heard of Jefferson's hatred of slavery but noted his dependence on slave labor. He was "crippled" with regard to slavery, one observed: "He wasn't courageous or strong enough to change it." This view comports with the conclusion of one historian, Paul Finkelman, who observed that James Madison sold land, rather than slaves, to settle his debts. Unlike George Washington, Finkelman also noted, Thomas Jefferson lived well beyond his means, and frequently resorted to selling slaves to maintain his extravagant lifestyle and cope with his chronic indebtedness. Jefferson shipped eighty-six large crates of artworks, furniture, china, and other luxury items back to Monticello from France, for example, and sold at least eighty-five slaves around the same time to pay his debts.[11]

A third narrative made Jefferson the country's primary abolitionist. According to this view, he tried to have slavery abolished, either in the Declaration of Independence or in the Constitution, but was thwarted by less progressive founding fathers. One visitor, apparently unaware of the actions of a few of Jefferson's neighbors, was convinced that had Jefferson "turned his slaves loose at the time," he'd have been "the only one to do it" and the freed slaves would have only been "enslaved all over again." Since freeing his own slaves would have been futile, this version contended, in an apparent reference to Jefferson's condemnation of the British slave trade in an early draft, that Jefferson attempted to abolish slavery in the Declaration of Independence but noted that this was unacceptable to the delegates from South Carolina and Georgia. Another called him the "first innovator" regarding slavery's abolition, the man who wrote his progressive thoughts and feelings into the Constitution (confusing the Declaration of Independence and the Constitution). Though he was unable to abolish slavery, this story went, he made differences that "ultimately helped the slaves," presumably by affirming his antislavery principles in the Declaration.

THE HOLLYWOOD VERSION OF HISTORY

More than two out of three visitors believed that Jefferson had fathered at least one child by Sally Hemings. Yet there was still some uncertainty about this aspect of their relationship, even after the reports of the DNA testing. Every person asked had an extremely positive view of the science of DNA testing, believing in the efficacy of science and often mentioning its value in criminal cases. Three people mentioned its use in the murder trial of O.J. Simpson and two in the identification of the remains of the family of the last Russian czar. All had faith in DNA testing in the courtroom, although one was skeptical of its use in historical study, and many doubted that it could give definitive results in the Jefferson-Hemings case. The unconvinced were likely to say that the results had been inconclusive, other Jefferson relatives were implicated, and more research was needed. A lone visitor (perhaps remembering the lack of DNA fit between descendants of Thomas Woodson and those of the Jefferson line) stood by the belief that the father of Hemings's child was definitely someone other than Jefferson, probably a European.

Visitors were most creative on the issue of Jefferson's relationship with Hemings, as there is virtually no historical evidence about its specific nature. A number of people mentioned having seen their story depicted on the Ken Burns television program *Thomas Jefferson*.[12] That program portrayed the relationship as one between "consenting adults," and most visitors generally accepted this. Some, however, were unsettled by their own speculations about the role of coercion or abuse, and one visitor did express shock that Sally Hemings was only fourteen years old at the time she went to Paris to serve Jefferson. The most frequent response was acceptance of the fact that such relationships between masters and slaves were common. "They all had black mistresses," according to one visitor, who observed that "a lot of slaves were white," having been fathered by their owners. Many found the relationship believable because, after all, "Thomas Jefferson was a man." Some took the DNA proof of a relationship as evidence of a long-standing lack of sexual inhibition in powerful men, mentioning Jefferson, George Washington, William J. Clinton, and John F. Kennedy as examples. There were a number of comparisons with the sexual behavior of President Clinton in which Jefferson was seen as flawed but not as bad as Clinton.

One narrative developed to explain the Jefferson-Hemings relationship centered on the idea that Sally Hemings wasn't so different from Thomas Jefferson. In this story, although a slave, she was practically a member of the family. The recognition of the fact that she was Jefferson's wife's half-sister was important to this construction. According to this story, Jefferson was depressed after his wife died, and forlorn because his wife had made him promise not to remarry. He was a lonely, devoted family man. Since Sally Hemings was only one-quarter black, she looked like the family and probably reminded him of his dead wife. If he loved his wife, her half-sister, he would certainly like Hemings, who was "birth white." "As wrong as slavery is," one visitor concluded, "one can see how Mr. Jefferson would end up in a relationship like that."

Another common narrative made Jefferson and Hemings into star-crossed lovers. As in the *Jefferson in Paris* scenario, they were just "two people who cared about each other." There was still some ambivalence about how she may have been treated, but generally people who subscribed to this view concluded that "he was caring," they were "attracted to each other," and "he loved her." One visitor concluded that he wasn't fooling around with other slaves, but was committed to Sally Hemings. They were "in love at a difficult time" for them, but in his favor, he wasn't afraid to be seen with her. A hint of doubt crept in as this person wondered if Jefferson couldn't have proved his love by freeing her, but then recalled that he had freed only five men in his will. In another ambivalent version of this story, the visitor found their love relationship "spiritually beautiful" but ethically questionable. A variation on this theme involved speculation that Jefferson found Sally Hemings intriguing because of her exoticism as a black woman, though the visitor also concluded that "he loved her dearly." If it wasn't illegal, another decided, Jefferson would have married Sally Hemings.

Following these narratives, many visitors concluded that the Jefferson family should accept Thomas Jefferson's black descendants. A number of people felt they were entitled to recognition, credited black oral histories claiming descent from Jefferson, and couldn't understand continuing denials. Others believed the DNA controversy was just unproven accusations about an issue that was not very important today. Some people expressed strong opinions that Hemingses should be included in any of the benefits of the Jefferson heritage. One went on to imagine Jefferson's reaction to the controversy and to the Monticello Foundation's reaction. Jefferson would scold them, this visitor believed, for being "narrow, bigoted, self-absorbed" and "conceited." After all, this person argued, "all of his slaves were a part of his family," not just property but people he cared for and loved.

SLAVERY AND AMERICAN HISTORY IN PUBLIC

Surprisingly, there were very few differences in the responses of white visitors and black visitors to Monticello on the issues of Thomas Jefferson and slavery. Even on the questions of the relationship between Jefferson and Sally Hemings and the parentage of her children, both blacks and whites were likely to credit black oral history or to express doubts about the definitiveness of DNA evidence. The greatest differences in visitors' views of whether or not it is important to talk about slavery at public sites and to discuss slavery as a part of American history were found among visitors in different age groups. Visitors sixty and older were less likely to see slavery as central, or even important, to America's story. They were also less likely to believe that the presentation of slavery was necessary at Monticello. The majority of visitors knew about and accepted at least the existence of American slavery as a shameful reality in American history. They were also aware of Thomas Jefferson's ambivalent position as slaveholder and author of the principles set forth in the Declaration of Independence. Fitting this Jefferson into the more commonly told American story of progress and moral uplift presented problems that people resolved by seeing slavery and Jefferson's slaveholding as only a "small part of the story" or by seeing him as a "man of his times," progressive but unable to escape his social world. Visitors expended the greatest energy and historical creativity in efforts to preserve Thomas Jefferson's iconic status in light of his relationship with Sally Hemings, a relationship scientific evidence has made more and more difficult to deny. In this connection visitors created the ubiquitous master-slave sexual relationship scenario, the all-in-the-family scenario, and the star-crossed lovers scenario to make the Jefferson-Hemings story truly an all-American one.

CONCLUSION

Scientific research on the DNA of descendants of Thomas Jefferson and Sally Hemings and the ensuing controversy over whether or not Hemings's descendants should be included in the prestigious Monticello Association of Jefferson descendants provided an opportunity for an examination of staff and visitor reaction to changes in the presentation of slavery at Monticello and an assessment of the impact of a generation of the social history of slavery on public perceptions. As one measure of historians' progress in integrating slavery into American history, the vast majority of respondents believed that learning about slavery was integral to understanding that history and the history of Monticello. The majority even believed that slavery was important for understanding Jefferson himself. The story of the Jefferson-Hemings relation raised questions for the visitors about the iconic status of the former president but seemed to do little to diminish their admiration for him. They emphasized his inventive genius, architectural creativity, and democratic principles while creating narratives to incorporate Sally Hemings into the story of the heroic Thomas Jefferson.

The placement of a statue of Abraham Lincoln seated on a bench with his young son Tad in Richmond, Virginia, the former capital of the Confederacy, was highly controversial. Some in the neo-Confederate movement opposed its placement, regarding it as symbolic of the defeat and humiliation of the Confederate South. Others, however, believe that this is "the most important statue of Lincoln in the world." COURTESY OF THE UNITED STATES HISTORICAL SOCIETY

8

Southern Comfort Levels: Race, Heritage Tourism, and the Civil War in Richmond

Marie Tyler-McGraw

As the twentieth century drew to its close, the city that was once the capital of the Confederacy tried again to revitalize its old central business district. Richmond, Virginia's downtown was a scene of classic urban blight—boarded-up department stores, fast-food franchises, and more blowing newspapers than pedestrians. Over decades the city had tried most of the nationally popular remedies for postindustrial blight, but to little avail. The strategy now adopted by city leaders was a riverfront development project, a popular form of urban renewal in the 1990s. Designed to draw tourists, developers, and retailers to the James River area at the heart of the city, the plan featured a James River canal walk, a Civil War exhibition and visitor center housed in a nineteenth-century iron works, and an outdoor recreational space. Partners in this new effort were the Richmond Historic Riverfront Foundation, a coalition of local businesses and government, and the Richmond National Battlefield Park of the National Park Service. The latter had a Civil War visitor center that was poorly located and seriously in need of funds for reinterpretation and renovation.

Park superintendent Cynthia MacLeod saw the riverfront project as an opportunity to enlarge and reinterpret the Civil War exhibition, adding current scholarship and better design, when the center was moved. The space for the expanded and updated exhibition, to be called the Richmond Civil War Visitors' Center, was a large renovated section within the old Tredegar Iron Works, famous for its contribution to the Confederate military. The riverfront outdoor recreational plan included a mile-long walk on the restored Kanawha Canal and murals depicting themes in Richmond's history. Intended to be tied to the floodwall that separated the James River from the Canal Walk, these murals were printed on thirteen vinyl panels that held a total of twenty-nine images. General Robert E. Lee was on the eleventh panel, under the heading of "war," sharing that section with Indian chief Powhatan, images of the burning of Richmond during the Civil War, and a World War I soldier. The design work was done by the well-known New York firm of Ralph Applebaum and Associates with the aid of a local historical interpretation committee.

Panel 11 was among the first to be put up, just before the official Memorial Day 1999 opening, and a newspaper photographer caught General Lee as he rose in lonely splendor over the Canal Walk. When this image appeared next morning in the local paper, black city councilman Sa'ad El-Amin called members of the Richmond Historic Riverfront Foundation, saying that Lee's image was offensive to African Americans and that its inclusion could precipitate a boycott and a protest. By the end of the day, it was down. Almost immediately, there was a general outcry among southern heritage groups, especially the Heritage Defense Committee of the Sons of Confederate Veterans. Still, the opening went on as planned, with most of Richmond's public officials in support of the Canal Walk and hoping for a compromise on the Lee image.[1]

On the day of the opening of the Canal Walk, with Lee's image still down, ex-governor Douglas Wilder, the first elected black governor of Virginia—or any state—was riding on a canal boat full of dignitaries that passed under the Fourteenth Street canal overpass. A contingent of the Sons of the Confederacy had stationed themselves on the overpass and draped the Stars and Bars over the side. In Wilder's words, "As the canal boat on which I was riding . . . was about to glide under a bridge draped with the stars and bars of the Confederacy, I rose, smiled and saluted the flag. The taunts, shouts and invective subsided . . . and we sailed on." Wilder later explained, "I acted to defuse the tensions . . . I believe in inclusiveness." But, he emphasized, white Richmonders needed to comprehend that "some things symbolize, to a degree unfathomable to persons who are not aggrieved parties, images of a past replete with segregation and subordination."[2]

Once again Richmond had a conflict that was irresistibly cinematic and thus attractive to national media under the general theme of race-based divisions over the interpretation of local history. The motto of the Richmond Chamber of Commerce is "Richmond: Still Making History," and it is so true as to be painful for local businesspeople who devoutly wish they could settle on a story of the city that would satisfy both black and white residents and—most of all—draw visitors and customers to the city's historic, cultural, and commercial sites. Richmond is just one of many postindustrial American cities that have, in the past three decades, turned to tourism as a strategy for overcoming the loss of an industrial base. But because it has a more dramatic and contentious history as the capital of the Confederacy, the dilemmas of heritage tourism as applied to the interpretation of race and slavery are more sharply drawn and more visible on the landscape.

Richmond's history is displayed on a terrain of monuments, memorials, plaques, buildings, cemeteries, and streetscapes that commemorate not just the ultrahigh drama of the Civil War years but a particular version of that event and its meaning. For one hundred years after the end of the Civil War, Richmond was the central site for the production and maintenance of the Confederate version of the causes of the Civil War, the nature of African American enslavement, and the postwar sufferings of the southern people. This version argued for the relatively benign nature of slavery, the states' rights origins of the Civil War, the ruthlessness of military Reconstruction and the necessity for keeping the races separate. It was a white, patrician and self-justifying narrative known collectively as the "Lost Cause."[3] This historical emphasis obscured Richmond's long history as a commercial and industrial city, and the tensions generated by a historical commitment to racial segregation threatened, by the late twentieth century, to delay the city's desired transformation into a New New South banking, business, and governmental center.

But a region could reach the New New South only by passing through the New South. In the decades after the Civil War and Reconstruction, Richmond's white leadership had several goals: to memorialize the Confederacy, to make Richmond part of the New South industrial economy, to embrace at least part of the 1890s City Beautiful urban design movement, and to effectively separate the city's black population from the white. Planning for public space was one city function that harmonized all these goals. The space that commemorated the Confederacy also staked out boundaries. Commemorative space was seen as part of the real city and as quality space for white people. A series of decisions about what to memorialize and where to place monuments and plaques defined the city's governmental and cultural sectors and was part of planning for elite new neighborhoods in the late nineteenth and early twentieth centuries.[4]

Memorialization of the Confederacy included Monument Avenue, a broad tree-lined expanse of large late-Victorian and colonial revival homes along an avenue of statues to Confederate heroes. While it was still a vast field, in the 1880s, the developers of the tract wisely offered a section of land for the statue of Robert E. Lee that was subsequently placed there and dedicated in 1890. As hoped, the developers saw the remaining land rise in value and be taken into the city. Downtown, near the state capitol and its growing complex of buildings with plaques honoring aspects of the Confederate capitol, other commemorative sites evolved. The Valentine Museum, founded in the 1890s and housed in an old mansion, displayed the collections and curiosities of local elite families and reflected their interests. Ultimately, it served the function of a celebratory city museum. Two blocks away, the Confederate Literary Memorial Society opened what is now the Museum of the Confederacy, with the wartime home of Jefferson Davis restored and opened next door as the Confederate White House.[5]

The 1919 celebration for the unveiling of the Stonewall Jackson equestrian monument marked the last of the constellation of Confederate heroes to be enshrined on Monument Avenue.[6] The imposing new homes that faced the monuments added weight to the avenue's effort at historic interpretation. At the same time that Monument Avenue was being constructed to center the new Richmond in harmony with the Lost Cause vision, another once-central neighborhood was becoming politically and historically peripheral. In the antebellum years, the downtown neighborhood of Jackson Ward had housed both black and white families. Following the Civil War, this community of large and solidly built freestanding dwellings and frame row houses became the acknowledged political and economic center of black Richmond. Slowly, after Reconstruction, black political representation was first confined to Jackson Ward and then effectively eliminated.

This manipulation of the political and cultural landscape did not efface the black presence. For generations before and after the Civil War, Richmond's black citizens constructed and preserved an alternative version of Richmond's townscape history that was expressed in parades, protests, oral traditions, counterinterpretations of historic sites and events, and a private mental geography of the city with its own sacred spaces. Black resistance to the dominant narrative in Richmond was a particularly herculean task, given the city's six generations as the center of the romanticized version of the Old South and the Civil War. The heightened historical awareness in Richmond, however, encouraged a more engaged and sophisticated black response to the city's efforts to control public space.

At the end of the Civil War, it was quickly apparent that ordinary black citizens understood the importance of claiming public space. As early as the summer after Robert E. Lee's April 1865 surrender, black Richmonders wrote to a New York newspaper about their inability to walk freely on the public streets without special passes reminiscent of slavery.[7] African Americans also quickly began to celebrate four holidays after the Civil War: New Year's Day, George Washington's birthday, April 3 as their own emancipation day, and the Fourth of July. Black militias paraded on these and other occasions, while black parades for occasions such as funerals and conventions were frequent occurrences, often featuring the uniformed members of various benevolent societies. By the beginning of the twentieth century, most of these activities had been restricted to black neighborhoods, although parades were known to march from one black neighborhood to another through the center of town.[8]

It was in this context of parallel histories that Richmond's civic leadership decided to promote heritage tourism. The Richmond Historic Riverfront Project, with its heritage tourism components, was not the city's first attempt at revitalization or preservation. Beginning in the 1950s, Richmond shared the fate of many of America's cities with an old industrial core, losing first its industrial base and then its commercial sector. Post–World War II federal housing and transportation policies and the Supreme Court desegregation decision made many American cities, including Richmond, lose middle- and working-class white population to black families restricted from buying in the suburbs. From the late 1950s onward, Richmond tried every form of urban planning, including whole-sale demolition of homes in the form of "slum clearance," a renewal strat-egy that characteristically destroyed African American neighborhoods and landmarks in order to put up such structures as civic centers, free-ways, and sports arenas. From the 1940s through the 1960s, white historic preservationists among local elites frequently allied with black families in the central city to oppose the destruction of central neighborhoods, but with little success.

By the late 1970s, Richmond had a black mayor, and the City Council was predominantly black. Integration of service industries, public facili-ties, and retail stores had seriously undermined downtown black busi-nesses, and the flagship department stores of once-proud Broad Street were failing. The suburbs were booming and stretching farther into the countryside. Black and white businessmen and politicians made their first efforts to work together to revive the downtown shopping area with the formation of Richmond Renaissance, a racially balanced public-private partnership to set priorities for downtown. Since the advent of Jim Crow, white Richmonders had shopped on one side of Broad Street, Richmond's main commercial thoroughfare, and black Richmonders had shopped on the other. One important effort sponsored by Richmond Renaissance in the 1980s linked the two sides of Broad Street with a symbolic overpass. Residents hoped it was a bridge between the black and white communities and a turn from the past to a new future.

Part of this effort was a festival marketplace, a popular urban solution of the 1970s and 1980s that frequently contained small shops and per-forming arts space. But in the late 1980s and early 1990s, in a final spasm of downtown department store, hotel, and small shop closings, the festi-val market closed, too. Near the James River, private entrepreneurial ef-forts with city assistance raised tall glass and steel insurance and banking buildings, too far from the old downtown for a lunch crowd. In the old to-bacco warehouse district and docks area, a restaurant district was slowly created, but the old downtown remained virtually empty. By the mid-1980s, the city's leaders had determined to put more emphasis on a mar-keting strategy for heritage tourism.[9]

Heritage tourism appeared more in harmony with the dominant history of Richmond, long on display, than with the research well under way by academic and public historians in 1980s Richmond. Indeed, it appeared at first that it might be a simple ratcheting up of Lost Cause history. Public monuments and displays are a form of civic education, and control of their sites, forms, and inscriptions is control of the meaning of local history. The right to create and participate in public discourse is at the heart of claims to public space, and these rights had been very effectively asserted by the Lost Cause advocates. How could Richmond, as a majority black city with a majority black city council, reconcile this Lost Cause landscape of tourism with the perspectives of the people they represented? How could heritage tourism be useful as an economic development strategy when blacks saw historicizing the city as a way of claiming it for whites and ignoring or destroying the physical representations of black history? To further complicate historic interpretation, many of the city's blacks saw any reference to slavery, or "subordination," as Wilder phrased it, as inherently embarrassing or shameful, reinvoking a sense of powerlessness, especially against wealthy and literate white elites.[10]

The city hoped to add African American history to the walking tours, site plaques, and memorials in the city, but not to erase the Lost Cause landscape that continued to draw tourists. African American tourism had become an important economic force, especially in the South, and it attracted both black and white visitors to sites.[11] Promoters of heritage tourism also assumed that adding African American monuments to the landscape would "heal wounds" and promote reconciliation. Perhaps the hard questions of interpretation, agency, and responsibility could be avoided in the rapid proliferation of monuments. And perhaps African American history and the Lost Cause could coexist in comfort in the interests of diversity and heritage tourism.

A remapping of the historic landscape by city museums began the process of modifying Confederate historiography. Local museums, long the conservators of a distinctly Lost Cause history, might seem unlikely frontline troops in an assault on tradition. But the New New South that arose after the civil rights movement of the 1950s and 1960s needed not only to revitalize downtown but to signal to the world of commerce that its racial conflicts were over, reconciliation had taken place, and nothing would interfere with the global transaction of business. The generally conservative white business progressives of most southern cities could find common cause with predominantly black city councils and business-men in an effort to create public memorials and a new city narrative that signaled an era of racial harmony.[12]

The museum of the history of Richmond, then the Valentine Museum and currently the Valentine Richmond History Center, produced contro-versial and well-documented exhibits on race issues in Richmond, and these exhibits attracted black Richmonders to the museum for the first time, won National Endowment for the Humanities awards, and re-ceived national notice. The Virginia Historical Society and the Museum of the Confederacy, with nationally important archives and a large visit-ing public, were also successful in obtaining public humanities grants for exhibits that employed national scholars and designers and engaged as-pects of southern and Virginia history previously unaddressed. By 1990, the director of the city museum had set his sights on an enlarged museum, one in which the entire physical city was used to tell the story of four cen-turies of a racially inclusive history.[13]

The black and white leadership of the city invested heavily in these plans and arranged a lease with the owners of the Tredegar Iron Works for a historical park and a cutting-edge exhibit center there that would be called Valentine Riverside. Valentine Riverside opened at the Tredegar in May 1994. The next February, it cut its days of operation from five to three per week, and it closed after Labor Day 1995. The entire concept failed in a swirl of accusations and counteraccusations about fiscal ac-countability. The fall of Valentine Riverside was due to an interplay of factors that included an overextension of its financial and intellectual re-sources, while attention was increasingly focused on public relations and marketing strategies. There was also a sense among many people that board members and financial backers had grown tired of supporting ex-hibitions that appeared to privilege African American history rather than simply include it. The city of Richmond took over the museum later that year, as part of a deal with Crestar Bank that included the assumption of the $9.1 million loan that the Valentine owed Crestar.[14]

Regrouping as the Richmond Historic Riverfront Foundation, a coali-tion of public and private organizations tried again with the Civil War ex-hibit and the Canal Walk. But as they organized, another major dilemma of public commemoration arose. In 1993, Arthur Ashe, the Richmond-raised tennis star, died prematurely. An ambitious local sculptor joined forces with an educational foundation created by Ashe to promote a statue of Ashe in the city. In 1995, the City Planning Commission decided to place the statue in the Confederate historic district of Monument Avenue, not in Jackson Ward or near the sports center dedicated to Ashe.[15] To this point, Jackson Ward had received such memorials to African Americans as the city offered. Progressive-era bank president and social reformer Maggie Walker's home was authorized as a National Historic Site in 1978, and the commemorative statue of Richmond-born and nationally known tap dancer Bill "Bojangles" Robinson was placed in Jackson Ward.

Efforts at inclusiveness and diversity in heritage tourism often depend on keeping the narrative very general or the conflicting stories geographically separate. Richmond was entering a period when these conventions would no longer work. In the public debate that followed the announcement that the Arthur Ashe statue was to go on Monument Avenue, four local positions and an aesthetic caveat were discernible. An African American weekly newspaper contended that Ashe was too good for "Rebels Row." One African American columnist for the city's leading paper, who first wrote that Ashe's statue on Monument Avenue would be "a symbol of racial reconciliation," changed his mind and concluded that Monument Avenue was "a painful reminder of black subjugation." Others argued that Ashe's accomplishments as a tennis player did not qualify him for Monument Avenue. Still others argued that such an inclusion would be good for the city and its image. Adding to the problem was the fact that there was no real review process for the Ashe statue, and many people thought that the sculpture was just bad art. Finally, largely outside these local assessments, those who argued that Monument Avenue was reserved for Confederate heroes were mostly members of southern heritage organizations, particularly the Heritage Defense Committee of the Sons of the Confederacy.[16]

Significantly, the *local* arguments were about placement and not about whether or not Arthur Ashe should have a statue. It would have been difficult for anyone to object to a statue of the high-minded and very talented Ashe.[17] While the city was ready for African American history, some were not ready to abandon segregated spheres of memorialization. In this, the city exemplified the American experience where residential neighborhoods remained racially segregated while work and public space were integrated. Black neighborhoods still seemed the logical place for African American history markers, as white neighborhoods were for the placement of markers to white heroes. Space such as the Canal Walk area was seen as neutral. With the Arthur Ashe statue, versions of inclusive history that had avoided direct confrontation for two decades appeared to collide in public space.

Still, when the Sons of Confederate Veterans (SCV) convened in Richmond a month after the dedication of the statue, they ignored the statue and direct confrontation by marching only beneath the generals. "We have no objection to the statue," was their public statement. "We aren't going anywhere near it. It's not one of our concerns." [18] The Virginia SCV did not want to appear to be attacking the idea of a statue to Ashe, but only marking off and protecting Monument Avenue's Confederate space. While the SCV was present at the margins of the Ashe statue controversy, that controversy remained a Richmond debate, with a local resolution reached through public hearings. But when the vinyl image of Robert E. Lee was removed from the neutral space of the Canal Walk, the southern heritage groups led a more visible protest. Southern heritage organizations from outside the local area and even outside the state soon became involved in Richmond's heritage tourism efforts at the Canal Walk. These groups were recently energized and politicized by efforts to remove Confederate symbols from state flags, and they had determined to confront what they defined as, at best, "revisionists" in Richmond.

To resolve the unexpected crisis of the Lee image, the city appointed a multiracial group of civic leaders—nine whites, nine blacks, and one Chickahominy—who agreed, within a month, on this compromise: Lee would return to the Canal Walk, but in civilian dress, and he would share space with two other images—a black Union soldier and Abraham Lincoln, who walked through Richmond two days after the Confederate departure from the city.[19] This compromise appeared to satisfy the Lee supporters in the city more than those who wanted the banner down. Two African American City Council members who voted for the compromise were briefly threatened with a boycott by a coalition of black church, political and civic groups.

Sa'ad El-Amin, the black city councilman who first protested it, did not accept the compromise. The most common complaint of black Richmonders was that even if they were not as militant as El-Amin, they were still tired of encountering Lee everywhere in the city. One black man spoke for many when he said, "We have too many things reminding us of General Lee." A poll showed that slightly more than half the city's African Americans favored taking down the vinyl banner, and 73 percent of white Richmonders wanted it up.[20] White Richmond tended to say that, like it or not, Lee was part of the city's history. The chairman of the Heritage Defense Committee of the Sons of Confederate Veterans was more positive: "it sounds great . . . I have no problem with the others . . . though I'm certainly not a Lincoln fan." One woman said, "As long as it's Robert E. Lee, I don't care if he's in his shorts."[21]

Professionals in urban studies and interracial civic groups in Richmond had another perspective on the removal of the Lee image. "We keep tripping over the same racial wire," said one, adding that the selection process for the images "was kept very private, isolated . . . we cannot do business like that." "We have to lower our defenses," said another, and talk openly about Richmond's history.[22] These comments echoed earlier complaints that decisions about the form and placement of the Arthur Ashe statue had been rushed through by the City Council without time for public comment on either the statue's depiction of Ashe or its placement.[23] The riverfront project had tried to avoid racial divisions by using an informed and diverse group of citizens and historians as the advisory committee for the Canal Walk images and the reinterpretation of Civil War history, but the perception in Richmond that the public had not been sufficiently involved remained.

The Sons of Confederate Veterans had a different interpretation of what removal of the Lee image meant. Just as freedmen in Richmond in 1865 understood the importance of freedom in public space, so the current SCV adopted the language of multiculturalism for their own ends and insisted that Confederate heritage was one more heritage within an overall diversity. They said that taking down the Lee mural was a violation of their right to celebrate their Confederate heritage, and the Southern Heritage Movement filed lawsuits and complaints alleging "heritage violations" for such actions. This was part of an effort to persuade Americans that they were just another self-respecting ethnicity and not motivated by racism.[24]

Since that 1999 compromise, the interpretation of Richmond's long history of slavery, the Civil War, Reconstruction, and Jim Crow segregation has remained contentious, unpredictable, and very public. The display and interpretation of historic symbols is as contested in the early years of the twenty-first century as at any other time since the end of the Civil War. Virginia currently celebrates Lee-Jackson-King Day in January, an effort to merge the old Lee-Jackson Day with the new Martin Luther King Jr. Day. Although awkward in phrasing, dysfunctional in its grouping, and pleasing no one entirely, it meets the state's need to have just one paid holiday in January. On Lee-Jackson-King Day in January 2000, arsonists torched the new banner with Lee's image. A new copy was soon up, and all public officials condemned the incident.[25] More positively, in June 2000 the new Richmond Civil War Visitor's Center opened. Sa'ad El-Amin visited the exhibition and declared himself "favorably impressed," saying that the center struck "a sensitive balance." Visitors commented that the exhibit had presented a balanced view of racial life and death in Civil War Richmond.[26]

In 2001 former Virginia governor Douglas Wilder announced that a National Slavery Museum would be built in Fredericksburg, Virginia, and Virginia governor James Gilmore declined to designate April as Confederate History and Heritage Month.[27] But the black mayor of Suffolk, Virginia, recognized Confederate History and Heritage Month. The mayor assured the president of the local NAACP that he had gone to the local library and looked it up and could say with assurance that slavery was not the defining issue in the Civil War.[28] In 2002, the new director at the Museum of the Confederacy put up the Confederate battle flag at the door as an "education piece." "We are going to be a professional proponent of Confederate history," the new director said, labeling his approach "inclusive."[29]

But it was the first major project of the twenty-first century that brought Richmond back into the national spotlight. In March 2002, the U.S. Historical Society, a nonprofit organization directed by local businessman Robert Kline, proposed a donation of a statue of Abraham Lincoln to the National Park Service (NPS) through the Richmond National Battlefield Park. The NPS accepted the statue as part of an outdoor interpretive exhibition on the grounds of the new Civil War Visitors' Center at the Tredegar Iron Works. The statue was to commemorate Lincoln's visit to Richmond two days after the city's surrender and to stress the healing words in his second inaugural address. The superintendent of the Richmond National Battlefield Park, Cynthia MacLeod, said the statue was intended as a tool for education and civic discussion.

Kline, who had earlier raised money for the Museum of the Confederacy, derived most of his income from the sale of small historic and patriotic replicas but was reported to lose money on his nonprofit. He saw the Lincoln statue as part of reconciliation and understanding, and, aware of the controversy over the placement of the Ashe statue, he made his offer to the National Park Service to avoid city jurisdiction. The artist commissioned, David Frech, minimized the monumental aspects by depicting a life-size Lincoln resting on a bench with his son, Tad, and looking pensive. The base of the statue would feature a quotation from Lincoln's second inaugural address: "to bind up the nation's wounds."

The statue's proposed placement on the site of the NPS Civil War Center had the opposite effect from what Kline desired. Much more than the Ashe statue or the Lee banner on the Canal Walk, the Lincoln statue proposal brought opposition from southern heritage groups. The negative response to the statue came largely from outside Richmond. Within the city, the statue drew support from the mayor and city council, from the conservative *Richmond Times-Dispatch,* and from the city's historical and cultural organizations. The Virginia Historical Society sponsored a half-day seminar on Lincoln and the Civil War. The *Times-Dispatch* responded to the placement of the statue with an editorial entitled "At Last!" Lincoln as a figure of reconciliation fit well with both the city's southern business progressives and most of its African Americans. Kline was among many businessmen who equated healing with commerce. The cost of the project was more than $675,000, and the U.S. Historical Society intended to raise funds by selling 750 miniatures of the statue at $875 each.[30]

The controversy came at an opportune time for various neo-Confederate historians, heritage groups, and fringe hate groups who decided in the 1990s to declare war on the image of Lincoln as the great moderate who would have prevented radical Reconstruction. This version had been a prominent part of Confederate history since its origins. But Lincoln as devious and dishonest fit the needs of those attempting to revive old arguments about states' rights as the cause of the Civil War, even as scholars appeared to have put that argument finally to rest. The archives at the Richmond National Battlefield Park contain some four hundred e-mails and letters, some letters painstakingly handwritten, that poured into the office of Superintendent MacLeod from all over the United States, but predominantly from the South outside Richmond. Most were very hostile to the idea of a statue of Lincoln in downtown Richmond and eager to explain why Lincoln was not a friend to the fallen South. Arguments that it was not on federal land, that it was a private donation, and that it was not a monument did little to mollify the protesters. Opponents said this privately funded statue was like placing a statue of John Wilkes Booth at Ford's Theater or Osama bin Laden in New York City.

There was a pattern to these communications. They argued first that secession was legal and "Lincoln's war" illegal. Just as damning in this indictment were Lincoln's motives: he was a "war criminal" who was no friend to blacks, seeking simply to deport them. They further argued that, as a former Whig and advocate of Henry Clay's American system, Lincoln served the interests of northern rich elites in declaring war. He "killed 620,000 Americans so rich Northern industrialists could get richer." Further, he was a "friend of 1848 communist revolutionaries in Europe."[31] All or some of these claims were repeated in most communications and were the product of a political effort among certain southern heritage groups to tap into white southern resentment of their perceived loss of political and cultural power since the late 1960s.

In addition to the true believers and romantics still deeply involved in the Lost Cause story, there was a political agenda, rooted in the southern strategy that had turned the solid Democratic South into the solidly Republican South over three decades.[32] Working-class resistance to African American civil rights included deep resentment at the power of the federal government to impose vast social changes and anger at a national media that frequently appeared to mock their cultural beliefs. Northerners, government employees, and highly educated people of any background were frequently seen as the natural enemies of their cultural truths. Southern heritage organizations frequently warn that the South will no longer put up with the "continued bigotry and hatred articulately expressed by the United States government and through [the] entertainment industry and the 'public' press."[33] They view southern heritage as an effort to "fight the centralization of power in Washington."[34]

On April 6, 2003, the Lincoln statue was dedicated in a ceremony in which speakers emphasized Lincoln's preservation of the Union and his desire to treat ex-Confederates with leniency. Overhead, a small airplane trailed a banner that read "Sic Semper Tyrannis." About eighty people, mostly Sons of Confederate Veterans, held a protest at the grave of Jefferson Davis in nearby Hollywood Cemetery, the site of the graves of thousands of Confederate dead. About two dozen people marched on to the dedication site, where they provided a background chorus of whistles and chants. No official from the Philadelphia or Washington regional offices of the National Park Service attended the ceremony.[35] The furor over the statue did not end with its dedication, and some months later, in January 2004, Waite Rawls, the director of the Museum of the Confederacy, who had earlier vowed to reemphasize the values of the Confederacy, resigned his membership in the Sons of Confederate Veterans over their stance against the Lincoln statue.

What may be learned from this chronicle of the last few decades in one racially divided southern city where both blacks and whites have long memories? First, the unintended consequences of a heritage tourism strategy for downtown revitalization continue. If the New South perceived its needs as industrialization and racial segregation, the New New South needs the appearance, at least, of racial healing in order to attract both business headquarters and tourists. Heritage tourism as a strategy is essentially commercial and seeks to both entertain and inform its audience. Its tendency is toward the popular or dominant story, often at odds with a minority perspective. Some cities, such as New York and San Francisco, can support the niche marketing of ethnic heritages, offering Chinese, Indian, Italian, or Nordic histories without infringing on another's narrative. But Richmond is perhaps the most dramatic example of an American city where multiculturalism has meant black and white, and the narratives and sites do overlap and contradict each other. In attempting to use heritage tourism as a revitalization strategy, Richmond learned the painful lessons of trying to make *unum* out of *pluribus* on the historic landscape as well as in the narratives.[36]

Currently in Richmond, "healing" remains an attractive thematic construct, still believed to be useful as both a reassurance to global business and a draw for heritage tourism. The latest effort at Civil War interpretation in Richmond, the proposed Tredegar National Civil War Center Foundation, promises to tell the story of Union, including African American, and Confederate Civil War soldiers at one site. The foundation has cultivated widespread local support and hired national scholars as consultants. Historian Charles Dew, one of the consultants, has said, "I can see the Tredegar National Civil War Center playing a healing role for our country by treating the history of this era in an open, forthright, and all-inclusive manner."[37]

The contrast between Richmond as "holy city" of the Confederacy and the city's gritty rust-belt realities and current majority black citizenry illustrates very clearly the need for strategies of commemoration that consider all the perceptions of important symbols, including what their placement says about ownership in the city. Every historical exhibition, walk, or talk inevitably draws on the cultural assumptions and resources of the people who make it and constitutes a contested terrain. No matter how it is organized, the subject matter is inevitably open to multiple interpretations, based on the cultural assumptions of the creators and viewers. Groups attempting to establish or maintain their own sense of community will challenge heritage tourism that overlaps with their concerns, will demand real power within such efforts, or will establish alternative institutions, memorials, and exhibits.[38]

The challenge for public historians is to negotiate between the "stakeholders," persons with some claim to the story being told, and the historic record. One task is to strengthen institutions that help individuals and groups exert control over the way they are represented, and another task is to provide expertise in the presentation of competing cultural claims. Community planning should take primacy over economic planning, and the community must be convinced that comprehensive and accurate research and data collection are at the core of the enterprise. Issues of cultural resources and site integrity must be negotiated and mediated. The community should be an informed and discerning "first tourist." This local support is essential, and locals usually have a clear understanding of how the promotion of certain sites will affect the economics of the neighborhood. If local historians have been part of the process of cultural inventory and have made their research methods known and accepted, there will be community benefits whether or not heritage tourism is profitable. Good-faith efforts to listen to historical informants and anticipated audiences are essential, but well-researched history will be useful during and after the current struggles over tourism destinations and real estate values are resolved.

Increasingly over three decades, Richmond has adopted some or all of these strategies. The city's residents have struggled to find a modest comfort level for the interpretation of their past, and they have succeeded to a significant extent. The goals of the southern heritage groups most recently involved in public history disputes were not the goals of the Richmond business progressives and the city government. For the most part, the latter groups had reason to feel that they had worked through their major interpretive issues and had reached at least a tentative accord. From former governor Douglas Wilder to Museum of the Confederacy director Waite Rawls, the black and white politicians and businessmen of the city had acknowledged their mutual concern and dependency.

The ongoing effort to interpret the Civil War in Richmond with due attention to the role of slavery and the perspectives of black and white leads to one overriding conclusion: heritage tourism cannot be a pilgrimage to an unchanging shrine, and sites are going to be forums, not temples. Faith in scholarship's ability to persuade communities that their interests lie in acknowledging complexity and diversity is the motivator for most of the research done by academic and public historians. But can it overcome cultural and political forces that do not accept the standards of interpretation used by historians and are primarily interested in history as a revenue enhancement or political strategy? There is reason for hope in the progress that Richmond has made in the last generation. The city has earned its higher level of local comfort with the interpretation of race. But there is also reason for concern in the national attention that Richmond's interpretive struggles now attract. Richmond is likely to remain an irresistible symbol for national controversy over the public historical interpretation of race and the Civil War so long as national political agendas have an important racial component.

Although it was not true at the outset, ultimately the Civil War became a war to end slavery, placing the federal government in the role of emancipator and protector of African American slaves. The symbolism of this role remains complex and controversial even a century and a half later. COURTESY OF THE NATIONAL MUSEUM OF AMERICAN HISTORY, SMITHSONIAN INSTITUTION

9

"A Cosmic Threat":

The National Park Service Addresses

the Causes of

the American Civil War

Dwight T. Pitcaithley

In a few years, the United States will mark yet another anniversary of the Civil War. How that event will manifest itself remains to be seen. Earlier celebrations (and they were, indeed, celebrations) focused on the themes of reconciliation and honor and bravery and a common remembering of a shared national experience. The centennial of the war (1961–1965), directed by a congressionally created commission chaired initially by U.S. Grant III, featured Civil War tours, battle reenactments, essay contests and other educational programs, and a variety of state-sponsored activities such as traveling exhibitions, history mobiles, and commemorative activities. In spite of coinciding with the modern civil rights movement, the centennial avoided the "emancipationist" memory of the war and stressed, instead, the "reconciliationist" memory.[1] The historian Allan Nevins, who followed Grant as chairman of the commission, noted the inability of the commission to embrace the civil rights aspects of the war:

> Southern leaders in the movement for [Civil War] commemoration formed an organization of their own, and made strenuous efforts to use it in bringing pressure upon the National Commission to take no stand on

the question of equal rights. In doing this, they came into collision with the announced purpose of the national Government to see that all federal agencies complied with the explicit requirements of the Fourteenth Amendment, and to see that the Negro was not only given full equal rights, but was welcomed to them.[2]

The separation of the causes and the meanings of the war from the 1960s national celebration was not something new. It grew out of a public memory of the Civil War that had been shaped and cultivated by former Confederates and their children through organizations such as the Sons of Confederate Veterans and United Daughters of the Confederacy.[3] Popular not only among southern whites, the "Lost Cause" interpretation of the war held that "slavery was a benign institution, that secession had been a last resort occasioned by fanatical abolitionist attacks on southern constitutional rights, and that Confederates had struggled bravely for four years to sustain those rights but finally had been beaten by a materially superior foe."[4] At least three respected historians, C. Vann Woodward, John Hope Franklin, and Oscar Handlin, noticed the centennial's failure to connect an understanding of the growing civil rights movement to the causes and consequences of the Civil War.[5] Noting that the war failed to confer complete freedom on African Americans and that any subsequent Civil War observance must acknowledge that fact, Franklin bitterly observed that "the marching of regiments of blue and gray, the pious declarations of orators, and the reenactment of Civil War battles may distract the unknowing observer. But it is well for us to remind him and ourselves that such observations do much to excite the imagination and stimulate certain kinds of loyalties. They do little, however, to set this nation on the urgent task of completing the work begun by the war."[6]

The conclusion of the centennial celebration at Appomattox in 1965 with an observance later described by Michael Kammen as extracting "a mythic Confederate moral victory from the facts of defeat, with histrionics and warped history as minor costs" also roughly coincided with an explosion of historical research throughout the country.[7] Labeled the "New Social History" (and later the "New American History"), this approach to analyzing and understanding the history of the United States resulted in a reexamination of the Civil War era that significantly altered and expanded existing scholarship.[8] While the scholarly discussion of the war over these years was rich and deep and led to a more complex and nu-anced interpretation of the relationship between the institution of slavery and secession and the failure of the United States to step up to the intent of the Fourteenth and Fifteenth Amendments to the Constitution, the new scholarship had little effect on the generations-old Lost Cause interpreta-tion of the war. The American public, especially white southerners, clung to a more comfortable understanding of the war that distanced the insti-tution of slavery from the coming of the war and embraced military honor as its most enduring legacy. Gaines Foster commented on this phe-nomenon:

> The rapid healing of national divisions and damaged southern self-image, however, came at the cost of deriving little insight or wisdom from the past. Rather than looking at the war as a tragic failure and trying to understand it, or even condemn it, Americans, North and South, chose to view it as a glorious time to be celebrated. Most ignored the fact that the nation had failed to resolve the debate over the nature of the Union and to eliminate the contradictions between its equalitarian ideals and the insti-tution of slavery without resort to bloody civil war. Instead, they cele-brated the war's triumphant nationalism and martial glory.[9]

Over the past several decades, Civil War–era historic sites and muse-ums, with few exceptions, have generally avoided all discussion of the causes of the war and its consequences, or they actively or passively em-braced the Lost Cause interpretation. The managers of historic planta-tions and battlefields determined that discussions of slavery in any but the most tangential way should be left to classrooms and other academic set-tings. The new scholarship, by and large, remained outside public presen-tations and discussions of the Civil War.[10] Beginning in the 1990s, however, African American history in general and slavery in particular has gained fuller discussion in the public arena, driven partly by this growing body of literature, partly by the growing number of museums and historic sites dedicated to African American history, and partly by the growth of a better-educated and more sophisticated cadre of historic-site and museum administrators.

The National Park Service experienced this changing environment through both external and internal forces. Congress played a major and somewhat surprising role in expanding the interpretation at historic sites. In 1989, through legislation affecting park boundaries at Fredericksburg and Spotsylvania County battlefields, Congress inserted language specifically instructing the secretary of the interior to interpret the park "in the larger context of the Civil War and American history, including the causes and consequences of the Civil War and including the effects of the war on all the American people, especially on the American South."[11] Similar legislation the following year imposed the same responsibility on the secretary for Gettysburg.[12] Boundary expansion legislation for Vicksburg National Military Park instructed the secretary to interpret the "campaign and siege of Vicksburg from August 1862 to July 4, 1863, and the history of Vicksburg under Union occupation during the Civil War and Reconstruction."[13]

Congress's expansive action must be understood in the context of other legislation passed during this decade. In 1991, Congress forced the National Park Service to reverse decades of management and interpretation at Custer Battlefield National Monument that had firmly established the park as a shrine to George Armstrong Custer. Over the years, the glorification of Custer had come at the expense of a deeper understanding of the Sioux, Cheyenne, and Arapaho who shared the battlefield with the Seventh Cavalry that summer day in 1876. (One exhibit label during the 1970s is reputed to have declared, "There were no survivors!" casually ignoring hundreds of victorious Indian survivors.) The legislation changed the name of the park to Little Bighorn Battlefield National Monument, required the secretary to create a more balanced interpretation of the event, and mandated that a memorial to the Indians who had fallen be erected. Other legislation passed during the decade included the creation of Manzanar National Historic Site (1992), Sand Creek Massacre National Historic Site (2000), Washita Battlefield National Historic Site (1996), *Brown v. Board of Education* National Historic Site (1992), Little Rock Central High School National Historic Site (1998), and Selma to Montgomery National Historic Trail (1996). In the creation of these parks, Congress sent a message not only to the National Park Service but also to the American public that a useful history must include both painful as well as prideful aspects of the past. This point was made manifest in a 1994 article by Yale professor of history Robin Winks entitled "Sites of Shame."

Education is best done with examples. These examples include that which we regret, that which is to be avoided, as well as that for which we strive. No effective system of education can be based on unqualified praise, for all education instructs people of the difference between moral and wanton acts and how to distinguish between the desirable and the undesirable. If this premise is correct, we cannot omit the negative lessons of history.[14]

The creation of these parks and Congress's interest in requiring parks to say something important about the past stood in stark contrast to the manner in which the National Park Service had traditionally interpreted the Civil War battlefields under its care. Until very recently, the causes and consequences of the Civil War were studiously avoided in NPS literature and exhibits. The National Park Service based its interpretation instead on a descriptive narration of battles devoid of any explanation of cause, context, or consequence. By 1998, it became apparent to most managers of Civil War battlefields that change was not only necessary but unavoidable. The visiting public deserved more at these special places than a mere recounting of the battle. Conceived and organized by the superintendents themselves, a meeting in Nashville in August 1998 fundamentally altered the National Park Service's interpretation of the Civil War. In addition to other common issues, the managers discussed the presentation of the parks to the public and came to the conclusion that "battlefield interpretation must establish the site's particular place in the continuum of war; illuminate the social, economic, and cultural issues that caused or were affected by the war, illustrate the breadth of human experience during the period, and establish the relevance of the war to people today."[15] Congress endorsed the battlefield managers' initiative a year later in the Department of Interior appropriations bill, charging the secretary to "encourage Civil War battle sites to recognize and include in all of their public displays and multi-media educational presentations the unique role that the institution of slavery played in causing the Civil War and its role, if any, at the individual battle sites."[16]

An examination of National Park Service–generated literature about the war reveals the degree to which the managers' decision represented a stunning break with National Park Service interpretive tradition. The most detailed explanation of the coming of the war up to that time was found in the park brochure for Fort Sumter, which began, "On December 20, 1860, after decades of sectional conflict, the people of South Carolina responded to the election of the first Republican president, Abraham Lincoln, by voting unanimously in convention to secede from the Union." [17] (Fort Sumter's brochure has since been revised to explain South Carolina's action through its 1860 Declaration of Secession, which justified secession on the basis of northern agitation against slavery.) Another National Park Service publication, *The Civil War at a Glance*, began its explanation for the war this way:

> Like a bolt of lightning out of a darkening sky, war burst upon the American landscape in the spring of 1861, climaxing decades of bitter wrangling and pitting two vast sections of the young and vigorous nation against each other. Northerners called it the War of the Rebellion, Southerners the War Between the States. We know it simply as the Civil War. [18]

Presenting parks within larger historical contexts is fundamental to National Park Service educational programs. Explaining that context occurs at sites as diverse as Women's Rights National Historical Park, site of the 1848 Women's Rights Convention; Marsh, Billings, Rockefeller National Historical Park, which commemorates the conservation movement in the United States; and the U.S.S. *Arizona* Memorial, which marks the Japanese attack on Pearl Harbor. But until 1998, the National Park Service avoided any mention of the causes of the Civil War. [19]

As news of the 1998 gathering and Congress's direction spread, heritage groups with particular interests in Civil War battlefields and the Lost Cause interpretation of the war began responding:

> Now, what I don't come to a National Battlefield Park for—to be subjected to yet another "piss-on-my-leg" story about slavery, having a not-so-thinly veiled purpose of disparaging, insulting, and slandering approximately half of the soldiers the park was built and staffed to honor. [20]

> I urge you Sir not to force our decent and honorable White Southern National Battlefield Park Rangers to, "repudiate their own great, if deeply flawed, regional culture." And, I urge you, Sir to rethink your "Black, good; White, bad" policy. [21]

It is not one of the functions of NPS to change history so that it is politically correct. When we do that, we ape the Soviet government of the 1930s through the 1960s.[22]

I do not believe the battlefield parks should become laboratories for sociological or "cultural" discussion and education. Issues of political, cultural, or ideological interest should be left to school classrooms all over the country. . . . Teaching is their job and not the job of the national military parks.[23]

I am completely disgusted with the National Park Service's new policy to post South-bashing propaganda about slavery at National "Civil War" Battlefield Parks. This mindless South-bashing has to stop if this nation is to continue being united. South-bashing propaganda sponsored by the federal parks will do nothing but increase the growing alienation of the Southern states from the rest of the nation. . . . I for one would rather see the parks defunded and turned over to the state governments to run, or closed completely, than see them used as South-bashing, hate-generating propaganda centers.[24]

The stridency of these letters, and hundreds of others received by the National Park Service, reflect the pressures from a group supporting battlefield preservation and from the Sons of Confederate Veterans. The first to register its displeasure with the National Park Service was HERITAGEPAC, a self-described "lobbying group dedicated to preservation of American battlefields." Written by Jerry Russell of Little Rock, Arkansas (who also served as national chairman for the Civil War Round Table Associates), the HERITAGEPAC newsletter for July 1999 incorrectly informed its readers that "the National Park Service, under the direction of Chief Historian Dwight Pitcaithley, has moved away from the 'military interpretation' of battlefields, toward a 'broader scope' of interpretation, completely ignoring the Congressional actions which established these national battlefield parks to commemorate battles."[25] Russell raised the alarm to his readers by stating that "at the risk of being overly dramatic, this could well be the most important letter HERITAGEPAC has ever sent out." He then continued to describe the National Park Service's new direction as a "cosmic threat to *all* battlefields in this country." "While the causes of the battle are certainly factors to be considered in the interpretation," he argued, "they should not—**must not**—supplant the interpretation of the military actions that were the battle." [26] While the intention of the superintendents was to enhance and broaden battlefield interpretation by providing a context for the battle and the war, Russell's hyperbole touched a nerve among Civil War fans and resulted in approximately one hundred letters protesting a perceived National Park Service slight of military history.

The Sons of Confederate Veterans sparked a larger response to the 1998 meeting by objecting to the Park Service's new direction in an article published in the *Confederate Veteran*. The article was accompanied by a preprinted postcard addressed to then secretary of the interior, Bruce Babbitt. The postcard contained two short paragraphs:

> It is my understanding that National Battlefield Park Rangers are being instructed to explain to visitors to sites of important battles of the War Between the States that the institution of slavery caused the War. I also understand that the role of slavery at individual battle sites is to be emphasized.

> I believe that the primary purpose of preserving battlefields is to understand the military actions which took place there and to remember the men who fought there. To attempt to change the way that a battlefield is interpreted to include social issues of the day does a great disservice to the military strategists and to the soldiers who sacrificed their all at these important battlefields. [27]

This campaign produced approximately 2,200 cards and letters of complaint. [28] Taken as a whole, the opinions expressed by those opposed to the Park Service's announced intention to place Civil War battlefields in historical context reveal how some Americans regard the national parks, the federal government, and the memory of the Civil War in contemporary society. Several initial generalizations can be drawn from these letters. First, they see the mere mention of slavery in connection with the Civil War as disparaging, insulting, slandering, South-bashing propaganda: "As a member of the Son's [*sic*] of Confederate Veterans and a reenactor, I am deeply offended at your attempt to discredit and dishonor our ancestors and hope that this practice will cease." [29] Second, they perceive incorporating current scholarship into park interpretive programs as ideological:

> I strongly urge you to join in the battle against the efforts of civil servants . . . to denigrate the military history of the United States and to hijack a vast heritage in the name of highly subjective, simplistic judgements about states' rights and slavery, some momentarily fashionable, politically correct, sensitive etc. ideology.[30]

Third, they believe national battlefield parks should only describe the course of battle and not discuss the reasons for the war:

> These Great Battlefields are the only means by which we true lovers of American History can get a full understanding and complete account of what actually took place in regard to the battle and the men who fought it. Why and how those two armies got to that battlefield is irrelevant at the point of the battle. The only thing that matters at that point is WHAT happened and not why. Allow the NPS to deal only with the facts about the battle and leave the why to the educators.[31]

The educational responsibility of national parks evident in the creation of the National Park Service in 1916 and the educational mandates embodied in the 1935 Historic Sites Act and the National Historic Preservation Act of 1966 went unrecognized by the Sons of Confederate Veterans and Jerry Russell.

When Congress began creating national battlefields during the 1890s, veterans were able to join forces precisely because they focused on common experiences and not on causes. Honor accorded to the vanquished as well as the victors was attained through the avoidance of any interpretation of the war, any mention of the war's causes, or any mention of slavery. The long tradition of the War Department beginning in 1890, followed by the National Park Service after 1933, in managing and interpreting national battlefields created a belief that battlefields, particularly national battlefields, existed only to interpret the moment of the battle and to honor those from both sides who fought and fell there. Honor, of course, is a fundamentally important function of any field of battle, whether it be Pearl Harbor or Little Bighorn. Honor was what President Lincoln appropriately emphasized at Gettysburg: "we can not consecrate—we can not hallow—this ground. The brave men, living and dead, who struggled here, have consecrated it, far above our poor power to add or detract."[32]

Honor, bravery, and nobility among veterans were the foundation upon which reconciliation and reunion were constructed. Celebrating the fraternity of combatants became the focus of Blue and Gray reunions. At Gettysburg, fifty years after the battle, the governor of Virginia both captured the evolving memory of the war and set the tone for battlefield interpretation in the future. "We are not here to discuss the Genesis of the war," he declared, "but men who have tried each other in the storm and smoke of battle are here to discuss this great fight." And then to make certain that none of his listeners missed his point, he continued, "We came here, I say, not to discuss what caused the war of 1861–65, but to talk over the events of the battle here as man to man."[33] Remembering the war only through the lens of personal valor and honor perpetuated the Lost Cause interpretation of the war by separating cause from action and consequence. Because of the interpretative tradition within military parks that abjured any discussion of secession, the introduction of the causes of the war was perceived as being ideologically motivated. Interestingly, the avoidance of a discussion of causes, which is equally ideological, was perceived as normal and ideologically neutral.

The theme of honor among soldiers as the principal interpretive focus at Civil War battlefields became Jerry Russell's primary argument. In his view, Congress established national battlefields during the 1890s exclusively to commemorate the battles and honor the soldiers who fought there. Indeed, Russell's criticism of the National Park Service evolved into a "zero-sum game" equation. "You only get so much of the visitors' time," he wrote, "if you add to the script, you must take something out of the script. And what they are taking out is honor, honor to the battle, honor to the men."[34] Russell reasoned that any time or space spent exploring the causes of the war would detract from the interpretation of the battle and diminish the dignity of the combatants. In spite of evidence to the contrary, that discussing causes of the war neither reduced time spent on the battle nor dishonored the battle's participants, Russell consistently tried to create the perception that a choice was being made between honor and blame. "Battlefields," he argued, "are not about 'blame' or any other political agendas or any sociocultural agendas or any arguments about political correctness. Battlefields are about honor."[35]

The earlier emphasis on honor, to the exclusion of any mention of historical cause or context, cleanly detached the battlefields from the environment in which the battles that occurred there were fought. Battlefields, over the years, became places where the chess game of war was explained in detail, but any explanation regarding why those armies were trying to kill each other was completely avoided. Fortunately, this avoidance of causality was not instituted at other and equally hallowed historic places. The interpretation at the U.S.S. *Arizona,* for example, explains the reasons for the Japanese bombing of Pearl Harbor. Likewise, interpretation at Little Bighorn provides a larger historical context so that visitors understand what George Armstrong Custer and the Seventh Cavalry were doing in the valley of the Little Bighorn. Setting battles within the social, political, and cultural context of their times is not only appropriate but essential. As the preeminent military historian Sir John Keegan observed, "an army is . . . an expression of the society from which it issues. The purposes for which it fights and the way it does so will therefore be determined in large measure by what a society wants from war and how far it expects its army to go in delivering that outcome."[36]

What is especially striking about the letters received from the Sons of Confederate Veterans and other Civil War devotees is the degree to which the Lost Cause interpretation continues to define much of their thinking about the war. In spite of three decades of new scholarship on the Civil War, scholarship that has probed every aspect of the war and examined its nonmilitary as well as military aspects, a certain segment of the public continues to reject the connection between slavery and secession.[37] In one sense, this is not surprising. Many historical events are accepted as acts of faith, and the popular memory of them cannot be dislodged by subsequent scholarship. Larry Gara's *The Liberty Line: The Legend of the Underground Railroad,* which focused on the role of African Americans in the Underground Railroad, for example, did little to change the public's perception that mainly whites operated the Underground Railroad. Likewise, Dan Kilgore's book *How Did Davy Die?,* which offered an alternative view of Davy Crockett's death at the Alamo based on an authenticated Mexican diary, was rejected by a public that clung to John Wayne's more heroic 1960 film interpretation of the battle.[38] The popular memory of these and other events in the nation's past serve to support social as well as political agendas and become powerful vehicles for constructing personal as well as national identities.

Within the National Park Service, the creation myth of Yellowstone National Park lived on long after it was determined to be false. Featuring an 1870 campfire conversation at the junction of the Gibbon and Firehole Rivers (Madison Junction) during which members of the Washburn Expedition proposed that the Yellowstone area be preserved as a national park, the myth became rooted in National Park Service lore, even prompting a diorama in the Department of the Interior building in Washington. Although the members of the expedition undoubtedly camped at Madison Junction, there is no evidence they conjured up national park status for Yellowstone that night. The myth grew out of claims by one member of the party in memoirs published almost thirty years later. Yet the story was so evocative that one high-ranking National Park Service official argued, "The campfire tradition is so important that if we did not have it we should have invented it for its fame is worldwide! Historical validity of the tradition is probably seriously in doubt, but this does not reduce the value of the tradition. We should continue to emphasize it as such and capitalize on it."[39] Good stories die hard.

When a Kentuckian writes, "I was taught the true history of the war from my grandparents. As a southerner, I can tell you, it wasn't about slavery," he writes with absolute sincerity and conviction.[40] For generations not only families but school systems interpreted the Civil War through the prism of the Lost Cause, a version of the past that involved an emphasis on battlefield heroism, the defeat of the Confederacy only by overwhelming numbers and resources, and the salvaging of a damaged self-respect through the retention of a doctrine of white supremacy. Confederates, according to this popular version of history, never fought for slavery, but only for the authentic legacy of the American Revolution and its defense of independence and state sovereignty.[41]

The continued reverence for the Confederacy is reflected in the continued popularity of books like *The South Was Right!; Was Jefferson Davis Right?;* and *Facts the Historians Leave Out: A Confederate Primer.*[42] "Nearly a century and a half after the war," write the authors of *Was Jefferson Davis Right?,* "the Confederacy still exists and an order of New Unreconstructed Southerners is calling for its reunification."[43] The contemporary revival of Lost Cause sentiments is best found in the republication of the writings of Mildred Lewis Rutherford, who held the august title of historian general of the United Daughters of the Confederacy during the early years of the twentieth century. Writing for almost forty years, between the 1890s and 1927, Rutherford articulated, perhaps better than anyone else during her era, the arguments of the Lost Cause, and her style has been emulated by many current neo-Confederate authors. Using unconnected quotes to bolster her arguments, Rutherford dealt with the relationship between slavery and the coming of the war, for example, by simply referencing Lincoln's First Inaugural Address statement that he had "no purpose directly or indirectly to interfere with the institution of slavery in the States where it exists."[44] The intricate and interwoven progression of Lincoln's thinking about slavery, the war, and abolition were reduced to a single quote from one address. Quoting from Lincoln's Second Inaugural Address, "all knew that this interest [slavery] was, somehow, the cause of the war," would, of course, have presented a different, more shaded, more complex history. Many of the letters received by the National Park Service reflect the tenacity with which their writers continue to embrace Rutherford's interpretation of the Civil War era.

If southerners have selectively remembered the war and its causes, so too have northerners. Just as southerners have separated slavery from the causes of the war, many northerners have conflated the end of the war with its beginning and believe the United States went to war in 1861 as a glorious moral crusade against the peculiar institution. The memory of the war was astutely examined during the war's centennial by the novelist and poet Robert Penn Warren, whose grandfather Penn fought for the Confederacy. Writing in 1960–61, Warren determined that the war gave the South the "Great Alibi," while it gave the North the "Treasury of Virtue." The former, wrote Warren,

> explains, condones, and transmutes everything . . . Even now, any common lyncher becomes a defender of the Southern tradition, and any rabble-rouser the gallant leader of a thin gray line of heroes. . . . By the Great Alibi the Southerner makes his Big Medicine. He turns defeat into victory, defects into virtue. Even more pathetically, he turns his great virtues into absurdities—sometimes vicious absurdities.[45]

The North's memory of the war, according to Warren, was likewise flawed. His "Treasury of Virtue" "may not be as comic or vicious as the Great Alibi, but it is equally unlovely. It may even be, in the end, equally corrosive of national, and personal, integrity." The "Treasury of Virtue" allows the northerner to forget the specifics of the war and revel only in the war's conclusion, the demise of slavery. Through this gauze of history northerners can forget that

> the Republican platform of 1860 pledged protection to the institution of slavery where it existed, and that the Republicans were ready, in 1861, to guarantee slavery in the South, as bait for a return to the Union. It is forgotten that in July, 1861, both houses of Congress, by an almost unanimous vote, affirmed that the War was waged not to interfere with the institutions of any state but only to maintain the Union.[46]

There is another important factor one must consider while attempting to understand the vehemence expressed in the letters received by the National Park Service. The furor over the removal of the Confederate battle flag from many southern state capitols was occurring at exactly the same time that the National Park Service was rethinking its interpretation at Civil War battlefields. Although unrelated, these occurrences were perceived by many as a larger pattern of animosity toward the South. "The South presently serves the United States in the role of whipping-boy for the national guilt trip over race relations," pronounced a Sons of Confederate Veterans Web page.[47] Indeed, this sentiment reoccurs repeatedly throughout these letters. According to one writer,

> Any Southerner who tries to honor his ancestors by preserving the songs and symbols under which they fought is declared a racist, simply because someone else does not like the symbols. . . . If . . . you are a Southerner, you are fair game for any abuse others decide to heap on you.[48]

"I feel that we, as white, Southern American's [sic]," said another, "are losing everything that we hold in memory relating to our Southern history. We can no longer have any semblance of the Confederate Battle flag for fear of offending some minority American."[49] Honor, of course, and sensitivity toward slights to personal or family honor were guiding features of southern society in the antebellum years. The same sense of honor that drove South Carolina congressman Preston Brooks to assail Charles Sumner on the floor of the Senate in 1856 propelled South Carolina to secede from the United States four years later.[50]

The action by the battlefield superintendents thus clashed, at least in some southern households, with a generations-long tradition of reverencing the war as a cause fought for high ideals and not for slavery, a war fought in defense of southern honor. Confederate monuments and memorials erected in the decades following the war all reflected causes designed to salvage self-respect and some degree of vindication in a shattered white South. The Confederate monument dedicated in 1903 on the Texas state capitol grounds is typical. Its inscription reads:

> DIED FOR STATES RIGHTS GUARANTEED UNDER THE CONSTITUTION. THE PEOPLE OF THE SOUTH, ANIMATED BY THE SPIRIT OF 1776, TO PRESERVE THEIR RIGHTS, WITHDREW FROM THE FEDERAL COMPACT IN 1861. THE NORTH RESORTED TO COERCION, THE SOUTH, AGAINST OVERWHELMING NUMBERS AND RESOURCES, FOUGHT UNTIL EXHAUSTED.[51]

This interpretation of secession carefully avoids any mention of the "grievances" listed in Texas's official declaration of secession, adopted on February 2, 1861. Specifically, Texas cited interference with the return of fugitive slaves, the northern demand for "the abolition of negro slavery throughout the confederacy," the action of abolitionists in "sowing the seeds of discord through the Union," stealing "our slaves," sending "seditious pamphlets and papers among us to stir up servile insurrection" and bringing "blood and carnage to our firesides," and hiring "emissaries among us to burn our towns and distribute arms and poison to our slaves for the same purpose." In summation of this list of grievances, the Texas secession convention concluded:

> In view of these and many other facts, it is meet that our own views should be distinctly proclaimed. We hold as undeniable truths that the government of the various States, and of the Confederacy itself, were established exclusively by the white race, for themselves and their posterity;

that the African race had no agency in their establishment; that they were rightfully held and regarded as an inferior and dependent race, and in that condition only could their existence in this country be rendered beneficial or tolerable.[52]

When Governor Sam Houston refused to take an oath of allegiance to the Confederacy, he was deposed. Earlier he had observed, "Our people are going to war to perpetuate slavery, and the first gun fired in the war will be the [death] knell of slavery."[53] In Texas, as well as elsewhere throughout the former Confederate South, the linkages between slavery and secession were forgotten as the Lost Cause interpretation became the dominant narrative of the war. It is not surprising, then, that the National Park Service's reintroduction of slavery into discussions on the war would be perceived as an attempt to rewrite the past.

The conflict between the National Park Service and those who wished to continue the separation of slavery and a discussion of the causes of the war from accounts of battles at Civil War battlefield parks is indicative of the distance between professional historians and nonacademic historians of the Civil War. The two groups rarely gather together to discuss findings and interpretations, and this separation feeds a growing sense of isolation from each other. The historical literature of the Civil War era generated over the past twenty years has been sophisticated and expansive and has offered a rich rendering of the intricate and complex, sometimes tortuous, history of the period. The growing body of popular neo-Confederate literature is based on a need to defend the Confederacy rather than present an objective reading of the evidence, and flows from small commercial publishers rather than from academic presses that employ the traditional peer review process. As a result, there is little association between the two groups. University based scholars disdain literature such as *The South Was Right!*, while pro-Confederate Civil War buffs demonstrate disdain for academic literature, labeling it "revisionist" and "politically correct."[54] Because both groups share a passion for history and an interest in its relevance to contemporary society, perhaps it would be worthwhile if they could engage in civil conversation. A model for this sort of interchange might be found in a gathering held in February 2003 among ranchers, environmental activists, and wolf experts on the reintroduction of the Mexican wolf into the American Southwest. While the issues are certainly quite different, the passions invoked are similar. Thoughtful meetings, formal and informal, between scholars and Civil War interest groups have the potential to shrink the distance between the two and place the popular discussion of the war on a firmer historical footing. At minimum, such gatherings would produce an interesting and lively exchange that, theoretically, would diminish the stereotypes each has about the other and lead to a richer and more substantive discussion about the Civil War and its memory.[55]

In spite of the assertion by the National Park Service that the introduction of interpretive material on the coming of the war grew out of a commitment to provide meaningful educational programs based on current scholarship, many argued that the federal government was simply being "politically correct" and intended to demean the memory and honor of those who fought for the Confederacy. Public reaction, however, to the several exhibitions, pamphlets, and booklets produced since 1998, has been overwhelmingly positive. The worst fears of HERITAGEPAC and the Sons of Confederate Veterans have not been realized. New exhibitions at Manassas, Richmond, Fort Sumter, Chickamauga and Chattanooga, Kennesaw, and Corinth; a new brochure at Fort Sumter; and a new booklet at Appomattox Courthouse (written by Edward Ayers, Gary Gallagher, and David Blight) have demonstrated that the causes and consequences of the war can be explored at Civil War battlefields without diminishing the honor and valor of Confederate soldiers. In fact, they demonstrate that without that larger perspective, the efforts of the armies of the United States and the armies of the Confederacy are rendered meaningless. The Civil War had causes and it had consequences, and we will be a better society when we can have a national conversation about the Civil War and its relationship to today without hyperbole and rancor.

As the United States prepares for the sesquicentennial of the Civil War, it would do well to reflect on the observations of Oscar Handlin during the last celebration. Writing in 1961 at the opening of the centennial and anticipating the flood of activities, programs, and books proposed for the subsequent four years, Handlin complained that "these retracings of familiar ground do little, however, to give Americans of 1961 an understanding of the struggle that tore their country apart a century ago. Rather they perpetuate myths that obscure the reality of the Civil War." He then proposed an alternative framework for the centennial of the war:

"An anniversary is an occasion for retrospective reconsideration. It affords an opportunity for analysis of what happened and why and for an estimate of the consequences that extend down to the present."[56] The Civil War is deserving, at long last, of the thoughtful analysis and public reflection suggested by Handlin. How the United States observes the sesquicentennial of the war will be a measure of how far the country has come in understanding the meaning of the war and its relationship to today's society.

10

In Search of a Usable Past:
Neo-Confederates and
Black Confederates

Bruce Levine

In June 1900, the U.S. Congress voted to set aside a section of Arlington National Cemetery as a burial site specifically for Confederate soldiers. The United Daughters of the Confederacy then pressed to have a large statue erected there, and the secretary of war granted that request. The cornerstone was laid in 1912, and the monument was finally dedicated in 1914. The commission to design it went to Moses Ezekiel, a world-famous sculptor who had seen action in the Civil War as a Virginia Military Institute cadet.[1]

Ezekiel covered his imposing, thirty-two-foot monument—which still stands—with vivid images. At its top is a woman crowned with olive leaves and bearing symbols of peace, commemoration, and reconciliation. Below her the sculptor placed representations of "the sacrifices and heroism of the men and women of the South."[2] Among these figures is the profile of a young African American man. The cemetery describes him as "a black slave following his young master."[3] But according to many modern-day champions of the Confederacy (the so-called neo-Confederates), Ezekiel here depicted a fully fledged black Confederate soldier.[4] For such people, this figure symbolizes the many thousands of loyal black combatants who, they claim, filled out the ranks of southern armies.

The organized modern campaign to memorialize such "black Confederates" began during the 1970s and picked up steam during the de-

FRANK LESLIE'S ILLUSTRATED NEWSPAPER.

PROSPECTS OF THE SOUTHERN SAMBO.

LEE—*"Hold on there, Driver, we want Sambo now to fight for Liberty and Independence. You can thrash him as much as you like when he comes back."*

This cartoon appeared in New York City's *Frank Leslie's Illustrated Newspaper* on March 25, 1865. It points out the hypocrisy of the Confederate move to enlist slaves in their military struggle to maintain the southern slave system. COURTESY OF THE LIBRARY OF CONGRESS cades that followed. During that time volumes entitled *Blacks in Blue and Gray, Black Southerners in Gray,* and *Black Confederates* have rolled off partisan presses, sold thousands of copies, and now adorn the shelves in bookstore chains and public libraries.[5] Web sites have proliferated, advancing the same arguments found in those books, often enough couched in identical language and invoking the same supporting evidence. The Sons of Confederate Veterans (SCV) and kindred organizations energetically promote the cause. "Most Americans do not know that there were thousands upon thousands of black soldiers who fought in the Confederate army and navy," declared SCV chaplain in chief Rev. Fr. Alister C. Anderson in 1999. Furthermore, he continued, "these black soldiers were integrated into the ranks of the army with the white soldiers. This was not the case in the Northern armies which segregated the black soldiers into colored units with only white commanders."[6] A group of southern Civil War reenactors styling itself the 37th Texas Cavalry aims "to educate others of the multi-racial and multi-ethnic makeup of the Confederate Armed Forces."[7]

The particulars of this claim vary. A relatively moderate version holds that between ten thousand and twenty thousand black combatants served the Confederacy. Others hold out for fifty thousand, and still others for a figure twice or even four times as big.[8] None of these claims is small. Ten thousand to twenty thousand soldiers would add up to ten to twenty infantry regiments. Fifty thousand soldiers would be enough to fill out four infantry divisions—more than a full corps. A hundred thousand soldiers was about twice as many as Robert E. Lee's whole Army of Northern Virginia boasted on the eve of Antietam. And two hundred thousand soldiers was more than the Confederacy had present for duty during much of the war. How is it that so enormous a body of southern black troops has remained unknown to most modern Americans? Because, we are told, historians of the Civil War have either neglected, dismissed, or deliberately concealed their existence.

Most of those who today make the Black-Confederate cause their own do so as part of a larger effort to vindicate the Confederacy and to honor their own southern ancestors. Ulysses S. Grant attempted to render a balanced judgment on the experience of wartime southern soldiers when he acknowledged that they had "fought so long and valiantly, and had suffered so much." Unfortunately, he also believed, they had done so for a cause that was "one of the worst for which a people ever fought," slavery and disunion.[9] Neo-Confederates reject that view. Not content with honoring southern soldiers' ability, courage, and sacrifice, they are determined also to justify the cause that those soldiers served. The Sons of Confederate Veterans thus holds that not the preservation of slavery but "the preservation of liberty and freedom was the motivating factor in the South's decision to fight the Second American Revolution."[10] Insisting on a massive black presence in southern armies aims to strengthen that assertion by demonstrating that African Americans identified with and were loyal to the Confederacy. The southern war effort thereby comes to appear as the cause not merely of slave owners, nor even of southern whites more generally, but of *all* southerners, white as well as black, free as well as slave.

The Black-Confederate campaign marks a tactical shift in the way the Confederacy and its war is depicted and justified. The civil rights movement of the 1960s and 1970s has left a deep imprint on society at large and on the South in particular. Among other things, it has changed the terms of acceptable public discourse. Emphasizing the supposedly biracial character of the southern army and war effort aims to make both the old Confederacy and the neo-Confederates more attractive to a modern audience. "By maintaining this false image of the Confederate Army as this sea of lily-white faces," explains Mississippian Michael Kelley (of the 34th Texas Cavalry reenactors), "the South can be demonized, and therefore it becomes very clear-cut. That way, they can say . . . that Southerners were fighting for slavery and racism, and Yankees were fighting to free the slaves. Which is false."[11] Painting the Confederate army as a sea of both white and black faces, it is hoped, will convey a very different impression of the war's significance. Recruiting a sprinkling of black members to modern Confederate heritage or reenactor groups is useful in the same way. "Obviously we'd like to have more black or minority members," Ben C. Sewell III, then executive director of the Sons of Confederate Veterans, told one reporter, "because the fact that we have minorities and welcome them deflects some of the criticism we seem to get" when championing the official public veneration of Confederate symbols.[12]

The bible of Black-Confederate advocates appeared about fifteen years ago: *Black Southerners in Gray,* by H.C. Blackerby, who prided himself on his "Confederate sympathies." [13] That volume promised to reveal the truth about "the blacks who worked and fought for the South as well as those blacks who were impressed by the thousands to support the North." [14] The implication that blacks fought eagerly for the South but only under compulsion for the Union was not accidental. "That most blacks supported the Confederacy is apparent," the author announced. [15]

Most of the books and essays that have appeared since then have hewn to the same line. "Contributions made by southern blacks," declared Charles Harper, "indicate that they did identify with the Confederacy with loyalty and fidelity both before and after peace was restored." [16] "The overwhelming majority of blacks during the War Between the States supported and defended with armed resistance the cause of southern independence," P. Charles Lunsford argued even more aggressively. [17] Although "they had it within their power to wreak wholesale havoc throughout the South," and even though they "could, with attendant risks, have escaped to nearby lines," Edward C. Smith has written, the fact remains that "few chose to do so and instead remained at home and became the most essential element in the Southern infrastructure to resisting Northern invasion." [18]

The claim of a massive black presence in southern armies is meant to accomplish something else as well: to demonstrate once and for all that the Confederacy did not stand and did not fight for slavery. [19] After all, the neo-Confederates ask, would so many blacks have so enthusiastically supported a war effort that was defined by such a goal? Of course not, they reply; both black and white southerners fought not to preserve bondage but simply "to defend their country." They stood ready "to shed their blood to establish their country's independence." [20]

Even as they hotly deny that the South fought for slavery, however, promoters of the black Confederate thesis commonly strive to improve slavery's reputation. Slaves were loyal to their southern masters, they argue, because masters were loyal to them, affording them security, social welfare, dignity, and affection. "Most Virginia planters . . . ," argues Edward C. Smith, "tended to be benign in their treatment of blacks." [21] In his own contribution to the *Black Confederates* volume, Maryland clergyman Edward C. Raffetto admonishes that slavery was not "inherently racist" and that "in the South the personal contact of black and white persons, even under the constraints of institutional slavery," was often "more constructive, more real, more human, than was possible in the 'free' North."[22]

A volume forthrightly entitled *The South Was Right!*, by James and Walter Kennedy, carries this argument a few steps further—in the process demonstrating that a change in neo-Confederate marketing strategy does not necessarily mean a change in mind-set. The Kennedys want it clearly understood that they are "not defending the system of slavery but rather seeking the truth about the history of that institution and of life in the Old South." The truth just happens to be that "in many ways, slavery was a positive institution for blacks"; it was a status "in which many blacks were happy and free from want and violence." So, the Kennedys demand to know, "how can anyone continue to believe the myth that Southern blacks were longing for Yankee-induced freedom?" In the 1850s, slavery's apologists insisted that blacks in southern bondage were better off than free blacks in the North. Taking a leaf from the same book, the Kennedys find the condition of antebellum slaves superior "in many ways" even to that of black Americans today. "One of the most frequently voiced requests made by blacks in the inner cities of America today," they write, "is the desire to be free from violence. Inner-city black crime is epidemic," whereas "crime was never a problem for the black community during the time of slavery." Nor, they continue, "has the family unit [ever] been stronger in the black community than it was during slavery days."[23] To be sure, the Kennedys acknowledge, not all enslaved southern blacks appreciated the benefits they enjoyed. Some did try to escape from their masters. But one should not jump to hasty conclusions about what such slave flight tells us. "Yes," the authors note, "some blacks ran away from home, just as some young people today run away from home . . ."[24]

Some claim that blacks fought for the Confederacy because they recognized that southern masters wished to improve black conditions even further and eventually to emancipate them outright. "Even before secession," according to H.C. Blackerby, "many of the blacks were under the wing of Southern groups working for the cause of Negro freedom. A number of slave owners contributed to these manumission societies, sometimes serving as officers in them."[25] "Black soldiers fought for the Confederacy because the United States government had enslaved them for over eighty years," according to the Confederate Memorial Chapel, whereas "the Confederate government took the first Constitutional action to end African slave trade."[26] Indeed, the Kennedys conclude, if the North had only left the South alone, slavery would have come to an end gradually and without bloodshed. Only the unrestrained attacks by "the rabid Yankee Abolitionist" derailed "any hope to bring a peaceful end to slavery."[27]

The Black-Confederates campaign also aims to reinforce a particular view of the postwar Reconstruction years. Just as abolitionists are to blame for slavery's survival into the 1860s, so the North bears responsibility for subsequent conflicts between southern whites and blacks—and even for legalized segregation and Ku Klux Klan terror. Wayne R. Austerman's contribution to the *Black Confederates* collection thus complains that "the emancipation and enfranchisement of former slaves, coupled with the ill-advised attempts by some radical reformers to overthrow long-standing social mores created the potential for conflict." Indeed, "Reconstruction and the crude attempt at social engineering that accompanied it drove a wedge between the races, inspiring far deeper bitterness and mistrust than ever had existed during the war. The appearance of hooded nightriders and the passage of Jim Crow laws were two of the results." And so it was that "even during the grimmest days of Yankee occupation, white and black Southerners recalled with pride the times when the gray ranks had swept forward to meet the enemy."[28]

As such words suggest, the celebration of black Confederates has become a mainstay of popular Civil War revisionism in the modern South. Like that revisionism, it serves a decidedly political purpose, helping to justify a particular view of today's world and an equally particular way of acting in it. The address that SCV chaplain in chief Anderson delivered at the 1999 Confederate Memorial ceremony (quoted earlier in this essay) illustrates the point. After lauding the memorial's supposed inclusion of a black Confederate soldier, Anderson insisted that the Confederacy had really been fighting the battles of humanity as a whole. Modern Americans should recognize that "the South, with all her inherited institutions and her embracing of religious and ethical values, was a continuation of the finest gifts and practices of European culture; and that the North had tragically deviated from that heritage." Surely the bitter fruits of the defeat of the South and its cause were now all too obvious: "We are degenerating into pantheism, hedonism, moral relativism, narcissism and worst of all, into socialism leading into nihilism and totalitarianism." The defense of the Confederate tradition has thus become inseparable from the modern struggle against all of those menacing evils. Conversely, "the anti-Southern and anti-Confederate demagoguery we witness today among bigoted people can be traced directly to our entire nation's abandonment of moral standards."[29]

A similar note is sounded by the League of the South, an organization that is smaller than the SCV (while sharing members with it) and more explicitly present-minded. Its stated goals include "turning back the tide of Cultural Marxism (otherwise known as Political Correctness), and otherwise standing firm against the liberal-leftist multicultural agenda that threatens to undo the South and all of America."[30] League members are prominent in the Black-Confederate campaign. One of them is Charles Kelly Barrow, coeditor of the *Black Confederates* volume, who previously served as the SCV's historian in chief. Another is P. Charles Lunsford, a contributor to *Black Confederates*.[31] A third is Walter Donald Kennedy, coauthor of *The South Was Right!* and past commander of the SCV's Louisiana Division; the League of the South's Web page identifies Kennedy as a senior advisor to its board of directors.[32] The Kennedy brothers' lengthy disquisitions about the past all lead up to a call for "a Southern political revolution" today, one to be led by "Confederate Freedom Fighters" that will "put an end to forced busing, affirmative action, extravagant welfare spending" as well as "the punitive Southern-only Voting Rights Act."[33]

A few African Americans have become involved in the Black-Confederate project, and they have naturally received a great deal of publicity. They explain themselves in various ways. For some the decision to participate reflects a more general endorsement of a strand of modern-day American conservatism that has made retrospective hostility to abolitionism and the early Republican Party a key article of faith.[34] Probably the best-known example here is economics professor Walter Williams of George Mason University, who waxes lyrical about "our patriotic black ancestors who marched, fought and died to protect their homeland from what they saw as Northern aggression."[35] Williams is glad that slavery was abolished, but (like former U.S. attorney general John Ashcroft) he nevertheless believes that the wrong side won the Civil War: "by destroying the states' right to secession, Abraham Lincoln opened the door to the kind of unconstrained, despotic, arrogant government we have today." [36]

Some other African Americans in the modern South apparently hope that adapting to the pro-Confederate sentiments of white neighbors will help to improve relations with them. It is thus a way of obtaining approval for one's ancestors and therefore for oneself. "Our grandfather fought with them," says the descendant of one Virginia slave who worked for the Confederate army, "so there will be some respect for us and for our family." [37] The most prominent representative of this current is Edward C. Smith, a professor at American University, whose 1990 essay, "Calico, Black and Gray: Women and Blacks in the Confederacy," has been enthusiastically welcomed and cited by virtually every Black-Confederate essay, book, and Web site that has subsequently appeared. In 1999 Smith joined in a ceremony in which the SCV honored the memory of a free black resident of wartime Virginia who had built breastworks for the Confederate army. "It's not that blacks today don't know this part of their history," a local newspaper quoted Smith on that occasion, "but they don't respect it." Perhaps now, he hoped, they had "turned a corner." According to the same account, indeed, "Smith called Saturday's event the fulfillment of the dream that Martin Luther King Jr. longed for. 'You see it, right here, today,' he said." [38]

In his published essays, Professor Smith presents himself as the true defender of Robert E. Lee's reputation and of the Lee tradition. He seems to think that stance will help him discredit virulent modern racism. "Unfortunately," Smith has thus written, "there are many Southerners who claim to cherish Lee and revere the flag for which he so nobly fought but still harbor rabidly racist sentiments towards blacks and their long delayed social progress. Such people do not honor Lee, instead they disgrace him." Smith asserts, quite inaccurately, that Lee "never owned a single slave, because he felt that slavery was morally reprehensible." [39] After Appomattox, Smith continues with just as little adherence to the record, Lee resolved "to embrace the new social order that the war had established and that the Constitution had codified through the addition of three new amendments." [40]

As students of the Old South will recognize, little more than window dressing distinguishes the version of history that most Black-Confederate supporters today defend from the one that the slave owners themselves advanced during the nineteenth century. And every one of the basic tenets of that story has repeatedly been exposed as a patently false, self-serving myth—first in the speeches, articles, and books published by black and white abolitionists before the Civil War; then, in life, by the dramatic events of the Civil War and Reconstruction; and finally, during the past fifty years, through conscientious historical research published in mountains of books and articles and more recently embodied in mass-distribution films such as *Glory!*

Slavery constituted the economic, social, and political foundation of the antebellum South. It was, first and foremost, a system of forced labor justified by racial ideology. It was profitable because the black slaves' status as racial pariahs and as private property allowed them to be worked harder, longer, and at a lower cost than free white workers could be driven.[41] The average slave's life was therefore one of exhausting labor, extreme poverty, physical punishment, personal humiliation, and wholesale attacks on family relationships.[42] And precisely because it was so profitable, there was no reason to expect that slavery would disappear from the South anytime soon, absent external compulsion. Since the days of Thomas Jefferson, masters in the Upper South had been voicing qualms about slavery's safety, utility, and morality. But they had also firmly and steadily resisted every practical attempt to bring it to an end.

That consistent pattern of slave-owner resistance, in fact, was the seedbed of secession. The rise of the Republican Party and the presidency of Abraham Lincoln threatened slavery's future. Republicans denounced slavery as "a relic of barbarism" and determined to prevent it from expanding into any additional territories or states. By thus containing slavery geographically, as Lincoln said in 1858, they also hoped to place it "in course of ultimate extinction."[43] This, as Jefferson Davis and hundreds of others made clear, was unacceptable to the slave-owning South. "With interests of such overwhelming magnitude imperiled," as Davis explained before the Confederate Congress, "the people of the Southern States were driven . . . to the adoption of some course of action to avert the danger" that Lincoln's 1860 electoral victory posed.[44]

That course of action included secession and a war to enforce it. And the Confederate war effort *did* require and make use of the labor of great numbers of black southerners, slave as well as free. As Georgia's governor

Joseph E. Brown accurately noted, "the country and the army are mainly dependent upon slave labor."[45] How could that not be true? Slaves made up more than a third of the Confederacy's population and a much larger proportion of its labor force. During peacetime, their labor yielded most of the South's commercial wealth, in the form especially of rice, sugar, tobacco, and cotton. Much of the work required to sustain the same society during war naturally fell on black shoulders as well. By drawing so many adult white men into the army, indeed, the war multiplied the importance of black labor. Slaves grew and prepared much of the army's food. They mined essential iron ore, coal, salt, and saltpeter. They fashioned horseshoes, nails, harnesses, bridles, collars, saddles, guns, and ammunition. They loaded, unloaded, and transported essential cargoes across land and water routes to southern armies. They tended horses, emplaced artillery, and built fortifications; they carried stretchers, drove ambulance wagons, and nursed the sick and wounded.[46]

Especially during the war's earlier stages, some slaves accompanied masters into the army and there continued to serve them. Few if any who did this came from the ranks of the hard-driven field workers who made up the great bulk of the South's black population. Such personal attendants came instead from among the better-off minority of slaves who worked as domestic servants. In the army, some of them wore the gray and carried their master's equipment, including his musket. Sometimes they went further still and fired such a weapon at Union troops, much to the delight and amusement of the Confederate soldiers they served.[47] These were the individuals about whom white Confederates boasted; these were the men that in later years Confederate army reunions lionized.

Southern free blacks often asserted their loyalty as well. A few of them had atypically managed to acquire substantial property and a degree of legal and even social toleration from their white neighbors, gains that were easier for those with light complexions. As one study of such people acknowledges, "these men took what can be seen as the final step of their acceptance or acculturation into the local white societies where they lived."[48] Other, perhaps less blessed, free blacks simply assumed that the Confederacy would win the war and hoped that public displays of fidelity would buy them some personal relief from the heavy legal and practical burdens that beset most nonwhites in the South. Even some slaves, as

Joseph T. Wilson noted, reasoned and acted that way. A black man born in Virginia, Wilson had made his way to Massachusetts prior to serving during the Civil War in the 2nd Regiment Louisiana Marine Guard (74th U.S. Colored Troops). "The negro who boasted the loudest of his desire to fight the Yankees," Wilson subsequently recalled, "who showed the greatest anxiety to aid the Confederates, was granted the most freedom and received the approval of his master."[49]

That approval—and the desire to hold up such conduct as an example for the rest of the South's black population—survived in the nostalgic cult of the loyal slave that lingered on long after the war was over. That cult, in fact, was the direct ancestor of modern veneration for so-called black Confederates. H.C. Blackerby dedicated *Blacks in Blue and Gray* "in the spirit of the following inscription on a monument at Fort Mill in South Carolina"—to "the faithful slaves who, loyal to a sacred trust, toiled for the support of the Army with matchless devotion."[50] Without a trace of irony, similarly, the *Black Confederates* collection reproduces other samples of such paternalistic postbellum eulogies. From a Georgia newspaper comes the 1907 death notice for "Uncle Gilbert," who "was a typical representative of the faithful slave . . . He gave obedience to his master and diligently performed the task he was given to do."[51] A 1929 obituary for Alabamian Calvin Scruggs recalled fondly that "during the period of reconstruction, where all slaves were freed, he chose to cast his lot in with that of the family to which he had previously belonged, and to which he remained faithful until his death."[52] Black South Carolinian Henry Brown also endeared himself to his obituary writer during Reconstruction when he distanced himself from the overwhelming majority of southern blacks and aligned himself with the white-supremacist Democrats. "His influence was marked among the negroes," Brown's obituary recalls wistfully if rather contradictorily. "He differed with them honestly and told them so squarely."[53]

The *Black Confederates* volume also features photographs of monuments erected since the Civil War in Mississippi, Georgia, and South Carolina in memory of "black loyalty to the Confederacy."[54] It could have added the stone that the Richmond Howitzers, a famous Virginia artillery unit, erected in 1913 in memory of Aleck Kean, a slave who accompanied his master into the army and remained after his master's death. The stone read: "In Testimony of this Admiration and Respect for a man who did his duty both in war and peace. 'Well done, good and faithful servant.' " One of that memorial's influential initiators publicly hoped that "it might stimulate some of the colored people of this day to emulate the life and character of this faithful and devoted member of their race."[55]

Neither old-time nostalgia for loyal slaves nor elaborate modern homage to black Confederates, however, can change the fact that from April 1861 through March 1865 the black men who actually served as Confederate soldiers never exceeded a small handful. Claims that thousands (much less tens of thousands and more) served rest on the same kind of wishful thinking, gullibility, and misuse and abuse of historical sources that characterize neo-Confederate Civil War revisionism in general. The evidence offered on their behalf is rife with unsupported anecdotes, demonstrably erroneous (and usually secondhand) accounts, wholesale misinterpretation, and quotations reproduced incompletely and/or out of context.

Here H.C. Blackerby's *Blacks in Blue and Gray* sets the standard. Attempting to document the existence of a large body of black Confederate soldiers, Blackerby recounts at one point that a "witness recorded that 'the streets of Richmond were filled with 10,000 Negroes who had been gathered at Camp Lee on the outskirts of Richmond.' " The witness, however, cannot be identified, and no further trace of those troops has ever again turned up. Blackerby similarly reports as fact that "an instruction camp for Confederate black soldiers was established near the Alabama River" but fails to note that the source of this intelligence was just one of many false rumors circulating among jittery Union troops.[56] *Blacks in Blue and Gray* quotes a letter published in the northern press in which an Indiana soldier reported hearing from others that "a body of seven hundred Negro Infantry opened fire on our men" in the fall of 1861.[57] But those seven hundred soldiers quickly disappeared, too. And the reader never learns that in January 1862 the Richmond *Dispatch* specifically cited and dismissed this secondhand account as "ridiculous and absurd."[58]

Much of the Black-Confederate literature that has appeared more recently proudly takes its stand on Blackerby's compendium of such "facts." More recently, in *Black Southerners in Gray,* Richard Rollins quotes from a memoir by the then-slave John Parker, who had been impressed into Confederate military service, in order to suggest Virginia slaves' support for the Confederacy in April 1861. Parker's recollections were meant to show (in Rollins's words) "the black population's excitement as the battle [of Bull Run] neared."[59] Not quoted was the following sentence in Parker's original account, although it might have helped explain that excitement: "We wish to our hearts that the Yankees would whip, and we could have run over to their side but our [Confederate] officers would have shot us if we had made the attempt." Similarly ignored was the fact that, shortly after Bull Run, Parker and his wife did succeed in escaping to Union lines.[60] A few pages later, while trying to prove blacks' enthusiasm for serving as Confederate soldiers, Rollins quotes an 1865 newspaper account of Virginia slaves' reaction to hearing that the Confederacy might soon invite them to join its armies after all. Rollins reproduces the following portion of that account: "After a cordial exchange of opinions it was decided with great unanimity, and finally ratified by all the auxiliary associations everywhere, that black men should promptly respond to the call of the rebel chiefs, whenever it should be made, for them to take up arms." Once again, the quotation is conveniently incomplete. The unsuspecting reader never learns what these would-be black Confederate soldiers planned to do (according to the same account) once they found themselves in battle—that is, to "raise a shout for Abraham Lincoln and the Union" and, with the help of Union troops on the field, to "turn like uncaged tigers upon the rebel hordes."[61]

In 1861, neither Washington nor Richmond would allow nonwhites to serve as soldiers. The Union, however, changed course. In 1862 it did form a few black units, and in 1863 it repudiated completely its earlier all-white policy. The Confederacy, in contrast, stood firmly by its ban on black troops until just a few weeks before its final defeat and destruction. The South wanted no slaves—indeed, no men at all who were not certifiably white—under arms. In July 1861 the chief of the Confederacy's Bureau of War typically informed one correspondent that the government was "not prepared to accept" any offers to raise black units.[62] Around the same time Jefferson Davis was explaining to one of his generals that the very idea was "stark madness" and "would revolt and disgust the whole South."[63]

It is true that a few individual southern communities (most notably New Orleans and Mobile, whose particular French and Spanish roots set them apart from most of the South) permitted some free people of color to serve in the home guard and other local defense units there.[64] But such units were confined to their own immediate vicinities, few saw action of any kind, and none was ever incorporated into the Confederate army. One prominent Mobile citizen did offer to raise "a battalion or regiment of creoles" to serve in the Confederate army. These men, he testified, were "mostly property-owners," including some slave owners, and were "as true to the South as the pure white race," even if they were "mixed blooded." That last detail, however, was quite sufficient for the War Department to reject the overture out of hand.[65] At the end of 1863, Major General Dabney H. Maury, of the Confederate Department of the Gulf, raised the idea again. But Secretary of War James J. Seddon remained adamant. Those Mobile Creoles who could "naturally and properly" be distinguished from blacks (that is, who were identifiably white) could be allowed to don the gray. Those who could not thus be "disconnected from negroes," however, could be used only as military laborers or for other types of "subordinate working purposes."[66] Tennessee's policy toward free blacks was far more typical of the Confederacy as a whole than was the city of Mobile's. In the middle of 1861, the Tennessee legislature moved to allow free blacks to enter the state militia, but only with the understanding that such recruits "shall be required to do all such menial service for the relief of volunteers as is incident to camp life, and necessary to the efficiency of the service."[67]

The Confederacy refused to allow nonwhites to become soldiers precisely because it was fighting to preserve African American slavery; the insistence that blacks were racially inferior (and would therefore make inferior soldiers) was the bedrock of slavery's ideological justification in the South. As Seddon put it in his letter to Maury, the stance that the Confederacy had taken both before "the North and before the world" would "not allow the employment as armed soldiers of negroes."[68]

These policies were effective. When a University of Virginia professor (and a captain in Charlottesville's home guard) inquired about them in the summer of 1863, the secretary of war investigated and affirmed that "no slaves have been employed by the Government except as cooks or nurses in hospitals and for labor."[69] The leading historians of the Civil War have reached parallel conclusions. James M. McPherson's exhaustive examination of soldiers' letters and diaries turned up no references to black Confederates in combat.[70] Robert K. Krick Jr., for many decades chief historian at the Fredericksburg and Spotsylvania National Military

Park, has examined the service records of at least one hundred thousand Confederate soldiers and found a total of twenty to thirty nonwhites among them.[71] Gary Gallagher agrees that only "a handful" of black men actually fought for the Confederacy, their number being "statistically insignificant."[72]

Even this proportionately tiny group of black Confederate troops, moreover, constantly risked (and often suffered) expulsion from army ranks. Few white Confederate soldiers would tolerate serving alongside those of darker hue; the rest helped the government enforce its policy of exclusion. In May 1862, for example, officers of Nelson's Battalion, South Carolina Volunteers, indignantly petitioned to have a small group of soldiers "removed from our midst on account of their not being white." The battalion commander agreed that because the men in question "are mulattoes" and "were so regarded in the neighborhood from which they came," they were therefore "a drawback to the company, preventing white men from joining it." The men were duly removed.[73]

Champions of the Black-Confederate cause have coped with such inconvenient facts and the flimsiness of their own documentation in various ways. Some deem it prudent to acknowledge (if hurriedly, in passing, almost under their breath) that "the number of armed black Confederates was always small."[74] Others try to rationalize their difficulties. "While engaged in fighting a war," explains one, "the Confederates had little time in which to record blacks' loyalty to them."[75] The General Nathan Bedford Forrest Camp #469 of the SCV blames a far-ranging conspiracy for the absence of better evidence to support its claims. "Because the victors—the north—needed to give the world the impression the War was fought over slavery," it intimates, "a concerted scheme was put into motion to suppress the figures by destroying records, thus giving credence to their 'the war was fought over slavery' mantra."[76]

Still others prefer simply to elide the distinction between soldiers and military laborers. Armed or not, fighting or not, they insist, all those involved in the Confederate war effort were Confederate soldiers—and certainly Confederate partisans. This tack helps explain a ceremony that took place not long ago in a cemetery in the small Virginia town of Rocky Mount. At its symbolic center was Creed Holland, a mid-nineteenth-century African American who had lived and labored on a nearby 732-acre farm owned by Thomas J. Holland. During the Civil War, Creed

Holland worked as a teamster for the Confederate army. Now, some 140 years later, the time had come (in the words of a local newspaper) "for Creed Holland to get the recognition he was due," since "he was a black slave, but also a Confederate soldier." So, on a Saturday in early September 2002, the Jubal Early chapter of the United Daughters of the Confederacy (UDC) dedicated memorial markers for Creed Holland and two other of Thomas J. Holland's slaves who had also worked for the Confederacy (one as an army cook, the other by building fortifications). All three were "Confederate heroes," declared the UDC's state president, "patriots who loved our Southland and suffered in its defense."[77]

Some sixty people attended this ceremony, mostly Confederate reenactors and members of either the UDC or the SCV. Also present was Linda Stanley of the local historical society, who at one point politely ventured to clarify the meaning of the Holland slaves' experience. During the war, six southern states (including Virginia) plus the Richmond government and various Confederate armies all compelled slave owners to lend some of their human property to the southern war effort.[78] Here was a fact, Stanley gently suggested, "possibly explaining the three Holland men's involvement in the war."

Given who had initiated this ceremony and why, her contribution had to be brushed aside; it could not be allowed to distract from the day's agenda of military-style funeral rites and southern-patriotic prayers, poetry, and speeches.[79] It did, however, point directly at the obvious problem with this variation on the Black-Confederate theme. Creed Holland and the two other men whose supposed southern patriotism was being celebrated that day worked for the Confederate army, just as they did for Thomas J. Holland, because they had no choice in the matter. The same was true, of course, of the thousands of other African American slaves impressed into Confederate labor service. (It was precisely to deprive them of choice, after all, that they were enslaved in the first place.)

Another attempt to gloss over the coerced nature of such labor came to grief a few years earlier and some one hundred miles eastward in Nottoway, Virginia. There, in 1993, the Sons of Confederate Veterans sought to have an additional marker placed at the foot of a Confederate monument already standing near the county courthouse. The new stone's inscription was to read, "Dedicated to over 400 Nottoway County African-Americans, free and slave, conscript and volunteers, who served

Virginia and the Confederacy from 1861–1865. The memory of their sacrifices will never perish." The county board of supervisors approved the project until members of the local black community mobilized in protest. Mae Tucker, an African American teacher at the local middle school, suggested that if there must be such a marker, it ought to say the following about the black laborers it referred to: "The irony of their plight was that though their bodies fought or served one side, their hearts and spirits perhaps prayed for the other." The board of supervisors soon decided to withdraw its approval from the original project.[80]

The issues that both Stanley and Tucker had raised were relevant to the experiences not only of slaves but of most southern free blacks as well. Freedom to choose whether to cooperate with the Confederacy was in short supply among them. Today's Black-Confederate advocates commonly cite wartime southern newspaper reports of free blacks loyally marching off to build military fortifications. They acknowledge far less often that southern governments at both the municipal, state, and Confederate levels regularly impressed not only slaves but also free blacks into such service.[81] Thus, when Confederate Tennessee recognized the value of having free blacks serve as "menials" with its state militia, it also decreed that if "a sufficient number of free persons of color to meet the wants of the State shall not tender their services, then the Governor is empowered, through the sheriffs of the different counties, to impress such persons until the required number is obtained."[82]

As Mae Tucker suggested, the vast majority of southern blacks forced to work for the Confederacy wished for the success of the Union. At first, Union policy did little to encourage such support. Washington's initial refusal to place emancipation on its banner or in many cases even to give sanctuary to slaves fleeing from Confederate masters confused and embittered sections of the South's black population. But two federal confiscation laws, enacted in 1861 and 1862, reversed those policies and renewed slaves' belief that the Union's triumph would mean their own deliverance. At that point, as Joseph T. Wilson recalled, "the slave negro went to the breastworks with no less agility, but with prayers for the success of the Union troops, and a determination to go to the Yankees at the first opportunity; though he risked life in the undertaking."[83] A witness with quite different sympathies acknowledged the same reality. Confederate general Joseph E. Johnston, who at one time or another held commands throughout the Confederacy, frankly admitted to a confidant that "we never have been able to keep the impressed Negroes with an army near the enemy. They desert." [84]

This was another reason why the Confederacy refused until the last minute to employ blacks (and especially slaves) as soldiers: it feared what such black troops would do. Masters and their spokesmen bragged about being able safely to leave their womenfolk and children in black hands, but this was whistling past the graveyard. Both slave owners and government officials did what they could to increase wartime surveillance and controls over all sections of their black populations. A month after the fall of Fort Sumter, the Tennessee legislature thus passed a law to raise "a Home Guard of Minute Men" whose duties included the responsibility "to see that all the slaves are disarmed; to prevent the assemblage of slaves in unusual numbers; to keep the slave population in proper subjection; and to see that peace and order is observed." [85]

During and after the war, Confederate apologists regularly pointed to the lack of open slave revolts as proof of black loyalty to their masters. As already noted, the same argument has recently been revived. But in fact, attempting an insurrection when nearly all white men were not only armed but also organized in the military would have been suicidal. Even trying to reach and join the Union army risked the most severe potential penalties.[86] As an insightful Georgia writer reminded his countryfolk early in 1865, "Evidences are not wanting to illuminate the ill suppressed discontent of many of our slaves." Because this discontent had not exploded in open revolts, he warned, some of his neighbors had grown "over secure." But "they should remember that the whole white population being under arms, any uprising of the negroes was more than ever impracticable." The South, he admonished, should not mistake the slaves' understandable caution for contentment.[87]

Mass black resistance to the Confederacy took the form not of isolated and doomed uprisings but of aiding and joining the Union army and navy and undermining the institution of slavery wherever and however possible. The dimensions of that resistance proved to the more perceptive and realistic southern whites that the vast majority of slaves were not loyal to their masters, much less to the Confederate cause, did aspire fervently to be free, and were prepared to act in pursuit of that aspiration. As one Virginia proslavery veteran acknowledged, "we see one-half of our entire population of no avail to us, but on the contrary ready at every opportunity to join the ranks of our enemies."[88]

The Confederate government began to modify its refusal to employ blacks as soldiers only at the eleventh hour. In November 1864, Jefferson Davis declared that it might after all prove necessary to arm some slaves and place them in Confederate service. In return for such service, he added, the South should promise freedom. In March 1865, only a month before Lee's battered Army of Northern Virginia surrendered, the Confederate Congress authorized the enlistment of black soldiers into its army, and the War Department set about recruiting them.[89]

Neo-Confederates commonly present this episode as the final, conclusive evidence for a number of their central propositions. In a flier entitled "Black History Month, Black Confederate Heritage," the Sons of Confederate Veterans' Education Committee triumphantly declares that "the CSA eventually freed slaves who would join the army and did recruit and arm black regiments."[90] Did this not show, among other things, that black southerners *did* support the Confederacy and take up arms on its behalf? Especially since as soon as the new law was passed "83% of Richmond's male slave population volunteered for duty"?[91] Did it not also demonstrate, once and for all, that the Confederacy fought for the right of southern independence and not for the preservation of slavery? After all, "if southerners had been primarily fighting to preserve slavery, as some have argued, then they would not have considered emancipation," nor would they have "assented to the raising of black Confederate regiments during the final months of the war."[92]

The truth about this intriguing story, however, tells not for but decisively against every one of the claims that neo-Confederates make about it. It demonstrates once again that between 1861 and the spring of 1865, no more than a handful of mulattoes could be found among Confederate troops.[93] It reveals that the belated policy's initiators planned to bestow only the most severely restricted version of freedom upon the black soldiers they hoped to enlist so that they could afterward return them and others to plantation labor. It shows that white resistance even to this very conservative plan was enormous and fierce and succeeded in stripping it of any emancipationist provision at all, no matter how minimal. It makes it clear, finally, that the policy proved a miserable failure in practice, frustrated by the resistance of both slave owners unwilling to part with their slaves and slaves unwilling to take up arms (and risk their lives) for the Confederacy.

The first important attempt to persuade Richmond to enlist black soldiers came in a memorandum written in December 1863 by General Patrick R. Cleburne of the Army of Tennessee. If any blacks were already serving in the ranks, Cleburne certainly knew nothing of them. He complained, on the contrary, that while the Union was successfully recruiting soldiers from among both free blacks and slaves, "our single source of supply is that portion of our white men fit for duty and not now in the ranks." At the same time, he continued, the South's own institution of "slavery is a source of great strength to the enemy in a purely military point of view" but "is our most vulnerable point, a continued embarrassment, and in some respects an insidious weakness." Cleburne's memorandum documented the slave population's active hostility to the Confederacy and its support for the Union. "All along the lines," he acknowledged, "slavery is comparatively valueless to us for labor, but of great and increasing worth to the enemy for information. It is an omnipresent spy system, pointing out our valuable men to the enemy, revealing our positions, purposes, and resources, and yet acting so safely and secretly that there is no means to guard against it." Cleburne understood very well why this was so; he entertained no illusions that slaves enjoyed their status or condition. The Union had won blacks' loyalty precisely because it promised them freedom, and "for many years, ever since the agitation of the subject of slavery commenced, the negro has been dreaming of freedom, and his vivid imagination has surrounded that condition with so many gratifications that it has become the paradise of his hopes."[94] It was therefore necessary both to enlist slaves as soldiers and to promise them freedom in exchange.

Jefferson Davis's government promptly and sternly rejected Cleburne's proposal. Placing blacks in the army, Davis declared, would immediately cause a public uproar throughout the South. So, for that matter, would public knowledge that army officers were even considering such a step. He therefore ordered an end to all such discussion in the army's ranks. Only after the fateful fall of Atlanta in September 1864 did Davis himself begin to reevaluate the matter. The results of this turnabout proved as revealing as the Cleburne episode, because once Davis decided that he *must* have black troops or be defeated, he also recognized that no appreciable number of slaves would ever fight for the South unless they were freed from bondage in return. Davis's closest advisor, Judah P. Benjamin, agreed. So did Robert E. Lee, who warned that "unless this freedom is guaranteed . . . we shall get no volunteers."[95] No more than Cleburne, in short, were any of these men under the impression that cheerful and contented (or ardently patriotic) slaves would agree to fight for the South so long as they remained in servitude.

Critics of Davis's new proposal opposed it on many grounds. First because it would destroy slavery, precisely that institution for the sake of which southern leaders had led their states into secession and war. When Davis's supporters indignantly replied that the war was not about slavery but only the right of southern whites to govern themselves, their opponents simply laughed them off the stage. What was the point of fighting for southern independence, critics jeered, if doing so would destroy the very foundation of southern society? Opponents of the measure also denounced it as utterly impractical, impolitic, and mortally dangerous. Blacks would make poor soldiers because blacks were inferior, they said. To say otherwise would undermine the whole rationale for keeping blacks in bondage. "The day you make soldiers of them is the beginning of the end of the revolution," cautioned Howell Cobb, one of the most influential men in the South. "If slaves will make good soldiers our whole theory of slavery is wrong."[96] Last but certainly not least, critics objected that arming slaves would prove suicidal, since black Confederate soldiers would certainly turn their weapons against the Confederacy itself.

How did the Richmond government and its supporters respond to such weighty arguments? Anyone familiar with modern Black-Confederate tracts might reasonably assume that Davis said something very much like this: "Are you gentlemen both deaf and blind? Or have you perhaps been asleep during these last three and a half years? All these objections of yours have been put to practical tests and have been refuted thousands of times over in the course of the war itself. How can you not know that fifty (or sixty-five or one hundred) thousand of our slaves have already proven themselves in action to be loyal, brave, and effective Confederate soldiers?" In fact, however, no such speech was ever made; no such newspaper editorial or letter to the editor was ever published; and no such private correspondence has ever come to light. It is hard to imagine a more thunderous refutation of the whole absurdly inflated Black-Confederates legend than this deafening silence.

To prove that slaves might be made to fight effectively and loyally for the South, Davis and his allies did not point to the record of fictitious black Confederate regiments (or brigades, or even companies) already in the field. Instead they quoted this or that body servant who had once supposedly offered to serve. Or they recalled the case of this or that personal attendant who had used his master's musket to shoot some Yankees. More often they rehearsed the claim that the absence of slave revolts in the Confederate rear proved slave loyalty, a claim wearing awfully threadbare by abrasion against the increasingly well-known record of slave support for and defection to the Union army. In fact, the fallback argument that Davis and his supporters most commonly employed was that the *Union* had already proved that blacks could make effective soldiers. If we offer our slaves freedom too, they asked, why should we expect to achieve any less success than the enemy?

Meanwhile, Davis, Lee, and like-minded members of the Confederate leadership showed (especially in correspondence among themselves) that the kind of freedom they envisioned for black soldiers would be a very partial one indeed. "The relation of master and slave, controlled by humane laws and influenced by Christianity and enlightened public sentiment," the supposedly antislavery Lee affirmed, was "the best that can exist between the white and black races." Unfortunately, he continued, events beyond the masters' control had now made the survival of that ideal relationship impossible; the war had already doomed slavery as such. Worse, the further penetration of Union forces into the Confederacy would eventually "destroy slavery in a *manner* most pernicious to the welfare of our people." And "whatever may be the effect of *our* employing negro troops, it cannot be as mischievous as this." Because even if the Confederacy's own use of black troops "ends in subverting slavery," at least that "will be accomplished by ourselves, and we can devise the means of alleviating the evil consequences to both races."[97]

Confederate secretary of state Judah P. Benjamin framed the issue in similar general terms but specified further the "means of alleviating the evil consequences." "We yield what we believe to be the best system on earth under protest," Benjamin said, "and take the next best system which could be obtained."[98] Under the new system the government had in mind, "ultimate emancipation" would come to southern blacks only after they had passed through "an intermediate state of serfage or peonage" of unspecified duration. So, "while vindicating our faith in the doctrine that the negro is an inferior race and unfitted for social or political equality with the white man," the South "might then be able" to "modify and ameliorate the existing condition of that inferior race" by affording it "legal protection for the marital and parental relations" and "by providing for it *certain* rights of property" and "a *certain* degree of personal liberty."[99] But no more.

At length, it was the prospect of the Confederacy's imminent collapse that determined the debate's outcome. In the second week of March 1865, the Confederate Congress passed a bill (by the narrowest of margins) authorizing the enlistment of three hundred thousand black troops, and Davis signed it into law. General Richard S. Ewell, already in charge of Richmond's defenses, assumed responsibility for implementing that law. Confederate officials and journalists loudly predicted massive enrollments. Union soldiers heard (and feared) rumors to the same effect. Some modern enthusiasts, as noted, boast that 83 percent of Richmond's black male slaves rushed to the colors (without ever feeling the need to substantiate this very precise claim); others talk knowingly about the swift formation of black Confederate regiments and even brigades in 1865.

The actual upshot of this furiously debated law was far, far smaller. A small company or two of black hospital workers was attached to a unit of home guard irregulars. The regular army managed to raise another forty to sixty men who were drilled, fed, and housed at military prison facilities in Richmond. General Ewell's longtime aide-de-camp later wrote of these soldiers that they "were the *first and only* black troops used on our side."[100] And one of the South's most popular and ardently pro-Confederate journalists wrote tellingly of how the rest of the capital's black population felt about the enterprise. As this small levy of soldiers marched in the streets of Richmond, he reported, "the mass of the colored brethren" of the city looked upon them "with unenvious eyes."[101]

Such extremely disappointing results reflected at least three underlying facts. First, most slave owners still refused to part with their slaves. Second, the Confederate government never granted freedom to a single prospective black recruit; the black-soldier law that it ultimately enacted explicitly left the relationship between slave owner and slave unchanged. Here, indeed, was an eloquent reminder of what the wealthiest and most powerful people in the South thought they had been fighting for since 1861. That fact, in turn, brings us to the third: few slaves or free blacks wanted any part of the Confederate cause, much less of the Confederate army. The too-little, too-late actions of the Confederate government in the spring of 1865 remind us why.

No matter how many fallacies are exposed, however, and no matter how many hard facts are put in their place, the most dedicated Black-Confederate devotees will not change their opinions. They are no more likely to do so, in any case, than they are likely to accept any of the other essential facts of the Civil War era—that slavery was the core of the antebellum South, that its impact was far from benign, that it lay at the root of the Civil War, that Reconstruction's real tragedy was its failure genuinely or enduringly to ensure racial equality, and that hopes for such equality, as for black-white amity, foundered on the rock of resurgent white racism. They will not acknowledge any of these things because they are determined not to do so.

It is necessary nonetheless to bring these truths to a wider audience, to the great mass of less ideologically driven individuals who, encountering the repetitive Black-Confederate propaganda, might otherwise be tempted to take it as good coin. It is important to disseminate the facts about these matters precisely because they are the facts—and because only an accurate understanding of history makes it possible to deal intelligently with the future. Nowhere is this truer than in the history of the American South, where, as William Faulkner famously observed, "The past is never dead. It's not even past." [102]

In 1897, Augustus Saint-Gaudens, an Irish-born sculptor who grew up in New York City, created this memorial to honor the African American soldiers of the Massachusetts 54th Civil War regiment and their white commander, Colonel Robert Gould Shaw, son of a New England abolitionist family. Saint-Gaudens imparted individuality to the soldiers by having black men pose as models. COURTESY OF JEFFREY NINTZEL PHOTOG-RAPHY

EPILOGUE: REFLECTIONS

Edward T. Linenthal

On June 5, 1960, during the Boston Arts Festival, Robert Lowell recited a poem, "For the Union Dead," honoring Robert Gould Shaw and the soldiers of the Massachusetts Fifty-fourth and calling attention to the Shaw Memorial on Boston Common, dedicated in 1897 but largely ignored in ensuing years. Lowell's elegy intimates that the ideals for which Shaw and his men died were as far from realization as they had ever been—for the nation as well as for the city of Boston—and, consequently, "the monument sticks like a fishbone in the city's throat."[1]

I thought of Lowell's powerful simile often while reading the provocative essays in this volume. Too often, in too many ways, the enduring legacies of slavery, the Civil War, Reconstruction, Jim Crow, and even the modern civil rights era stick like a fishbone in the nation's throat, and every page of this book is stark evidence of the fishbone's enduring presence.

Every nation has its own set of indigestible narratives, its "fishbone" stories. In Australia, for example, Denis Byrne, manager of the Cultural Heritage Research Unit at New South Wales Parks and Wildlife Service in Sydney, observes that resistance to remembering violent relations with Aboriginal peoples is accomplished through "erasure by substitution." The Australian landscape, he writes, "is replete with traces of our relationship with Aborigines over the last two hundred years, including traces of impoverishment, massacres, and institutionalization. . . . We look through or around this landscape in order to see instead an indigenous historical landscape populated with traces or sites of pre-contact 'authentic' Aboriginal presence." For some Japanese, a focus on victimhood as a result of Hiroshima and Nagasaki displaces a need to confront Japanese atrocities in China and in the Pacific War. In Germany a traveling exhibition, "War of Extermination: Crimes of the Wehrmacht 1941 to 1944," engendered fierce opposition in the mid-1990s. "The effect," wrote historians Omer Bartov, Atina Grossmann, and Mary Nolan, "was shock, dismay, disbelief, and rage." The exhibition asked visitors to jettison a cherished belief that the Wehrmacht, the German army, was innocent of complicity in the Holocaust. "Within the German Bundestag it sparked a highly emotional debate about both personal and national relationships to and responsibility for the Third Reich. In Munich there were street demonstrations against the exhibit; in Saarbrucken the site was firebombed."[2]

All of these essays assume the historical and moral importance of engaging America's indigestible stories. I was struck by the number of action words used in these essays to characterize engagement with the sites and stories considered here. There are terms that speak of processes of erasure: *marginalizing, suppressing, concealing, masking.* It seems one strategic stance toward the fishbone is denial: deny its presence, minimize its seriousness, and ignore its enduring scars. Consequently, sites and stories can deny the significance of slavery, deny its reality as a violent and brutal economic and cultural system, deny it had anything to do with the Civil War, deny its harsh reality and lasting legacy throughout the life of the nation. Or if not denial, then transformation into something benign, through a minefield of monumental memory to the "faithful slave" and "black mammy," the *Gone with the Wind* fiction of slavery, or transformation through, as Bruce Levine observes, an invented tradition of slaves fighting for an equal-opportunity Confederacy, or, as Dwight Pitcaithley informs us, a Civil War landscape where battle tactics, troop movements, characteristics of armaments, and casualties crowd out any talk of causes or consequences. (It is hard to imagine after appreciating the enduringly bitter battles over the meanings of the Civil War—including battles over the war's name—that anyone could continue so easily to use simpleminded rhetoric about winners writing the history that endures.)

On too many tours of plantations and historic homes, slaves, if recalled at all, become "servants." Their lives do not often resonate with the dominant "we"—the mostly white visitors—who have little or no interest in imagining themselves back into the skin of or the world of slaves. This public wants to come in the front door and see the house from the perspective of those who lived there. Their imagining is not of coming in the back door, of emptying chamber pots, of working in the kitchen making someone else's meals, of looking at the Big House from slave quarters, or of living every minute with the wrenching vulnerability of one's body or one's family. No, comfortable imaginings situate most visitors at the dinner table, eating the meal. It focuses on, as Joanne Melish writes, the "aesthetic approach to objects." If slaves are mentioned at all, their stories are usually segregated on "special" (add-on) tours, or marginalized and contained in circumscribed interpretive space. If we avoid telling integrated stories, we are left, argues Denis Byrne, with the "fiction of pure, unalloyed, and separate cultures." "Can we be comfortable," he asks, "with such an arrangement, one that evokes the horror of miscegenation that informed nineteenth century racism and the bogies of racial deterioration and cultural contamination that informed the White Australia [and, certainly, American] policy?"[3]

The enduring hunger for redemptive narratives smooths any rough edges in these indigestible stories, insisting that other, more positive stories about slavery be told in the service of "balance." (To be consistent about such "balance" in the telling of history, I suppose tours of concentration camps, massacre sites, and the like should find some positive stories to tell as well.) It takes work and a willingness to trouble our stories (and who wants to do this on vacation, after all?)—to make these lives count, to integrate, to complicate, to put flesh and blood on the stick-figure stories still told too often at too many American sites.

But, of course, it is not simply a white problem. As John Michael Vlach observes, for some African Americans stories of slavery should be erased as well because they are shameful and better forgotten. For, they argue—echoing in some measure Alexander Crummell's disagreement with Frederick Douglass—such stories are likely to disempower contemporary generations of African Americans. Like their neo-Confederate brethren who believe—mistakenly, in my view—that admitting slavery as a root cause (or even a secondary cause) of the Civil War will lead to the dishonoring of their ancestors, African Americans who objected to the "Back of the Big House" exhibition or to the slave auction at Colonial Williamsburg wanted to inhabit a therapeutic history that would support their strictly circumscribed sense of acceptable identity for themselves as well as their ancestors. And if there is a past that may be, in fact, subversive of such cherished identities, erasure, denial, transformation, and intentional consignment to oblivion are called for.

These essays, however, also contain terms that describe processes of restoration: *excavation, uncovering, remapping, reconstructing.* Because African Americans had been read out of American history for so long in so many insidious ways, these acts of restoration—the excavation of the President's House in Philadelphia, the expansion of the boundaries of Thomas Jefferson's family, the efforts to tell stories from slave quarters, to add African American names to monuments, to gain a symbolic presence in the cityspace of the former capital of the Confederacy—become litmus tests for the integrity of memory. What stories are we prepared to tell, and what stories are we willing to hear, without transforming them into preferred narratives that make no demands on our comforting illusions about the relationship between slavery and freedom in the life of the nation?

All of these case studies illustrate a steady expansion of what counts as worthy of inclusion on the American historic landscape. New National Park Service sites, for example, often reflect the challenge voiced in 2000 by historian John Hope Franklin, who served as chairperson of the National Park System Advisory Board. "The places that commemorate sad history," he argues, "are not places in which we wallow, or wallow in remorse, but instead places in which we may be moved to a new resolve, to be better citizens. . . . Explaining history from a variety of angles makes it not only more interesting, but also more true. When it is more true, more people come to feel that they have a part in it. That is where patriotism and loyalty intersect with truth."[4]

As Dwight Pitcaithley observes, some of these sites expand the National Park Service's African American historic landscape: Cane River Creole National Historic Park, Little Rock Central High School National Historic Site, Selma to Montgomery National Historic Trail, Tuskegee Airmen National Historic Site, for example. And beyond the expansion of the National Park Service landscape, there has been a dynamic marking of the African American landscape in many ways.

Processes of archival and material restoration offer one kind of marking. The Greenwood area of Tulsa, Oklahoma, almost completely destroyed in the Tulsa race riot of 1921, offers visitors few clues to its former life as a vibrant home to a well-established African American community. Through the meticulous work of the Tulsa Race Riot Memorial Commission and the Oklahoma Historical Society, the site of Greenwood has been re-created on maps, through the oral histories of survivors, and through discovery of photographs that had never been made public. The commission's final report informs readers that "old records have been re-opened, missing files have been recovered, new sources have been found." This work was an act of both historical reconstruction *and* memorialization, bringing to symbolic life a destroyed community.[5]

Material restoration and commemoration of relics, both painful and inspiring, allow people to "touch" the past viscerally, much as they do through the powerful material presence of relics at the United States Holocaust Memorial Museum: a railcar, a part of a women's barracks from Auschwitz, a casting of the Warsaw Ghetto wall, and the intimate mass of personal detritus left from the killing process: shoes, eyeglasses, photographs of women's hair shorn from victims before gassing and used in the German war effort. How powerful is a slave auction block in Fredericksburg, Virginia, the old slave mart in Charleston, South Carolina, the ballpark and monument in Daytona Beach, Florida, where Jackie Robinson broke the color barrier in modern baseball on March 17, 1946, the bus on which Rosa Parks was arrested and which is now restored and on display at the Henry Ford Museum in Dearborn, Michigan!

The horror of the Middle Passage can begin to be recalled by viewing a life-sized model of a slave ship in the Museum of African American History in Detroit, Michigan, or glass beads used to trade for slaves, or a hundred pairs of shackles for adults and children recovered from the sunken slave ship *Henrietta Marie*. For *Washington Post* reporter Michael H. Cottman, diving on the ship became a ritual of remembrance. At the dedication of the monument at sea on November 15, 1992, Cottman was "struck by the sight of the black divers dropping effortlessly onto a site of soggy planks of wood that had once made up a ship that hauled my ancestors into slavery." The power of the ship and the stories it contained led him to visit Goree Island, the slave prison off the coast of Senegal.[6]

These West African sites are surely an extension of the African American landscape. Like Cottman, the late historian Nathan Irvin Huggins felt about these places as a pilgrim visiting a charged site, in his case one transformed—haunted still—by an immensity of human suffering. For Huggins, the slave forts and castles off the coast of Ghana were "points of departure, not arrival, places of despair rather than liberty. . . . They are the few physical remains of the traffic in human beings that brought many Americans, black Americans, to the United States," and, he observes, they are "as much a part of our nation's history as Plymouth Rock."[7]

As for visitors to the Holocaust Museum transfixed and transported by small and intimate relics, so too for Huggins. At Cape Coast Castle "the floors are dirt and . . . have absorbed some part of everything that has passed over them. Scratching in the dirt, it is not hard to find the pitiful legacy of the slave trade: beads from women's clothing, pottery, bones. The place gives one the feeling that nothing ever left except the people. Their odors, their breath, their tears, their blood have seeped into the earth: they sweat through the stones of the walls." The stories straining to be told from this site are, for Huggins, not contained in a safe place called the past. They are alive and toxic. "To see the urban ghetto in its fullest perspective," writes Huggins, "one must walk in the Cape Coast dungeon. To really understand Attica prison, one must know the meaning of Elmina, and the others, too." These kinds of stories, writes Kathleen Stewart, "reopen the American story." They provide a valuable "back talk to America's mythic claims." They are rooted in places where—as she writes about the coal mining regions of West Virginia—"the story of 'America' grows dense and unforgettable in re-membered ruins and pieced-together fragments." These stories are what historians, to be worthy of the name, must insist upon including in—and thereby forever changing—triumphal or redemptive or progressive narratives. Resistance to their inclusion in our national stories allows the continuance of immature renderings of our past and an invitation to insidious forgetfulness.[8]

African American heritage trails, museums and exhibitions, monuments, and memorial sites increasingly mark the historical landscape.

Adam Goodheart captures some of this energy, observing, "Savannah is building a slave monument at its harbor. A slave dwelling in Brooklyn is being investigated and restored. Montpelier, the Virginia home of James Madison, owned by the National Trust, hosted a family reunion for hundreds of descendants of the plantation's black families. Even Robert E. Lee's Stratford Hall is holding a conference on African-American history."[9]

The naming of the nation's physical features is also undergoing change. Until recently, too many geographical features used the murderous, racist term *nigger* ("Nigger Creek" or "Nigger Run," for example) until Congress changed all such names to *negro* or, writes *New York Times* reporter Jon Nordheimer, "removed [such names] altogether." Some historic sites express sensitivity to the use of the term *slave*. Laura Gates, NPS superintendent of Cane River Creole National Historical Park, writes that their interpreters refer to "enslaved people," not "slaves," "thus putting the emphasis on the concept of the enslaved as people rather than property." Historian Peter H. Wood objects to the familiar and inviting term *plantation*. "Beyond the carefully maintained elegance and cultivation of the big house," Woods argues, southern plantations were "privately owned slave labor camps, sanctioned by the powers of the state, that persisted for generations." (It might be interesting to write about the reaction of guardians of plantation mythology to Wood's suggestion that these places should more accurately be classified as "gulag.") And some African Americans who have served in the armed forces during America's wars now have their names listed on memorials—the African American Civil War Memorial in Washington, D.C., for example, lists 209,145 names—an important way in which the memorial landscape bears witness to their service and sacrifice.[10]

This landscape is also transformed by stories resurrected by the work of oral history, from the remembrances of former slaves to the National Park Service's collection of oral histories of the Tuskegee Airmen and the tidal wave of autobiographies and oral history collections about the civil rights movement. Writing about another racial landscape in words that resonate powerfully in the United States, Denis Byrne declares, "The heritage of segregation—like the rules governing its enforcement—remains mostly in the realm of the unspoken." Byrne offers compelling examples of how the landscape "forgets" stories. Writing about a segregated theater, for example, he observes that Aboriginal peoples first remember "the humiliation of having to sit in those front rows and of only being allowed in after the lights went down. For them this is what the Boomerang Theatre means. But that meaning has no direct physical expression in the fabric of the place and would only become visible through an assessment of the place's historical or social significance." [11]

These essays also pushed me to think about the challenge of memorializing sites of the more recent civil rights era. Movement veteran and congressman John Lewis spoke to the importance of such places: "At this site is where the Freedom Riders were beaten. . . . Here is the place where children faced police dogs. . . . On this bridge we shed a little blood to replenish the foundations of our democracy. . . . This movement gave birth to the nonviolent movement for civil rights." Historian Robert Weyeneth's categorization of types of sites is helpful: sites of protest, sites of organizing, sites of marches, sites of incarceration, sites of racist violence, sites of legal activity, and sites of black power and white resistance. This last category, he observes, is almost completely effaced from the landscape. Echoing Weyeneth, Jim Carrier's *A Traveler's Guide to the Civil Rights Movement* informs readers that the movement's landmarks are "remarkably ordinary: a Woolworth's lunch counter, a bus stop, a bridge, modest homes and schools . . . Many are unmarked. Too many are falling down. None has been glorified with pillars and statues." [12]

Gradually, however, recognition of even painful sites of violence is finding a place in the memorialized landscape. The motel in Memphis, Tennessee, where the Reverend Dr. Martin Luther King Jr. was assassinated, has been transformed into the National Civil Rights Museum. In Birmingham, Alabama, Kelly Ingram Park, the site of demonstrations that riveted television viewers around the world, and the Sixteenth Street Baptist Church, where four young girls were killed by a terrorist bombing on September 15, 1963, are popular sites on the city's civil rights landscape. Through Tougaloo College, which now owns the property, it is possible to make appointments to tour Medgar Evers's home in Jackson, Mississippi, where he was murdered in his driveway as his family watched on June 11, 1963. In August 2004, at the sites of the firebombings of two homes and a store, three markers were erected in Indianola, Mississippi, part of a three-day program welcoming back civil rights workers who had risked their lives in order to establish Freedom Schools for African American young people during the Freedom Summer of 1964.[13]

Sometimes the very lack of memorial attention to marking certain acts of racist violence on the landscape calls attention to such places for that very reason: previously ignored sites become significant because they have been ignored. Several years ago, while attending the annual meeting of the Organization of American Historians in Memphis, Tennessee, I participated in a daylong tour of civil rights sites in Mississippi's Delta region. We visited the ruins of the store in Money, Mississippi, where on August 24, 1955, fourteen-year-old Emmett Till, visiting relatives from his home in Chicago, Illinois, said something, whistled, somehow fatally stepped out of his assigned place in the strict racial hierarchy of Mississippi with Carolyn Bryant, wife of the store's owner. Several days later, Roy Bryant and his half-brother J.W. Milam kidnapped Till, tortured and murdered him, and when brought to trial were quickly declared not guilty. While an enormously important event at the time—Till's open-casket funeral in Chicago drew tens of thousands—there has been no marking at the store, nor any marking at the courthouse site of the trial in Sumner. And yet the ruins of the store in Money figure prominently in two recent books about the intricacies of memory work in the South.

Shortly after finishing college, Richard Rubin accepted a job as a sports reporter in Greenwood, Mississippi, in order to find and understand "the South," an exploration he writes about in *Confederacy of Silence: A True Tale of the New Old South.* "I had always known that things were different in the South," he observes, "but my mind could not wrap itself around the notion that there might be room in my America for a place where two men could, with impunity, murder a fourteen-year-old boy for saying 'Bye, Baby,' or anything else." (Rubin's incomprehension about what there is room for in America, or anywhere else for that matter, is assuredly a testament to the enduring power of American innocence, stunning in its hold on so many, especially after the body counts of the last century.)[14]

Rubin's fascination with the Till story centered on the store in Money. He would often drive from Greenwood to sit in his car and stare at "the loose screen pocked with holes, the sagging second-story enclosed porch, the rusty sign that had become partially detached and limped out from the wall like a flag. . . . I would search the dirt on either side of the front steps, trying to discern where the tables had been, tables upon which someone had once set out checkerboards and around which Emmett Till and his cousins and their friends had gathered that afternoon. . . . And after a short while I would slowly and with a false and shallow calm saunter on into the store itself and greet the clerk behind the counter and engage in meaningless conversation for no other purpose than to allow me to study the counter and silently postulate: she stood there, a little to the left, probably, and he stood here, right on this spot where I am right now, right here." [15]

He felt himself surrounded by the living presence of the event. Someone pointed out a member of the jury to him at a high school basketball game, one of the defense attorneys came to the newsroom where he worked, and someone at a county board of supervisors meeting pointed out the man who owned the gin fan that took Till's body to the bottom of the Tallahatchie River. Rubin also found out—the year was 1989—that Bryant was still alive and ran a store in Ruleville. Walking into it, he imagined, "I was about to get close to some sort of pure historical evil, the kind that people read about for many centuries afterward but can never really hope to understand or even envision. . . . I wanted to get as close to it as I could." He went into the store, met Bryant—then legally blind—and bought two Moon Pies and a Coke. Returning to his car he "tossed that bag, with the bottle of Coke and the two Moon Pies, onto the floor behind the passenger's seat. It lay there, just like that, not moved or even touched, until I left Mississippi for good a few months later." [16]

I recognize more of myself in Rubin's visceral attraction to the site and his fascination with the personification of evil in the figure of Bryant than I am comfortable with: a touch of voyeurism, a sprinkle of tourism, a dash of pilgrimage, a pinch of consumerism. The conviction is that somehow places speak, and places where extreme events were carried out (or began) speak even more importantly—more problematically, that our memories of such events will be as powerful, as enduringly constructive, as the enduringly destructive event itself. What an interesting place—the ruins of the Bryant store—to make its way onto the national historic landscape! Not Emmett Till's grave site, not the banks of the river where his body, with a face battered beyond recognition, was recovered, not the private property on which he was tortured in a barn, not even the courthouse in Sumner, but the ruins of this store. Surely, part of its power is that it is *not* remembered in any official way, but its ruins are horribly intimate—they allow people to approach without competing interpretive voices placed in their way.

The Bryant store also figures prominently in Paul Hendrickson's *Sons of Mississippi*. Like Rubin, Hendrickson offers his readers a detailed, visceral description of the ruins and characterizes it as "its own kind of American shrine. . . . Nearly every Mississippi story sooner or later touches this one, ends up—in some spiritual, homing way—right here, in absurdly misnamed and depopulated Money, along this ribbon of Illinois Central railroad track, on this backcountry asphalt, before this tottering and yet somehow beautiful and abandoned building where fatback and bamboo rakes and Lucky Strikes and lye soap and BC headache powder and so many other simple, needed goods and wares and staples were once sold to locals." Hendrickson also imagines the past at the courthouse in Sumner: "It's the place where, if you squint, you can see straw-bottom chairs in a second-floor courtroom, the lone overhead fan, the widening moons of sweat beneath the rows of armpits." [17]

Pilgrimage is, in part, a physical and spiritual journey to a place of power in order to "touch" transforming power, to get, as Rubin wrote, "as close to it as I could." Rubin's and Hendrickson's vivid descriptions of the ruins, their imaginative time travel to the days of the event, and Rubin's wary encounter with an aging Bryant suggest that this place is, indeed, a particular kind of shrine—not a sacred place, certainly, but a place that holds the memories of a shattering event, memories to be recalled most powerfully at the site. It is a pilgrimage site because it is, as Hendrickson observes, a place at the center of so many Mississippi stories, a place that offers moral and historic orientation, a place where one can see and hear the memories of this foundational event of the civil rights era.

There are other sites of lynching just beginning to become visible on the nation's historic landscape. From October 3 to 6, 2002, I took part in a conference at Emory University entitled "Lynching and Racial Violence in America." During the conference, we had the opportunity to confront and struggle with—*visit* does not seem the appropriate term—the exhibition "Without Sanctuary: Lynching Photography in America," housed at the Martin Luther King Jr. National Historic Site in Atlanta. Before we left, Frank Catroppa, superintendent of the site, told some of us that not long before, a ranger asked him to come and talk with someone outside the small room where the exhibition was located. Catroppa saw an elderly black gentleman who, the ranger told him, had been standing there for a long time. In talking with him, Catroppa discovered that as a young boy this gentleman had seen his father lynched. He had come to the exhibition to see if it contained a photograph of his father. "Nothing is ever escaped," James Baldwin cautions us, and the presence of people such as this gentleman make these acts of historical excavation profound acts of moral remembrance.

Throughout the nation, from Minnesota to Georgia, interracial groups of reconciliation are caring for long-forgotten grave sites of those murdered, placing names on gravestones, holding ceremonies of remembrance, creating "living memorials" of scholarships for students, asking for posthumous pardon for those lynched after being "convicted" by juries on no evidence, and calling for prosecution of those still alive who perpetrated such atrocities.

There are still too many voices, particularly strong in an age of triumphal and coarse nationalism, that argue against the public representation of these "fishbone" stories. They open old wounds, some argue; they are evidence of contemporary historians' hatred for America, transforming our sacred past into something dark and gloomy. Cheerleading court history, however, is not a sign of intellectual or moral maturity. Neither does populating the historic landscape with these searing stories consign the nation's history to one of shame. It is the case, as some critics argue, that we are not responsible for events long past, but we are responsible for the preservation and presentation of them to coming generations. Conscientious remembrance is more than a necessary expansion of the nation's narrative. It is an act of moral engagement, a declaration that there are other American lives too long forgotten that count. Edward Ball, author of *Slaves in the Family,* writes, "Reconciliation is not about being nice. It's not about pretending that things were other than they actually were. This kind of reconciliation, based upon misrepresentation and the softening of the realities, is not true reconciliation and will not last. Reconciliation is about being able to look the tragedy of American history in the eye. It's about coming to terms with the violence and suffering, chaos and anger and fear in our heritage, and saying: 'We accept this, and together we will transcend it.' " These essays are an important step in this process of historical transcendence.[18]

NOTES

Introduction (James Oliver Horton and Lois E. Horton)

1. Ellen Gibson Wilson, *The Loyal Blacks* (New York: Capricorn Books, 1976), 2–3.
2. Abigail Adams to John Adams, Sept. 22, 1774, in Lyman H. Butterfield, ed., *Adams Family Correspondence* (Cambridge, MA: Harvard University Press, 1963), 1:162, 13–14.
3. Thomas Jefferson, *Notes on the State of Virginia,* ed. William Peden (New York: W.W. Norton, 1954 [1787]), 143, 142.
4. Quoted in Paul Finkelman, *Slavery and the Founders: Race and Liberty in the Age of Jefferson,* 2nd ed. (Armonk, NY: M.E. Sharpe, 2001), 132.

1. Coming to Terms with Slavery in Twenty-First-Century America (Ira Berlin)

1. Henry Louis Gates Jr., *Wonders of the African World* (New York: Knopf, 1999), and "Wonders of the African World," http://www.pbs.org/wonders (Jan. 1, 2002) with subsequent discussion on H-AFRICA; Peter Applebome, "Can Harvard's Powerhouse Alter the Course of Black Studies?" *New York Times,* Nov. 3, 1996; Lynn B. Elber, "PBS' Film 'Africans in America' Examines Roots of Slavery," Associated Press, Oct. 16, 1998; Michael O'Sullivan, " 'Shadrach': A Museum Piece," *Washington Post,* Oct. 16, 1998; "Unchained Memories: Readings from the Slave Narratives," dir. Ed Bell and Thomas Lennon, Home Box Office (HBO), Feb. 10, 2003, also became a book of the same title edited by Henry Louis Gates Jr. and Cynthia Goodman (Boston: Bulfinch, 2002). For information on the *Amistad* monument, see Ken Ringle, "Sailor on History's Seas," *Washington Post,* Mar. 23, 2000; David M. Herszenhorn, "A Slave Ship Reborn into History," *New York Times,* Mar. 26, 2000; "*Amistad* Friendship Tour 2003," www.amistad america.org/new/main/html/schedule.html (Oct. 19, 2003). Also see David Brion Davis, "Free at Last: The Enduring Legacy of the South's Civil War Victory," *New York Times,* Aug. 26, 2001.
2. For information on the Clinton apology, see William Douglas, "We Were Wrong," New York *Newsday,* Mar. 25, 1998; and on conservative reaction see Leonard Pitts Jr., "Slavery Apology Fitting and Proper," *Baltimore Sun,* Apr. 9, 1998. For Bush's speech at Goree, see "President Bush Speaks at Goree Island," www.whitehouse.gov/news/ releases/2003/07/print/20030708-1.html (Oct. 19, 2003); "White House Initiative on Race," www.acenet.edu/bookstore/descriptions/making_the_case/works/national.cfm#house (Oct. 19, 2003); Editorial Writer's Desk, "Race Panel's Lost Chance," *Los Angeles Times,*

Sept. 21, 1998. See also Scott La Fee, "Grave Injustice," *San Diego Union-Tribune,* Sept. 15, 1999; Mel Tapley, " 'Dem Dry Bones' Get Belated Respect," *Amsterdam News,* Oct. 19, 1991. See Stephan Salisbury and Inga Saffron, "Echoes of Slavery at the Liberty Bell Site," *Philadelphia Inquirer,* Mar. 24, 2002; Stephan Salisbury, "Discussing Slavery at Liberty Bell Site," *Philadelphia Inquirer,* Apr. 25, 2002, 1; Stephan Salisbury, "Liberty Bell's Symbolism Rings Hollow for Some," *Philadelphia Inquirer,* May 26, 2002, 1; "Liberty Bell Center Exhibit Preview Now on Independence National Historical Park Website," data2.itc.nps.gov/release/Detail.cfm?ID=326 (Oct. 19, 2003). See Jesse Leavenworth and Kevin Canfield, "To Be Sold," *Hartford Courant,* July 4, 2000; Ross Kerber, "Aetna Regrets Being Insurer to Slaveowners," *Boston Globe,* Mar. 10, 2000; Peter Slevin, "In Aetna's Past: Slave Owner Policies," *Washington Post,* Mar. 9, 2000. Regarding California's actions, see Tamar Lewin, "Calls for Slavery Restitution Getting Louder," *New York Times,* June 4, 2001; Slavery Era Insurance Registry Report to the California Legislature, www.insurance.ca.gov/SEIR/SlaveInsuranceReporttoLeg.htm (Oct. 20, 2003); *Washington Post,* May 2, 2002. For a similar action by the Chicago City Council, see "Chicago City Council Seeks Slavery Records," Reuters, Oct. 2, 2002. On Jefferson and Hemings, see Eugene Foster et al., "Jefferson Fathered Slave's Last Child," *Nature* 396 (Nov. 1998): 27–28; Annette Gordon-Reed, *Thomas Jefferson and Sally Hemings: An American Controversy* (Charlottesville: University Press of Virginia, 1997); Jan Ellen Lewis and Peter S. Onuf, eds., *Sally Hemings & Thomas Jefferson: History, Memory, and Civic Culture* (Charlottesville: University Press of Virginia, 1999); Jan Lewis, Joseph J. Ellis, Lucia Stanton, Peter S. Onuf, Gordon Reed, Andrew Burstein, Annette-Gordon Reed, Fraser D. Neiman, "Forum: Thomas Jefferson and Sally Hemings Redux," *William and Mary Quarterly* 57 (Jan. 2000): 121–210; Roy L. Brooks, ed., *When Sorry Isn't Enough: The Controversy over Apologies and Reparations for Human Injustice* (New York: New York University Press, 1999).

3. Steven Deyle, *Carry Me Back: The Domestic Slave Trade in American Life* (New York: Oxford University Press, 2005); James L. Huston, *Calculating the Value of Union: Slavery, Property Rights, and the Economic Origins of the Civil War* (Chapel Hill: University of North Carolina Press, 2003).

4. Leonard L. Richards, *The Slave Power: The Free North and Southern Domination, 1780–1860* (Baton Rouge: Louisiana State University Press, 2000); Don E. Fehrenbacher with Ward M. McAfee, *The Slaveholding Republic: An Account of the United States Government's Relations to Slavery* (New York: Oxford University Press, 2001).

5. *New York Times,* Aug. 29, 2004.

6. Washington *City Paper,* Nov. 5, 2004.

7. Clipping from the *New York Herald Tribune,* Feb. 13, 1865, "Negroes in Savannah," Consolidated Correspondence File, ser. 225, Central Records, RG 92, National Archives.

8. Louis B. Wright and Marion Tinling, eds., *The Secret Diary of William Byrd of Westover, 1709–1712* (Richmond, VA: Dietz, 1941), 112, 117. For Carter, see Lancaster County, Virginia, Order Book #5, 1702–13, 185; Robert Carter to Robert Jones, Oct. 10, 1727, Carter Papers, University of Virginia Library, Charlottesville. Thomas Jefferson, *Thomas Jefferson's Farm Book* ed. Edwin M. Betts (Princeton, NJ: Published for the American Philosophical Society by Princeton University Press, 1953), 11.

9. Orlando Patterson, *Slavery and Social Death: A Comparative Study* (Cambridge, MA: Harvard University Press, 1982); David Brion Davis, "Looking at Slavery in Broader Perspective," *American Historical Review* 105 (2000): 451–66.

10. Ira Berlin, *Generations of Captivity: A History of African American Slaves* (Cambridge, MA: Harvard University Press, 2000).

11. Ira Berlin, *Many Thousands Gone: The First Two Centuries of Slavery in North America* (Cambridge, MA: Belknap Press, 1998), pt. 1.

12. Ibid., 29–45; J. Douglas Deal, *Race and Class in Colonial Virginia: Indians, Englishmen,*

and *Africans on the Eastern Shore of Virginia During the Seventeenth Century* (New York: Garland Publishers, 1993), 217–50. Also useful are T.H. Breen and Stephen Innes, *"Myne Owne Ground": Race and Freedom on Virginia's Eastern Shore, 1640–1676* (New York: Oxford University Press, 1980), ch. 1.

13. Quoted in Berlin, *Generations of Captivity,* 37.
14. Ibid., ch. 1.
15. Quote in Marion Tinling, ed., *The Correspondence of the Three William Byrds of Westover, Virginia, 1684–1776,* 3 vols. (Charlottesville: University Press of Virginia, 1977), 2:487.
16. Ibid., ch. 5.
17. In addition to the above, see Winthrop D. Jordan, *White over Black: American Attitudes Toward the Negro, 1550–1812* (Chapel Hill: University of North Carolina Press, 1968), pt. 2, especially ch. 6. Quotation in Hugh Jones, *The Present State of Virginia, from Whence Is Inferred a Short View of Maryland and North Carolina,* ed. Richard L. Morton (Chapel Hill: University of North Carolina Press, 1956), 36–38.
18. Jordan, *White over Black,* pt. 2.
19. Berlin, *Many Thousands Gone,* pt. 3; also Sylvia R. Frey, *Water from the Rock: Black Resistance in a Revolutionary Age* (Princeton, NJ: Princeton University Press, 1991).
20. Frey, *Water from a Rock;* Ira Berlin, *Slaves Without Masters: The Free Negro in the Antebellum South* (New York: Pantheon, 1975), ch. 3.
21. In 1772, Lord Mansfield, chief justice of England, ruled that a slave named James Somerset who had been brought to England from Virginia was free, declaring that "as soon as ever any slave set his foot upon the soil of England, he became free." The Somerset decision is generally viewed as the beginning of the end of slavery in the British Empire. After Mansfield's decision, Somerset became a popular name among free blacks.
22. Thomas Jefferson, *Notes on the State of Virginia,* ed. William Peden (New York: W.W. Norton, 1972), Query 8.

2. If You Don't Tell It Like It Was, It Can Never Be as It Ought to Be (David W. Blight)

This article is based on a talk given at a conference on Yale and Slavery at Yale University, New Haven, Connecticut, Sept. 26, 2003.

1. Gabriel García Márquez, *One Hundred Years of Solitude,* trans. Gregory Rabassa (New York: Avon, 1970), 50–57.
2. Saint Augustine, *Confessions,* trans. Edward Bouverie Pusey (New York: Book of the Month Club, 1996), 240–41.
3. Daniel L. Schacter, *Searching for Memory: The Brain, the Mind, and the Past* (New York: Basic Books, 1996) 11.
4. Robert Hayden, "Middle Passage," in Abraham Chapman, ed., *Black Voices: An Anthology of Afro-American Literature* (New York: New American Library, 1968), 444–49.
5. Nathan Irvin Huggins, *Black Odyssey: The African American Ordeal in Slavery* (New York: Vintage, 1990 [1977]), 26–27.
6. W.E.B. Du Bois, *The Suppression of the African Slave Trade to the United States of America, 1638–1870* (Cambridge, MA: Harvard University Press, 1896), 196.
7. Ibid., 197.
8. John Lukacs, *Historical Consciousness or the Remembered Past,* (New York: Schocken, 1985 [1968]), 33.
9. Bernard Bailyn, "Considering the Slave Trade: History and Memory," *William and Mary Quarterly* 58 (Jan. 2001): 250.
10. See Edward T. Linenthal and Tom Engelhardt, eds., *History Wars: The Enola Gay and Other Battles for the American Past* (New York: Henry Holt, 1996).
11. Maurice Halbwachs, *The Collective Memory* (New York: Harper and Row, 1950), 52.

12. See John R. Gillis, "Memory and Identity: The History of a Relationship," in John R. Gillis, ed., *Commemorations: The Politics of National Identity* (Princeton, NJ: Princeton University Press, 1994), 5.

13. Cynthia Ozick, "Metaphor and Memory," in *Metaphor and Memory: Essays* (New York: Vintage International, 1991), 281.

14. See David W. Blight, *Race and Reunion: The Civil War in American Memory* (Cambridge, MA: Harvard University Press, 2001), 300–37.

15. *Christian Recorder,* Apr. 25, 1878, Sept. 29, 1887; Kelly Miller, "The Negro's Part in the Negro Problem," in *Race Adjustment: Essays on the Negro in America* (New York: Arno Press, 1968 [1908]), 99.

16. "The Need of New Ideas and New Aims for a New Era," address to the graduating class of Storer College, Harpers Ferry, WV, May 30, 1885, in Alexander Crummell, *Africa and America: Addresses and Discourses* (New York: Atheneum, 1969 [1891]), iii, 13–15.

17. Ibid., 18.

18. Frederick Douglass, "Speech at the Thirty-third Anniversary of the Jerry Rescue," 1884, Frederick Douglass Papers, Library of Congress, reel 16.

19. Frederick Douglass, "Thoughts and Recollections of the Antislavery Conflict," speech undated, but it is at least as late as the early 1880s; "Decoration Day," speech at Mt. Hope Cemetery, Rochester, NY, May 1883, Douglass Papers, Library of Congress, reel 15.

20. See Blight, *Race and Reunion,* 315–18.

21. Crummell, "The Need of New Ideas and New Aims for a New Era," 19, 13; W.E.B. Du Bois, *The Souls of Black Folk* (Boston: Bedford Books, 1997 [1903]), 38; Toni Morrison, *Beloved* (New York: New American Library, 1987), 273.

22. Mary Frances Berry, "Reparations for Freedom, 1890–1916," *Journal of Negro History* 57, no. 3 (1972): 222.

23. Ibid., 223, 229.

24. Ibid., 230.

3. Slavery in American History:
An Uncomfortable National Dialogue (James Oliver Horton)

1. John F. Kennedy, Presidential Inaugural Address, Jan. 20, 1961.

2. Mary-Christine Phillip, "To Reenact or Not to Reenact," *Black Issues in Higher Education,* Nov. 3, 1994, 26.

3. The encounter took place in the Old Granary Burial Ground at the Park Street Church in Boston, Apr. 23, 2004.

4. For an important discussion on this complex issue, see Paul Finkelman, "The Centrality of Slavery in American Legal Development," in Paul Finkelman, ed., *Slavery and the Law* (Madison, WI: Madison House, 1997), 3–26.

5. John Dickinson, *Letters from a Farmer in Pennsylvania to the Inhabitants of the British Colonies* (Philadelphia, 1768), 38, quoted in F. Nwabueze Okoye, "Chattel Slavery as the Nightmare of the American Revolutionaries," *William and Mary Quarterly,* 3rd Ser., 37, 1 (Jan. 1980): 3.

6. Josiah Quincy Jr., *Observations on the Act of Parliament Commonly Called the Boston Port-Bill; with Thoughts on Civil Society and Standing Armies* (Boston, 1774), 69, quoted in Okoye, "Chattel Slavery as the Nightmare of the American Revolutionaries," 5.

7. George Washington, General Orders, July 2, 1776; *The Writings of George Washington from the Original Manuscript Sources, 1745–1799,* ed. John Fitzpatrick (Washington, DC: Government Printing Office, 1932), 5:211.

8. James Otis, *The Rights of British Assured and Proved* (Boston: Edes and Gill, 1765), 37.

9. Arthur Zilversmit, *The First Emancipation: The Abolition of Slavery in the North* (Chicago: University of Chicago Press, 1967), 118.
10. Jean R. Soderlund, *Quakers and Slaves: A Divided Spirit* (Princeton, NJ: Princeton University Press, 1985); Gretchen Holbrook Gerzina, *Black London: Life Before Emancipation* (New Brunswick, NJ: Rutgers University Press, 1995).
11. "Thomas Jefferson to John Holmes, Monticello, April 22, 1820," in Philip B. Kurland and Ralph Lerner, eds., *The Founder's Constitution* (Chicago: University of Chicago Press, 1987), 1:575. Thomas G. West, *Vindicating the Founders* (New York: Rowman and Littlefield, 2001).
12. Louis Agassiz as quoted in James Ford Rhodes, *History of the United States from Compromise of 1850 to the Final Resolution of Home Rule in the South in 1877* (New York: Macmillan, 1906–1919), 6:37.
13. *My Country* (1948), quoted in *Social Studies Review* 7 (winter 1991): 10.
14. Samuel Eliot Morrison and Henry Steele Commager, *The Growth of the American Republic* (New York: Oxford University Press, 1950), 521.
15. Richard M. Ingersoll and Kerry Gruber, "Out-of Field Teaching and Educational Equality," National Center for Education Statistics, United States Department of Education, Oct. 1996, 24. Other states with high percentages of non-history-trained high school history teachers include Maryland (72 percent), Arizona (71 percent), South Dakota (70 percent), and Mississippi (70 percent). New York and Wisconsin had the lowest percentages with 32 percent each.
16. Kenneth Jackson, "Divisions, Real and Imagined," *OAH Newsletter,* Aug. 1997, 3–4.
17. Diane Ravitch, "The Educational Backgrounds of History Teachers," unpublished paper, 1998, 10.
18. Gerald W. Bracey, "Record-Level SATs: Course Related; Scholastic Aptitude Test," *Phi Delta Kappan* 76, 7 (Mar. 1995): 566.
19. Roy Rosenzweig and David Thelen, *The Presence of the Past: Popular Uses of History in American Life* (New York: Columbia University Press, 1998), 21, 32.
20. James Oliver Horton, "Confronting Slavery and Revealing the Lost Cause," *Cultural Resources Magazine* 21, no. 4 (1998).
21. Essays in this book by Dwight Pitcaithley and Gary B. Nash focus in greater detail on some of these projects and other Park Service cooperative efforts and reactions to attempts at updating historical reinterpretation at National Park Service sites.
22. Jesse L. Jackson Jr., "A More Perfect Union," in Robert K. Sutton, ed., *Rally on the High Ground: The National Park Service Symposium on the Civil War,* 4.
23. Some of the most significant recent studies of the culture wars include Edward T. Linenthal and Tom Engelhardt, eds., *History Wars: The Enola Gay and Other Battles for the American Past* (New York: Metropolitan Books, 1996); Lawrence W. Levine, *The Opening of the American Mind: Canons, Culture, and History* (Boston: Beacon Press, 1996); Gary B. Nash, Charlotte Crabtree, and Ross E. Dunn, *History on Trial: Culture Wars and the Teaching of the Past* (New York: Alfred A. Knopf, 1997).
24. "Slavery 'Abhorred,' Gilmore Says," *Washington Post,* Apr. 10, 1998.
25. Ibid.
26. Larry L. Beane II, "Gov. Gilmore's 'Denigration Proclamation,' " www.angelfire.com/biz/hpadva/edlb.html (Apr. 1998).
27. "Slavery 'Abhorred.' "
28. Tony Horwitz, *Confederates in the Attic: Dispatches from the Unfinished Civil War* (New York: Pantheon Books, 1998), 99.
29. *Boston Globe,* Mar. 9, 1997.
30. Interview with Stephanie Batiste-Bentham, Washington, DC, Mar. 3, 1998.
31. Phone interview with Rex Ellis, former director of Williamsburg African American Department, May 14, 1998.
32. Christy Coleman Matthews, director of Colonial Williamsburg's African American De-

partment, quoted in the *Washington Post,* Oct. 11, 1994. Marie Tyler-McGraw kindly provided me with material from her Jan. 20, 1997, interview with Matthews at Colonial Williamsburg, which has provided information and a context for much of this discussion.

33. Phillip, "To Reenact or Not to Reenact," 25.
34. *Washington Post,* Oct. 8, 1994.
35. *New York Times,* Oct. 11, 1994.
36. Phillip, "To Reenact or Not to Reenact," 26.
37. Rex Ellis, "An Open Challenge of Educators," unpublished manuscript, July 1989, 1.
38. Phone interview with Rex Ellis, former director of Williamsburg African American department, May 14, 1998.
39. Ellis interview; Phillip, "To Reenact or Not to Reenact," 26.
40. Telephone interview with Liz Cherry Jones, Feb. 18, 1999.
41. Donald R. Kinder and Lynn M. Sanders, *Divided by Color: Racial Politics and Democratic Ideals* (Chicago: University of Chicago Press, 1996), 270.
42. The 1998 outrage of whites as well as blacks at the horrible dragging murder of black Texan James Byrd at the hands of white supremacists and the death sentence of John William King, the first white man so sentenced for murdering an African American in Texas history, are grisly evidence of this change. For a comparison of southern tolerance of violence and even murder of blacks by whites, see Leon F. Litwack, *Trouble in Mind: Black Southerners in the Age of Jim Crow* (New York: Alfred A. Knopf, 1998).

4. The Last Great Taboo Subject: Exhibiting Slavery at the Library of Congress (John Michael Vlach)

1. James Loewen, *Lies My Teacher Told Me: Everything Your American History Textbook Got Wrong* (New York: New Press, 1995), 134.
2. Jennifer L. Eichstedt and Stephen Small, *Representations of Slavery: Race and Ideology in Southern Plantation Museums* (Washington, DC: Smithsonian Institution Press, 2002), 3, 271–75.
3. John Michael Vlach, *Back of the Big House: The Architecture of Plantation Slavery* (Chapel Hill: University of North Carolina Press, 1993), 16.
4. Cited in George P. Rawick, ed., *The American Slave: A Composite Autobiography* (Westport, CT: Greenwood Press, 1972), 6 (pt. 1): 385.
5. Those who are interested in viewing this exhibition for themselves can find it on the following Web site: www.gwu.edu/~folklife/bighouse.
6. Norman R. Yetman, *Life Under the "Peculiar Institution": Selections from the Slave Narrative Collection* (New York: Holt, Rinehart, and Winston, 1970), 96.
7. Booker T. Washington, *Up from Slavery* (New York: Penguin Books, 1986 [1901]), 19–20.
8. Cited in Eric Foner, *Reconstruction: America's Unfinished Revolution, 1863–1877* (New York: Harper and Row, 1988), 77.
9. See Gail Fineberg, "$8.5 Million Cook Payout Cleared," *The Gazette* (Library of Congress) 7, no. 44 (Nov. 29, 1996): 1, 10–14 for a summary of this court case, which was litigated for twenty-one years. One year after the announcement of the settlement, Anna Buchanan, one of the original complainants in this case, noted that the library had yet to honor fully the court-ordered agreement. That the payout continues to be a troubling issue is signaled on the Web site of the group known as Blacks in Government—Library of Congress Chapter. On the opening page of the site the "Cook Case Archives" is highlighted (see www.bigloc.gov).
10. Mark Fischer, "Library of Congress Scraps Plantation Life Exhibit," *Washington Post,* Dec. 21, 1995.

11. "Letter to the Editor," *The Gazette* (Library of Congress), Jan. 19, 1996.
12. "The Costs of Cultural Blackmail," *Washington Post,* Dec. 24, 1995.
13. Karen Lange, "Library of Congress Fracas Spotlights UNC Press Book," *Chapel Hill Herald,* Dec. 22, 1995, 1.
14. "A Library on Tiptoe," *Washington Post,* Dec. 22, 1995.
15. Kate Mulligan, "Life on Plantations as Lived by the Slaves: Controversy Fades as Exhibit Is Big Hit at MLK Library," *Washington Times,* Feb. 1, 1996; Mary Ann French, "Slavery Show Shut Down at Library Congress Seen with New Eyes," *Washington Post,* January 18, 1996; Lee Rosenbaum, "Slavery Abolished by Feds, Rises Again," *Wall Street Journal,* Jan. 25, 1996.
16. These aims are expressed on the opening page of each issue of the society's journal, *Washington History.*
17. John Michael Vlach, "Evidence of Slave Housing in Washington," *Washington History* 5, no. 2 (1993–94): 64–74.
18. The pre-capital period of Washington is addressed in considerable detail by Don Alexander Hawkins in "The Landscape of the Federal City: A 1792 Walking Tour," *Washington History* 3, no. 1 (1991): 10–33, and Priscilla W. McNeil, "Rock Creek Hundred: Land Conveyed for the Federal City," *Washington History* 3, no. 1 (1991): 34–51; in the latter, see especially the map by Don Hawkins that reconstructs early Washington, 42–43.
19. See John W. Reps, *Washington on View: The Nation's Capital Since 1790* (Chapel Hill: University of North Carolina Press, 1991), 13, 20.
20. Since a census taken in 1798 reported that Notley Young owned only sixty-one slaves within the District of Columbia, the larger total of 265 must include African Americans held on several of his farming and milling enterprises elsewhere in Maryland. See Bob Arnebeck, *Through a Fiery Trail: Building Washington, 1790–1800* (Lanham, MD: Madison Books, 1991), 20.
21. Reps, *Washington on View,* 26. The Duddington Manor house was under construction just as L'Enfant was laying out the line for Washington's streets. When L'Enfant found that Carroll's house intruded a few feet into the path of New Jersey Avenue, he had the building, unbeknownst to Carroll, torn down. The resulting argument led not only to Congress paying to rebuild the house on a different site, but also to L'Enfant's dismissal. The house and its grounds were carefully mapped to ensure that there would be no further problems.
22. Howard Gillette, ed., *Southern City, National Ambition: The Growth of Early Washington, D.C., 1800–1860* (Washington, DC: Center for Washington Area Studies, 1995).
23. Mary Ann French, "Behind Freedom's Facade," *Washington Post,* Mar. 5, 1996.
24. Cited in Carl Abbott, *Political Terrain: Washington, D.C., from Tidewater Town to Global Metropolis* (Chapel Hill: University of North Carolina Press, 1999), 57.
25. Peter H. Wood, "Slave Labor Camps in Early America: Overcoming Denial and Discovering the Gulag," in Carla Gardina Pestana and Sharon V. Salinger, eds., *Inequality in Early America* (Hanover, NH: University Press of New England, 1999), 222, 228–230.

5. For Whom Will the Liberty Bell Toll?
From Controversy to Cooperation (Gary B. Nash)

Versions of this essay were given at the New Jersey Council for History Education, Dec. 6, 2002, Princeton University; at Christ Church, Philadelphia, Jan. 25, 2003; and at the George Wright Society Annual Meeting, San Diego, Apr. 17, 2003. I am indebted to the audiences at all three venues for probing comments and questions.

1. For a history of the bell and its home in Independence Hall, see Charlene Mires, *Inde-*

pendence Hall in American Memory (Philadelphia: University of Pennsylvania Press, 2002).

2. Jill Ogline, " 'Creating Dissonance for the Visitor': The Heart of the Liberty Bell Controversy," *The Public Historian* 26 (2004): 52.

3. Martha Aikens, "Summary of Final General Management Plan/Environmental Impact Statement," National Park Service, Denver, Co, 1997, 1.

4. Ibid., 50.

5. Edmund S. Morgan, *American Slavery, American Freedom: The Ordeal of Colonial Virginia* (New York: W.W. Norton, 1975), 5.

6. The 1997 General Management Plan took pride that INHP "lies at the heart of a great American city—a living museum of historic sites, significant events, and diverse cultures" and pledged that INHP would work with the community to "foster opportunities for experiences that promote reflection, learning, and enjoyment" (*Summary of Final General Management Plan,* 1).

7. A review of these debates of the early 1990s can be found in Edward T. Linenthal and Tom Engelhardt, eds., *History Wars: The Enola Gay and Other Battles for the American Past* (New York: Henry Holt, 1996); Mike Wallace, *Mickey Mouse History and Other Essays on American Memory* (Philadelphia: Temple University Press, 1996); and Gary B. Nash, Charlotte Crabtree, and Ross E. Dunn, *History on Trial: Culture Wars and the Teaching of the Past* (New York: Alfred K. Knopf, 1997).

8. The history of the Morris mansion is provided by Edward Lawler Jr., "The President's House in Philadelphia: The Rediscovery of a Lost Landmark," *Pennsylvania Magazine of History and Biography* 126 (2002): 5–96 (9–18 for its various occupants up to 1781). One of Morris's slaves, Hero, had fled to the British just before they occupied the city in September 1777. See Gary B. Nash, *Forging Freedom: The Formation of Philadelphia's Black Community, 1720–1840* (Cambridge, MA: Harvard University Press, 1988), 47–48.

9. For Washington's modifications and additions to the Morris property in order to house his large domestic staff, see Lawler, "The President's House," 23–28. Without conclusive evidence, it appears that slaves lived in different parts of the main house and outbuildings rather than in separate slave quarters.

10. Lapsansky to Nash, Mar. 1, 2002; Nash to Lapsansky, Mar. 2, 2002; Nash to Pitcaithley, Mar. 7, 2002; Lapsansky to Nash, Mar. 8, 2002.

11. *First City,* 325–27.

12. Troy Johnston to Martha Aikens, July 17, 1995, quoted with permission of Superintendent Aikens.

13. The Radio News interview and call-in responses can be heard on http://www.whyy.org/91FM/philaslaves.html. Edward Lawler had been unable to interest the *Philadelphia Inquirer* in publishing his op-ed essay "A Forgotten National Landmark," which dealt with INHP's unwillingness to deal with these issues in its new Liberty Bell exhibits. Lawler to Nash, Mar. 13, 2002.

14. *Philadelphia Inquirer,* Mar. 24, 2002. At one time or another, nine Washington slaves lived and worked at the President's House. Mostly lost in the story are more than eighty white servants, indentured and free, who labored there.

15. The first to join were Philip Lapsansky; Ed Lawler; Charlene Mires; Howard Gillette, director of the Mid-Atlantic Humanities Center; Sharon Ann Holt, editor of the *Pennsylvania Magazine of History and Biography;* Rosalind Remer, professor of history at Moravian College and director of museum planning and programming at the National Constitution Center from 1997 to 1999; David Moltke-Hansen, director of the Historical Society of Pennsylvania (HSP); Michael Benjamin, an African American lawyer who sits on the council of HSP; and Ken Finkel, head of cultural programming at WHYY. Joining shortly thereafter were Emma Lapsansky, professor of history at Haverford College; Robert Engs, professor of history at the University of Pennsylvania; Ted Carter, librarian of the American Philosophical Society; Richard Dunn and Mary Maples Dunn,

codirectors of the American Philosophical Society; Roger Moss, director of the Philadelphia Athenaeum; and John Van Horne, librarian of the Library Company of Philadelphia.

16. *Philadelphia Inquirer,* Mar. 26, 2002.

17. Ibid., Mar. 27, 2002.

18. Gary B. Nash and Randall M. Miller, "Don't Bury the Past: Honor Liberty by Including the Stories of All"; Charlene Mires, "Park Service's Task: Making History Accessible," *Philadelphia Inquirer,* Mar. 31, 2002.

19. Ibid. On Apr. 2, 2002, Acel Moore, an African American columnist for the *Philadelphia Inquirer,* chimed in with advice that "full knowledge of all of American history would benefit all citizens of this nation. It might even foster better understanding, respect, and tolerance." By now the issue had caught the attention of the Pew Charitable Trust, which with extraordinary nimbleness for a large foundation announced that it would sponsor a workshop, "Interpreting the President's House: Moving Beyond Antiquarianism." Moore published another column in the *Inquirer* on Apr. 14, 2002. On Apr. 15, the *Philadelphia Daily News* ran an op-ed piece by William C. Kashatus supporting our position. Readers can view dozens of news stories and letters to the editor at the Independence Hall Association Web site (www.ushistory.org). Included is an unpublished letter from the Independence Hall Association chiding Aikens for evading the central issues that had been raised. See www.ushistory.org/presidentshouse/controversy/aih2.htm.

20. Martha Aikens, "Park Tells the Story of Slavery," *Philadelphia Inquirer,* Apr. 7, 2002; see also Martha Aikens to Nancy Gilboy, Oct. 11, 2001, at www.ushistory.org/presidents house/quotes3.htm.

21. Ad Hoc Historians to Martha B. Aikens, Apr. 18, 2002. Miller hand-delivered the letter to Aikens.

22. Dinitia Smith, "Slave Site for a Symbol of Freedom," *New York Times,* Apr. 20, 2002.

23. Aikens to Randall Miller, Apr. 22, 2002.

24. Pitcaithley to Aikens, Apr. 3, 2002, quoted with Pitcaithley's permission.

25. Scheduled for a new assignment in Washington shortly, Aikens delegated her responsibilities regarding the Liberty Bell exhibits to Deputy Superintendent Dennis Reidenbach by late April 2002.

26. Pitcaithley to Reidenbach, May 2, 2002; quoted with Pitcaithley's permission.

27. Ibid.

28. INHP staffers present included Chris Schillizzi, chief of interpretation and visitor services; Mary Reinhart, interpretative planner; Joe Becton, supervisory park ranger; Doris Fanelli, chief of the Cultural Resources Management Division; Coxey Toogood, INHP historian; and Katie Diethorn, supervisory museum curator.

29. Stephan Salisbury, who covered the controversy from the beginning for the *Philadelphia Inquirer,* reported the breakthrough on May 14, 2002, in an article entitled "Liberty Bell's new home will address slavery."

30. Those who agreed to review a revised script included Eric Foner, whose book on the various meanings of freedom made him a logical choice; Edward Linenthal, who had worked with NPS on many contested historical sites; Fath Davis Ruffins, Smithsonian Institution curator on African American history; Spencer Crew, director of the National Museum of American History; and James Horton, who had been a leading advisor to NPS on African American topics.

31. *Philadelphia Inquirer,* May 14, 16, and 26. The *New York Times* covered the meeting on May 15, 2002.

32. The entire exhibit text can be viewed at www.nps.gov/inde/lbc.html.

33. Remer to Ad Hoc Historians, May 30, 2002.

34. Stephan Salisbury, "Slavery's Story to Be Part of Bell Site," *Philadelphia Inquirer,* Aug. 11, 2002.

35. Stephan Salisbury, "A Protest Today Seeks Memorial to Slaves," *Philadelphia Inquirer,* July 3, 2002; Nora Achrati, "500 Seek Slave Memorial at Liberty Bell," ibid., July 4, 2000.

36. Martha Washington had promised Oney Judge as a marriage gift to her granddaughter Eliza Custis, who wed Thomas Law in Virginia in March 1796. It is possible that Judge decided to leave after hearing that Eliza and Thomas Law were invited to honeymoon in Philadelphia and stay at the President's House. In any case, she fled just before the Washingtons prepared to leave in June for Mount Vernon, where the transfer of Judge to the Laws would have taken place. I am indebted to Edward Lawler Jr. for this information.

37. Evelyn Gerson, "Oney Judge Staines: Escape from Washington," www.seacoastnh .com/blackhistory/ona.html; two articles from New Hampshire newspapers in the 1840s on Oney Judge Staines's life can be read at www.ushistory.org/presidents house/slaves.

38. www.ushistory.org/presidentshouse/slaves.

39. The quote is from George Washington Parke Custis, Martha Washington's grandson; www.ushistory.org/presidentshouse/slaves/hercules. For more on Hercules, see Henry Wiencek, *An Imperfect God: George Washington, His Slaves, and the Creation of America* (New York: Farrar, Straus and Giroux, 2003), 314–20.

40. I have treated the thickening of free black life in the city in the 1790s in *Forging Freedom: The Formation of Philadelphia's Black Community, 1720–1840* (Cambridge, MA: Harvard University Press, 1988), chs. 3–5.

41. The Hercules story and documentation are available at www.ushistory.org/presidents house/slaves.

42. These newspaper pieces can be viewed at www.ushistory.org/presidentshouse/news. Through July 2005, the *Philadelphia Inquirer* alone published more than seventy news articles, op-ed essays, and editorials on the Liberty Bell Pavilion and President's House site.

43. A series of articles on the design and the design itself can be viewed at www .ushistory.org/presidentshouse/plans/jan2003/index.htm.

44. The oil portrait of Hercules, presumed to be by Gilbert Stuart, can be viewed at www.ushistory.org/presidentshouse/slaves.

45. Bomar's previous NPS assignment, superintendent of the new Oklahoma City National Memorial, prepared her well for emotion-laden issues and contests over public memory.

46. A minority report from Edward Lawler Jr. quickly followed. Both documents can be viewed at www.ushistory.org/presidentshouse/controversy/minority.htm.

47. Letters written in Sept. and Oct. 1790 between Washington and his secretary Tobias Lear discuss the accommodations for the presidential family (including two grandchildren), the office staff, about fifteen white servants, and eight slaves to be brought from Mount Vernon. The letters are in George Washington Papers, Series 4, General Correspondence, 1741–1799, George Washington Papers, Library of Congress, as cited in Lawler, "President's House in Philadelphia," 25, n. 58; 33, nn. 77, 78.

48. The panel consisted of INHP superintendent Mary Bomar, Charlene Mires of the Ad Hoc Historians group, architectural historian Edward Lawler Jr., Michael Coard of the Avenging the Ancestors group, local African American historian Charles Blockson, and local activist Sacaree Rhodes. The forum was sponsored by INHP, the Historical Society of Pennsylvania, the Mid-Atlantic Regional Center for the Humanities, and other civic partners.

49. Dwight Pitcaithley's essay in this book explicitly addresses this change in NPS interpretive policies.

50. "How We Got Here: An Overview of the Development of the Civic Engagement Initiative at NPS," www.nps.gov/civic.

51. "The National Park Service and Civic Engagement" can be viewed at www.nps .gov/civic. Case studies of implementing the civic engagement initiative can be viewed at

www.nps.gov/civic/casestudies. The American Association of Museums added momentum with its *Mastering Civic Engagement: A Challenge to Museums* (Washington: American Association of Museums, 2002).

52. Ogline, " 'Creating Dissonance for the Visitor,' " 55–56.
53. The phrase is Ogline's (ibid., 55). For further discussion, see Jennifer Eichstedt and Stephen Small, *Representations of Slavery: Race and Ideology in Southern Plantation Museums* (Washington, DC: Smithsonian Institution Press, 2002), and James O. Horton, "Presenting Slavery: The Perils of Telling America's Racial Story," *Public Historian* 21 (Fall 1999): 19–38.
54. Edward T. Linenthal, "Can Museums Achieve a Balance Between Memory and History?" *Chronicle of Higher Education,* Feb. 10, 1995. A decade ago, Robin Winks argued in a Park Service journal that chapters of the American past that we are not proud of should be openly discussed at historic sites and that erasing shameful parts of the past is the work of authoritarian regimes. See "Sites of Shames: Disgraceful Episodes from Our Past Should Be Included in the Park System to Present a Complete Picture of Our History," *National Parks,* Mar./Apr. 1994, 22–23.

6. Recovering (from) Slavery:
Four Struggles to Tell the Truth (Joanne Melish)

1. Vincent Harding, "Beyond Chaos," in John A. Williams and Charles F. Harris, eds., *Amistad 1* (Washington, DC: Howard University Press, 1970), 286.
2. For a comprehensive analysis of the struggles and results of introducing the "new" social history and attempting to move from an objectivist to a constructionist approach at an important historic site, see Richard Handler and Eric Gable, *The New History in an Old Museum: Creating the Past at Colonial Williamsburg* (Durham and London: Duke University Press, 1997).
3. Promotional brochure, "The Rhode Island Historical Society's John Brown House Museum," n.d., n.p.
4. Scott MacKay, "Slavery in R.I.: Shameful Origin, Heroic Opposition," *Providence Journal,* Feb. 24, 2002.
5. Karen Davis, "Acknowledgment of 'House That Slavery Built,' " *Providence Journal,* Aug. 1, 2002.
6. J. Stanley Lemons, "John Brown House Is Not 'House That Slavery Built,' " *Providence Journal,* Aug. 12, 2002.
7. Richard Lobban, "The Struggle for the Truth About Rhode Island, John Brown, and the Slave Trade," *The Anchor,* Dec. 10, 2002, 1.
8. Ibid., 2.
9. Jay Coughtry, *Notorious Triangle: Rhode Island and the Slave Trade* (Philadelphia: Temple University Press, 1981), 39–40.
10. "Plantation Complex," by Sylvia Soares. Written and performed as part of the "Rhode Island Slavery and Its Legacies" project undertaken by a consortium of five historical societies—Newport Historical Society, Pettaquamscutt Historical Society, Rhode Island Black Heritage Society, Rhode Island Historical Society, and Smith's Castle, with support from the Rhode Island Council for the Humanities under its "What Does Freedom Mean" initiative, and from the Rhode Island Foundation, Joanne Pope Melish, consulting historian.
11. The question of whether separate, focused treatments by themselves actually serve to celebrate African American history or to marginalize it is a matter of much debate, of course.
12. Barbara Jeanne Fields, *Slavery and Freedom on the Middle Ground: Maryland During the Nineteenth Century* (New Haven: Yale University Press, 1985), 90.

13. Waveland's Web site is at www.state.ky.us/agencies/parks/wavelan2.htm.
14. "My Old Kentucky Home: Federal Hill, Bardstown, Kentucky," promotional brochure published in 2000 and available at the site, 9, 24.
15. See www.state.ky.us/agencies/parks/kyhome.htm.
16. U.S. Office of the Census, Fifth Census.
17. This and subsequent references to Eric Browning's experience in changing the script at My Old Kentucky Home, unless otherwise noted, are documented in Eric Browning, "The Rest of the Rowan Story: A Beginning to the Retelling of the History of Federal Hill—the Unheard Voices and Unseen Faces of My Old Kentucky Home," submitted Apr. 22, 2003, to me as Eric's "Memory Project," a requirement in the second half of my two-semester introductory course, History/Afro-American Studies 260 and 261: Afro-American History to 1865 and from 1865 to the Present. His efforts to rewrite the script began the preceding fall, in conjunction with his work in the first half of the course.
18. E-mail from Eric Browning to Brooks Howard, Mar. 10, 2003; e-mail from Brooks Howard to Eric Browning, Mar. 13, 2003.
19. E-mail from Eric Browning to Joanne Pope Melish, Apr. 9, 2003.
20. Faxed communication from Eric Browning to Joanne Pope Melish, Sept. 30, 2004.
21. *Brown Daily Herald,* March 13, 2001, 6.
22. See, for example, the *Boston Globe,* Apr. 17, 2001, 1; NBC's *Weekend Today,* Apr. 18, 2001.
23. The entire incident is fully described by Norman Boucher in "The War over Words: Race, Speech, and Community in Conflict," *Brown Alumni Magazine,* May/June 2001, 35–39; for the sidebar, see 38. In it, I, as a Brown Ph.D. and visiting scholar, am quoted as saying that although "the direct connections are oblique or minimal . . . Brown and the Browns were suspended in a web of trade and a domestic institution that is very, very significant in the commercial and social development of Rhode Island and New England."
24. See, for example, Keith W. Stokes, "Debating Slavery Reparations in R.I.," *Providence Journal,* Mar. 29, 2001; Paul Braverman, "Slavery Strategy: Inside the Reparations Suit," *Rhode Island Law Tribune,* July 11/17, 2001, 12 (which discussed the plans of the national "Reparations Coordinating Committee); "The Reparations Scam," a derisive editorial in the *Providence Journal* that described the "drive for slavery reparations" as "yet another plot devised by trial lawyers to keep the victim industry humming and themselves rich," Aug. 21, 2002.
25. *"A Special Report:* Slavery, the Brown Family of Providence and Brown University," press release, Brown University News Service, July 2001 (News_Service@brown.edu).
26. Subscription List for the Rhode Island Baptist College, by Hezekiah Smith, 1769, Rhode Island Historical Society Miscellaneous Manuscripts.
27. Ibid.
28. Conference Program, "Yale, New Haven, and American Slavery," Sept. 26–28, 2002, Yale Law School, sponsored by the Gilder Lehrman Center and Yale Law School, 1.
29. Ruth Simmons to selected faculty members, administrators, and students, Apr. 30, 2003.
30. Letter from the University Steering Committee on Slavery and Justice publicly e-mailed to "announce.all.oncampus," Mar. 13, 2004. Draft circulated Jan. 27, 2004.
31. Pam Belluck, "Brown U. to Examine Debt to Slave Trade," *New York Times,* Mar. 13, 2004.
32. Ibid.
33. Jennifer D. Jordan, "Unearthing the Past: Brown University, the Brown Family and the Rhode Island Slave Trade," *Providence Journal,* Mar. 15, 2004.
34. Jennifer D. Jordan, "Should Brown Make Amends for Its Ties to the Slave Trade?" *Providence Journal,* Mar. 5, 2004.
35. Jordan, "Unearthing the Past."
36. Conrad Leslie, "What About My Family's Reparations?" letter to the editor, *Providence Journal,* Mar. 16, 2004.

37. Thomas Sowell, "Slavery Reparations: Simmons's Hypocritical Race Hustling," *Providence Journal,* Mar. 26, 2004.

38. Frank Newman, "Simmons Embraces Civic Responsibility," *Providence Journal,* Apr. 10, 2004.

39. John Tessitore, "Maybe Simmons Just Wants to Start a Debate," *Providence Journal,* Mar. 31, 2004.

40. William Atwater, "Slavery: America Has a Special Burden," *Providence Journal,* Apr. 16, 2004.

41. Ruth J. Simmons to Brown parents and alumni, Apr. 2004.

42. The committee's program of sponsored events, along with a list of the members, the president's charge to the committee, and other information can be found on its Web site, www.brown.edu/Research/Slavery_Justice/.

43. *Brown Daily Herald,* Sept. 30, 2004, 1.

44. Private conversation with James T. Campbell, Nov. 7, 2004.

45. Anthony Walker, *So Few the Brave: Rhode Island Continentals 1775–1783* (Newport, RI: Seafield Press, 1981), 50–54; Sidney S. Rider, *An Historical Inquiry Concerning the Attempt to Raise a Regiment of Slaves by Rhode Island During the War of the Revolution. With Several Tables Prepared by Lt.-Col. Jeremiah Olney, Commandant* (Providence: S.S. Rider, 1880). This history is summarized in a paragraph headed "Historical Significance" in a letter from Edmund T. Parker Jr., chief engineer, Rhode Island Department of Transportation, to William F. Bundy, director, Rhode Island Department of Transportation, Jan. 18, 1995. This and all other correspondence on the project subsequently cited are archived at the Rhode Island Preservation and Heritage Commission (RIHPHC), Providence.

46. Review of this history in Vincent J. Palumbo, principal civil engineer, RIDOT, to Edward F. Sanderson, executive director, RIHPHC, Apr. 22, 1996.

47. Parker to Bundy, Jan. 18, 1995; telephone interview with Richard Greenwood, Project Review Coordinator, RIHPHC, Sept. 1, 2004.

48. Parker to Bundy, in a paragraph headed "Current Status," Jan. 18, 1995.

49. See Ruth Wallis Herndon and Ella Wilcox Sekatau, "The Right to a Name: The Narragansett People and Rhode Island Officials in the Revolutionary Era," *Ethnohistory* 44 (Summer 1997): 443–62. I have made this argument in "(Re)Placing the Indians, (Re)Inventing the Negroes" and "The Vernaculars of Slavery and Race in New England," unpublished papers.

50. Following the signing into law of the Intermodal Surface Transportation Efficiency Act of 1991 (ISTEA), the Rhode Island Department of Transportation (RIDOT) early in 1992 began to formulate policy and prepare for implementation and administration of provisions of the act requiring expenditures for transportation enhancement activities. The ISTEA requires that 10 percent of a state's Surface Transportation Program (STP) funds be spent on "transportation enhancements" emphasizing historic sites. Harold J. Neale, Charles R. Anderson, Barbara M. Shaedler, "A Historical Review of the TRB Review Board A2A05 Committee: Landscape and Environmental Design Committee. Prepared for 70th Anniversary Celebration at the Mid-Year Meeting, Topeka, Kansas, August 2002," 11.

51. Parker to Bundy, Jan. 18, 1995.

52. Paul L. Gaines, chair, Patriots' Park Development Committee, to Vincent J. Palumbo, principal civil engineer, RIDOT, June 30, 1999.

53. Louis E. Wilson to Derek Bradford, June 27, 1999, letter explaining the coding, covering the complete list; Derek Bradford to Mike Hebert, Historical/Archaeological Office, RIDOT, July 19, 1999.

54. Section 106 Documentation Form, Patriots' Park Enhancement Project, Portsmouth, Rhode Island—RIC No. 99103, RIFAP No. STP-ENHR (203), May 1, 2001. Individual letters from Vincent J. Palumbo, chief civil engineer, Rhode Island Department of

Transportation, dated Nov. 30, 1999, to John B. Brown, III, tribal historic preservation officer, Narragansett Indian Tribe, and Matthew Vanderhoop, natural resource director and THPO, Wampanoag Tribe of Gay Head (Aquinnah); individual letters from Vincent Palumbo dated Dec. 16, 1999, to: Maurice Foxx, tribal chairman, Mashpee Wampanoag; Linda Elderkin-Degnan, president, Pokanoket Wampanoag Federation/Wampanoag Nation; Bela Joaquina Teixeira, executive director, Rhode Island Black Heritage Society; Paul Gaines, chair, Patriots' Park Development Committee, Newport County NAACP; Kevin O'Malley, regional manager, Colt State Park; Herbert Hall, president, Portsmouth Historical Society; Robert G. Driscoll, Portsmouth town administrator.

55. Edward S. Szymanski, chief transportation projects engineer, to Edward Sanderson, Mar. 9, 2001.

56. Re-draft July 5, 2001; agreement communicated to all parties by Edward S. Szymanski, chief transportation projects engineer, Office of Environmental Programs, RIDOT, in letters dated Sept. 18, 2001.

57. "Patriots Park Dedication Wall Text," with attached memo from Edward Sanderson to Richard Greenwood, Feb. 16, 2001.

58. Ibid.

59. Albert T. Klyberg to Edward S. Szymanski, Apr. 16, 2001.

60. John Brown to Paul L. Gaines, Mar. 22, 2001, quoted in Edward S. Szymanski to Melisa L. Ridenour, division administrator, Federal Highway Administration, June 23, 2002.

61. "Draft Text, Front Panel, Patriots Park Monument," enclosed with letter from Edward F. Sanderson to Edward S. Szymanski, June 14, 2001.

62. Edward S. Szymanski to Edward Sanderson, Aug. 24, 2001.

63. Edward Sanderson to Edward S. Szymanski, Sept. 14, 2001; Paul L. Gaines, NAACP, to Edward S. Szymanski, Sept. 10, 2001; Linda Elderkin-Degnan, sachem, to Mike Hebert, RIDOT chief preservation officer, Sept. 9, 2001; Paul A. Weeden to Edward S. Szymanski, Sept. 20, 2001.

64. "Draft Text, Front Panel Patriots Park Monument," enclosed with letter from Edward Sanderson to Edward S. Szymanski, Sept. 14, 2001; Mark D. Harding, deputy THPO, Wampanoag Tribe of Gay Head (Aquinnah), Oct. 3, 2001; Sanderson to John Brown, Oct. 11, 2001; John Brown to Edward Sanderson, Oct. 22, 2001; and John Brown to Melisa Ridenour, division administrator, Federal Highway Administration, Mar. 18, 2002.

65. Minutes of Mar. 11, 2002, meeting, RIDOT, chaired by Edward S. Szymanski, Mar. 21, 2002.

66. J. Michael Butler, Environmental Officer, Federal Highway Administration, to Edward Sanderson, RIHPHC, Aug. 15, 2002; "Front Panel, Patriots Park Monument" appended to the letter.

67. Edward F. Sanderson to Edward S. Szymanski, Sept. 12, 2002.

68. John Brown to Edward S. Szymanski, Oct. 4, 2002; Richard Greenwood memo recording telephone conversation with John Brown, May 1, 2003; Richard Greenwood interview with the author.

69. The Pokanoket/Wampanoag Federation/Wampanoag Nation did not concur with the wording but, probably because the Pokanoket are not a federally recognized tribe with standing in Rhode Island, the Federal Highway Administration directed the RIDOT to explain to the Pokanoket that the new text represented a relative consensus. J. Michael Butler, Federal Highway Administration, to James R. Capaldi, director of RIDOT, Apr. 27, 2004.

70. Telephone interview with Richard Greenwood, project review coordinator, RIHPHC, Sept. 1, 2004; Alex Kuffner, "Revolutionary War's Black Regiment—Memorial Will Honor Service in the Battle of Rhode Island," *Providence Journal* (East Bay Edition), Aug. 31, 2005.

71. Text headed "(NITHPO Revised copy): Front Panel, Patriots Park Monument," appended to letter from Edward F. Sanderson to Edward S. Szymanski, Apr. 16, 2004.

72. Private conversation with Keith Stokes on June 29, 2004, at Rhode Island Council for the Humanities luncheon.

73. Linda Crotta Brennan, *The Black Regiment of the American Revolution* (North Kingstown, RI: Moon Mountain Publishing, 2004), 5.

74. Harding, "Beyond Chaos," 286.

7. Avoiding History:
Thomas Jefferson, Sally Hemings, and the Uncomfortable Public Conversation on Slavery (Lois E. Horton)

With gratitude to graduate student interviewers Stephanie L. Batiste, Paul R. Gardullo, Denise D. Meringolo, and Michele A. Gates Moresi, and to James Oliver Horton, with whom I worked in conducting this study and whose Center for the Study of Public History and Culture at George Washington University supported it. With special thanks to Lucia Stanton, Dianne Swan Wright, and the rest of the administration and staff of Monticello, whose gracious cooperation and assistance made the study possible. An earlier version of this paper was presented at the European Association for American Studies, Bordeaux, France, March 22–25, 2002.

1. James Oliver Horton and Lois E. Horton, *In Hope of Liberty* (New York: Oxford University Press, 1997); Ira Berlin, *Many Thousands Gone* (Cambridge, MA: Harvard University Press, 1998).

2. Lucia Stanton, *Free Some Day: The African-American Families of Monticello* (Charlottesville, VA: Thomas Jefferson Foundation, 2000), 17–18.

3. Paul Finkelman, *Slavery and the Founders* (Armonk, NY: M.E. Sharpe, 1996), 136, 112; Ira Berlin, *Slaves Without Masters* (New York: Pantheon, 1974), 46–50; Peter Kolchin, *American Slavery, 1619–1877* (New York: Hill and Wang, 1993), 78; Lucia Stanton, *Slavery at Monticello* (Charlottesville, VA: Thomas Jefferson Memorial Foundation, 1996), 13.

4. Peter Kolchin, *Unfree Labor* (Cambridge, MA: Harvard University Press, 1987), 51.

5. See, for example, Dumas Malone, *Jefferson and His Times*, 6 vols. (Boston: Little Brown, 1948–81); Scot A. French and Edward L. Ayers, "The Strange Career of Thomas Jefferson: Race and Slavery in American Memory, 1943–1993," in Peter S. Onuf, ed., *Jeffersonian Legacies* (Charlottesville: University of Virginia Press, 1993), 418–56.

6. Finkelman, *Slavery and the Founders*, 129–31. Two of Sally's children, both daughters, died in infancy.

7. Annette Gordon-Reed, *Thomas Jefferson and Sally Hemings: An American Controversy* (Charlottesville: University of Virginia Press, 1997).

8. E.A. Foster, M.A. Jobling, P.G. Taylor, P. Donnelly, P. de Knijff, R. Mieremet, T. Zerjal, and C. Tyler-Smith, "Jefferson Fathered Slave's Last Child," *Nature* 396, no. 6706 (Nov. 5, 1998): 27–28; Eric S. Lander and Joseph J. Ellis, "DNA Analysis: Founding Father," *Nature* 396, no. 6706 (Nov. 5, 1998): 13–14.

9. Typescript, Thomas Jefferson Memorial Foundation DNA Study Committee Minority Report, April 12, 1999, Monticello Foundation, Charlottesville, Virginia.

10. Five black visitors were questioned by white interviewers, and two were questioned by black interviewers. Thirty-seven of the remaining people were questioned by a white interviewer, and forty-two were questioned by a black interviewer.

11. Finkelman, *Slavery and the Founders*, 107, 150.

12. The Ken Burns three-hour documentary film *Thomas Jefferson* was aired on PBS in Feb. 1997. In 1995 the Merchant-Ivory feature film *Jefferson in Paris* had received only modest attention.

8. Southern Comfort Levels: Race, Heritage Tourism, and the Civil War in Richmond (Marie Tyler-McGraw)

Thanks to Cynthia MacLeod, Gregg Kimball, and James O. Horton for thoughtful comments, corrections, and clarifications.

1. Gordon Hickey, "Park Service Seeks Center at Riverfront," *Richmond Times-Dispatch,* Jan. 14, 1998; Gordon Hickey, "Lee Absent for Canal Walk's Opening," *Richmond Times-Dispatch,* June 5, 1999; Craig Timberg, "Confederate Image Casts Shadow," *Washington Post,* June 4, 1999.

2. L. Douglas Wilder, "Let's Stop Fighting a 134-Year-Old War," *Washington Post,* June 19, 1999.

3. Grace M. Hale, *Making Whiteness: The Culture of Segregation in the South, 1890–1940* (New York: Vintage Press, 1999), 51–67; David Blight, *Race and Reunion: The Civil War in American Memory* (Cambridge, MA: Belknap Press, 2001), 255–84.

4. Catherine W. Bishir, "Landmarks of Power: Building a Southern Past in Raleigh and Wilmington, NC, 1885–1915," in W. Fitzhugh Brundage, ed., *Where These Memories Grow: History, Memory and Southern Identity* (Chapel Hill: University of North Carolina Press, 2000), 139–68; Dell Upton, "Memorials to the Second Civil War: Commemorating the Civil Rights Movement," paper presented at the Tulane-Cambridge Civil Rights Conference, New Orleans, April 2001, copy in possession of Marie Tyler-McGraw, 17.

5. Jay K.B. Williams, *Changing Views and Unforeseen Prosperity* (Richmond: privately published, 1969), 30, 35–37, cited in Marie Tyler-McGraw, *At the Falls: Richmond, Virginia and Its People* (Chapel Hill: University of North Carolina Press, 1994), 207–8; John M. Coski and Amy R. Feely, "A Monument to Southern Womanhood: The Founding Generation of the Confederate Museum," in Edward D.C. Campbell Jr., ed., *A Woman's War: Southern Women, Civil War, and the Confederate Legacy* (Charlottesville: University Press of Virginia, 1997).

6. In 1929, a statue of Matthew Fontaine Maury, explorer and admiral, was added to the upper section of Monument Avenue. Maury was not a Confederate hero.

7. A.A. Taylor, "The Negro in the Reconstruction of Virginia," part 1, *Journal of Negro History* 11, no. 2 (Apr. 1926): 282–83; John T. O'Brien, "Reconstruction in Richmond: White Restoration and Black Protest, April-June, 1865," *Virginia Magazine of History and Biography* 89 (July 1981): 259–81.

8. See Elsa Barkley Brown and Gregg D. Kimball, "Mapping the Terrain of Black Richmond," in Kenneth W. Goings and Raymond A. Mohl, eds., *The New African American Urban History* (Thousand Oaks, CA: SAGE Publications, 1996), 66–115, for a thoughtful interpretation of many aspects of African American construction of space in Richmond.

9. Tyler-McGraw, *At the Falls,* 276–311; Edward Slipek, "The Suburbanization of Downtown," *Style Weekly,* Oct. 29, 1991; Jon C. Teaford, *The Rough Road to Renaissance: Urban Revitalization in America, 1940–1985* (Baltimore: Johns Hopkins University Press, 1990), chs. 6 and 7.

10. Gregg D. Kimball, "African, American, and Virginian: The Shaping of Black Memory in Antebellum Virginia, 1790–1860," in W. Fitzhugh Brundage, ed., *Where These Memories Grow: History, Memory, and Southern Identity* (Chapel Hill: University of North Carolina Press, 2000), 57–58; Upton, "Memorials," 14–15.

11. Robert Weyeneth, "Historic Preservation and the Civil Rights Movement of the 1950s and 1960s," study in possession of author at Applied History Program, University of South Carolina, Columbia, SC.

12. Upton, "Memorials," 14–15.

13. "Valentine Museum Long-Range Plan for the 1990s," internal memo, Valentine Museum, Oct. 4, 1990, copy in possession of author.

14. Gordon Hickey, "Park Service Seeks Center at Riverfront," *Richmond Times-Dispatch,* Jan. 14, 1998.

15. John Kneebone, "Location, Location, Location: The Arthur Ashe Monument and Monument Avenue," *Cultural Resources Magazine* 9 (1999): 1–5. Available at CRMOnline at crm.cr.nps.gov/archives/22-9/22-09-01.pdf.

16. Quotations from Michael Paul Williams, *Richmond Times-Dispatch,* June 26, 1995, and July 3, 1995, in Kneebone, "Location."

17. Efforts to commemorate Gabriel, the slave instigator of Gabriel's Rebellion in 1800, as a "freedom fighter" have met a much more negative response.

18. *Washington Times,* cited in Kneebone, "Location," 5.

19. *Richmond Times-Dispatch,* June 15, 1999; *Washington Post,* July 1, 1999.

20. Michael Paul Williams, "Renaissance in Thinking Must Be First," *Richmond Times-Dispatch,* June 7, 1999.

21. Craig Timberg, "Views of New Lee Image: Closer to a Compromise," *Washington Post,* July 7, 1999.

22. *Richmond Times-Dispatch,* June 5, 1999.

23. *Richmond Style Weekly,* cited in Kneebone, "Location."

24. "Battle Brews for Soul of Confederate Group," *Washington Post,* Dec. 14, 2001.

25. Deborah Fitts, "Lee Portrait Burned in Richmond," *Civil War News,* April 2000.

26. Rob Morano, "A Civil Action," *Richmond Style Weekly,* June 13, 2000, 13.

27. Although other Virginia cities better known for slavery, such as Richmond, had lobbied to get the site, Wilder was apparently swayed by the donation of thirty-five acres by a development company. The company is planning a 2,100-acre tract that will be commercial, residential, and recreational. The museum will reportedly be next to a golf course. *Washington Post,* Dec. 31, 2001.

28. Richard Just, "Confederate Flap," *American Prospect,* June 17, 2002, 25–27.

29. "Battle Flag: Museum's Director Has Unfurled a Debate," *Richmond Times-Dispatch* online, March 22, 2002.

30. Lance Gay, "Lincoln Statue Ignites Confederate Passion," Scripps-Howard News Service, Feb. 15, 2003, in Lincoln Statue file, Richmond National Battlefield Park Archives, Richmond, VA; "At Last!" *Richmond Times-Dispatch* editorial, April 18, 2003.

31. Michael W. Masters and Susan Lee Masters, Fredericksburg, VA, to Supt. Cynthia MacLeod, January 1, 2003, in Richmond National Battlefield Park Archives. Obtained through FOIA request.

32. Bob Moser, "Lincoln Reconstituted," *Intelligence Report* (Southern Poverty Law Center) 110 (Summer 2003): 9–14. Thanks to Laura Feller for providing this copy.

33. Tim D. Manning, Stokesdale, NC, to Supt. Cynthia MacLeod, Jan. 5, 2003, in Richmond National Battlefield Park Archives.

34. John Quinn, former editor of *Southern Partisan,* cited in Michael Powell, "The Rebels of the Right," *Washington Post,* Jan. 16, 2001.

35. Michael D. Shear and Peter Whoriskey, "Lincoln Statue Heightens Old Pains," *Washington Post,* Apr. 6, 2003; Michael Buettner, "Virginia Unveils Controversial Lincoln Statue," *Newsday,* Apr. 5, 2003, in Richmond National Battlefield Park Archives.

36. This is changing in Richmond as people of every possible background move to the city.

37. Charles B. Dew in Tredegar National Civil War Center Foundation, draft case statement, 2001, 1, copy in possession of author.

38. Ivan Karp and Steven D. Lavine, eds., *Exhibiting Cultures: The Poetics and Politics of Museum Display* (Washington, DC: Smithsonian Institution Press, 1991).

9. "A Cosmic Threat": The National Park Service Addresses the Causes of the American Civil War (Dwight T. Pitcaithley)

1. The historian David Blight has observed that the memory of the Civil War can be classified into three visions: the reconciliationist, the white supremacist, and the emancipationist, all of which collided and then combined into what came to be labeled the Lost Cause. David W. Blight, *Race and Reunion: The Civil War in American Memory* (Cambridge, MA: Belknap Press, 2001).

2. Quoted in Michael Kammen, *Mystic Chords of Memory: The Transformation of Tradition in American Culture* (New York: Alfred A. Knopf, 1991), 602.

3. The most recent and comprehensive treatment of this subject is Blight, *Race and Reunion*.

4. Robert Cook, "(Un)furl That Banner: The Response of White Southerners to the Civil War Centennial of 1961–1865," *Journal of Southern History* 68 (Nov. 2002): 881.

5. C. Vann Woodward, "Reflections of a Centennial: The American Civil War," *Yale Review* 50, no. 4 (June 1961): 481–90; John Hope Franklin, "A Century of Civil War Observance," *Journal of Negro History* 47, no. 2 (Apr. 1962): 97–107; Oscar Handlin, "The Civil War as Symbol and as Actuality, *Massachusetts Review* 3 (Autumn 1961): 133–43.

6. Franklin, "A Century of Civil War Observance," 107.

7. Kammen, *Mystic Chords,* 603.

8. See Eric Foner, ed., *The New American History* (Philadelphia: Temple University Press, 1990). For scholarship on the Civil War, see Catherine Clinton, *Civil War Stories: Actual Accounts of the War's Impact on Women and Children, Black and White, on Both Sides of the Conflict* (Athens: University of Georgia Press, 1998), and *Tara Revisited: Women, War, and the Plantation Legend* (New York: Abbeville Press, 1995); Catherine Clinton and Nina Silber, eds., *Divided Houses: Gender and the Civil War* (New York: Oxford University Press, 1992); William J. Cooper, *Jefferson Davis, American* (New York: Alfred A. Knopf, 2000); William C. Davis, *Look Away!: A History of the Confederate States of America* (New York: Free Press, 2002); M. Thomas Emory, *The Confederate Nation: 1861–1865* (New York: Harper and Row, 1979); Drew Gilpin Faust, *The Creation of Confederate Nationalism: Ideology and Identity in the Civil War South* (Baton Rouge: Louisiana State University Press, 1988), and *Mothers of Invention: Women of the Slaveholding South in the American Civil War* (Chapel Hill: University of North Carolina Press, 1996); Eric Foner, *Reconstruction: America's Unfinished Revolution, 1863–1877* (New York: Harper Collins, 1989); William W. Freehling, *The Reintegration of American History: Slavery and the Civil War* (New York: Oxford University, 1994); Gary W. Gallagher, *The Confederate War: How Popular Will, Nationalism, and Military Strategy Could Not Stave Off Defeat* (Cambridge, MA: Harvard University Press, 1997); Peter Kolchin and Eric Foner, eds., *American Slavery: 1619–1877* (New York: Hill and Wang, 1994); Leon F. Litwack, *Been in the Storm So Long: The Aftermath of Slavery* (New York: Alfred A. Knopf, 1979); James Marten, *The Children's Civil War* (Chapel Hill: University of North Carolina Press, 1998); James M. McPherson, *Battle Cry of Freedom: The Civil War Era* (New York: Ballantine Books, 1988); Peter J. Parish, *Slavery: History and Historians* (New York: Harper and Row, 1989); Maris A. Vinovskis, ed., *Toward a Social History of the American Civil War: Explanatory Essays* (New York: Cambridge University Press, 1990); Garry Wills, *Lincoln at Gettysburg: The Words That Remade America* (New York: Touchstone Books, 1992); Charles Reagan Wilson, *Baptized in Blood: The Religion of the Lost Cause, 1865–1920* (Athens: University of Georgia Press, 1980). See also Joe Gray Taylor, "The White South from Secession to Redemption," in John B. Boles and Evelyn Thomas Nolen, eds., *Interpreting Southern History: Historiographical Essays in Honor of Sanford W. Higginbotham* (Baton Rouge: Louisiana State University Press, 1987), 162–98.

9. Gaines M. Foster, *Ghosts of the Confederacy: Defeat, the Lost Cause, and the Emergence of the New South* (New York: Oxford University Press, 1987), 196.

10. See James Oliver Horton and Spencer R. Crew, "Afro-Americans and Museums: Towards a Policy of Inclusion," in Warren Leon and Roy Rosenzweig, eds., *History Museums in the United States: A Critical Assessment* (Urbana: University of Illinois Pres, 1989), 215–36.

11. Public Law 101–214, Dec. 11, 1989.

12. Public Law 101–377, Aug. 17, 1990.

13. Public Law 101–442, Oct. 18, 1990.

14. Robin Winks, "Sites of Shame," *National Parks,* March/April 1994, 22.

15. National Park Service, "Holding the High Ground: Principles and Strategies for Managing and Interpreting Civil War Battlefield Landscapes," unpublished proceedings, 1998 conference of battlefield managers, 11.

16. Department of the Interior, FY 2000 Appropriations, "Joint Explanatory Statement of the Committee of Conference," Title I, 96.

17. *Fort Sumter National Monument,* brochure (Washington, DC: GPO, 1997).

18. *The Civil War at a Glance,* brochure (Washington, DC: GPO, 1991).

19. The single exception to this statement is a set of exhibits installed at Fort Sumter in 1995 that specifically linked the coming of the war to slavery. The exhibits engendered no negative reaction. See John Tucker, "Interpreting Slavery and Civil Rights at Fort Sumter National Monument," *The George Wright Forum* 19, no. 4 (2002): 15–31.

20. Privacy Act requirements prevent the full citation of correspondence received unsolicited by a federal agency. Correspondence of this sort will be cited as follows: Correspondence to Secretary of the Interior, Sept. 10, 2000, Lake Jackson, TX, in "SCV General-1" file, Park History Subject Files, National Park Service, Washington, DC.

21. Correspondence to Secretary of the Interior, Sept. 3, 2000, Spain, in "SCV General-1" file, Park History Subject Files, National Park Service, Washington, DC.

22. Correspondence to Secretary of the Interior, Oct. 22, 1999, Sarasota, FL, in "Civil War General-2" file, Park History Subject Files, National Park Service, Washington, DC.

23. Correspondence to Associate Director for Cultural Resources Stewardship, Nov. 20, 1999, Palo Alto, CA, in "Civil War General-2" file, Park History Subject Files, National Park Service, Washington, DC.

24. Correspondence to Senator John B. Breaux, Sept. 18, 2000, Iowa, LA, in "Civil War General-2" file, Park History Subject Files, National Park Service, Washington, DC.

25. HERITAGEPAC, July 1999.

26. Ibid.

27. Collin Pulley, "Forward the Colors: A Report from the Heritage Defense Committee," *Confederate Veteran* 4 (2000): 8.

28. If the total membership of the SCV is 29,000, as advertised on its Web site, www.southern messenger.org/scv_camps.htm, fewer than 10 percent of SCV members responded to the organization's plea to lobby the secretary.

29. Correspondence to Secretary of the Interior, n.d., Indianapolis, IN, in "SCV General-1" file, Park History Subject Files, National Park Service, Washington, DC.

30. Correspondence to Representative Frank Wolf, Jan. 17, 2000, Front Royal, VA, in "Civil War General-2" file, Park History Subject Files, National Park Service, Washington, DC.

31. E-mail correspondence, Jan. 9, 2000, Richmond, VA, in "Jerry Russell" file, Park History Subject Files, National Park Service, Washington, DC.

32. Garry Wills, *Lincoln at Gettysburg: The Words That Remade America* (New York: Simon and Schuster, 1992), 263.

33. Governor William Hodges Mann's speech was reprinted in *Fiftieth Anniversary of the Battle of Gettysburg: Report of the Pennsylvania Commission, December 31, 1913* (Harrisburg, PA: n.p., 1915); quoted in Blight, *Race and Reunion,* 9.

34. Jerry Russell, "Refighting the Civil War: Park Service Wants to Talk About the Causes," *Arkansas Democrat Gazette,* Oct. 20, 2002.

35. Ibid.

36. John Keegan, *The Mask of Command* (New York: Penguin Books, 1987), 2.

37. For recent scholarship on the coming of the war, see Gabor S. Boritt, ed., *Why the Civil War Came* (New York: Oxford University Press, 1996); John Patrick Daly, *When Slavery Was Called Freedom: Evangelicalism, Proslavery, and the Causes of the Civil War* (Lexington: University Press of Kentucky, 2002); Charles B. Dew, *Apostles of Disunion: Southern Secession Commissioners and the Causes of the Civil War* (Charlottesville: University Press of Virginia, 2001); Drew Gilpin Faust, *The Creation of Confederate Nationalism: Ideology and Identity in the Civil War South* (Baton Rouge: Louisiana State University Press, 1988); William W. Freehling, *The Reintegration of American History: Slavery and the Civil War* (New York: Oxford University Press, 1994) and *The Road to Disunion: Secessionists at Bay, 1776–1854* (New York: Oxford University Press, 1990); Maury Klein, *Days of Defiance: Sumter, Secession, and the Coming of the Civil War* (New York: Alfred A. Knopf, 1997); Bruce Levine, *Half Slave and Half Free: The Roots of the Civil War* (New York: Hill and Wang, 1992); William A. Link, *Roots of Secession: Slavery and Politics in Antebellum Virginia* (Chapel Hill: University of North Carolina Press, 2003); James M. McPherson, *Battle Cry of Freedom: The Civil War Era* (New York: Ballantine Books, 1988); William Lee Miller, *Arguing About Slavery: The Great Battle in the United States Congress* (New York: Alfred A. Knopf, 1996); Michael A. Morrison, *Slavery and the American West: The Eclipse of Manifest Destiny and the Coming of the Civil War* (Chapel Hill: University of North Carolina Press, 1997); Kenneth M. Stampp, ed., *The Causes of the Civil War* (New York: Touchstone, 1991).

38. Larry Gara, *The Liberty Line: The Legend of the Underground Railroad* (Louisville: University Press of Kentucky, 1996 [1961]); Daniel Edmond Kilgore, *How Did Davy Die?: Essays on the American West* (College Station: Texas A&M University Press, 1978).

39. Paul Schullery and Lee Whittlesey, *Myth and History in the Creation of Yellowstone National Park* (Lincoln: University of Nebraska Press, 2003), 51.

40. Correspondence to Secretary of the Interior, Sept. 18, 2000, Louisville, KY, in "SCV General-1" file, Park History Subject Files, National Park Service, Washington, DC.

41. David W. Blight, "A Confederacy of Denial," *Washington Post,* Jan. 29, 2001. The degree to which the Lost Cause interpretation of the war became accepted nationally as the dominant narrative of that era can be seen in the *U.S. News & World Report* article "The Untold Story of the Civil War: After 100 Years—A Look at the Facts," April 17, 1961, 61–69.

42. James Ronald Kennedy and Walter Donald Kennedy, *The South Was Right!* (Gretna, LA: Pelican Publishing, 1994 [1991]); James Ronald Kennedy and Walter Donald Kennedy, *Was Jefferson Davis Right?* (Gretna, LA: Pelican Publishing, 1998); and John S. Tilley, *Facts the Historians Leave Out* (Nashville: Bill Coats, 1951).

43. Kennedy and Kennedy, *The South Was Right!,* from flyleaf.

44. Mildred Lewis Rutherford, *Truths of History* (Atlanta: Southern Lion Books, 1998), 54.

45. Robert Penn Warren, *The Legacy of the Civil War* (Lincoln: University of Nebraska Press, 1998 [1961]), 54–55.

46. Ibid., 53–66.

47. See www.southernmessenger.org/scv_camps.htm, May 30, 2001.

48. Correspondence to Secretary of the Interior, n.d., Duluth, GA, in "SCV General-1" file, Park History Subject Files, National Park Service, Washington, DC.

49. Correspondence to Senator Shelby, December 24, 2002, Hartselle, AL, in "SCV General-2" file, Park History Subject Files, National Park Service, Washington, DC. The relationship between public memory of the Civil War and southern identity has been well chronicled in Tony Horwitz's *Confederates in the Attic: Dispatches from the Unfinished Civil War* (New York: Pantheon Books, 1998) and David Goldfield's *Still Fighting*

the Civil War: The American South and Southern History (Baton Rouge: Louisiana State University Press, 2002).

50. For a detailed analysis of honor in the antebellum South, see Bertram Wyatt-Brown, *Southern Honor: Ethics and Behavior in the Old South* (New York: Oxford University Press, 1982).

51. Sanford Levinson, *Written in Stone: Public Monuments in Changing Societies* (Durham: Duke University Press, 1988), 55.

52. Ernest Wallace and David Vigness, eds., *Documents of Texas History* (Austin, TX: Steck, 1960), 195–96.

53. John H. Reagan, "A Conversation with Governor Houston," *Texas Historical Association Quarterly* 3, 4 (Apr. 1900): 280. Jefferson Davis appointed John H. Reagan postmaster general of the Confederacy, a position he held throughout the war. With the fall of Richmond, Reagan abandoned the city with President Davis and was captured with him on May 10, 1865, near Irwinville, Georgia. See John H. Reagan, *Encyclopedia of the Confederacy* (New York: Simon and Schuster, 1993), 3:1311–13.

54. See review of *Was Jefferson Davis Right?* in *Journal of American History* 86, 2 (Sept. 1999): 784–86.

55. See Marsha L. Weisiger, "The Debate over El Lobo: Can Historians Make a Difference," *The Public Historian* 26, no. 1 (winter 2004): 123–44; John M. Coski, "Historians Under Fire: The Public and the Memory of the Civil War," *CRM* 25, no. 4 (2002): 13–15.

56. Handlin, "The Civil War as Symbol and as Actuality," 134.

10. In Search of a Usable Past: Neo-Confederates and Black Confederates
(Bruce Levine)

Thanks to James Oliver and Lois E. Horton for their advice in revising this essay and to John Coski for his invaluable archival guidance.

1. Ponsford, Ltd., "Confederate Memorial," www.statueconservation.com/flash_site/confederate2.htm; Arlington National Cemetery, www.arlingtoncemetery.org/visitor_information/Confederate_Memorial.html.

2. Moses Jacob Ezekiel, *Memoirs from the Baths of Diocletian,* ed. Joseph Gutmann and Stanley F. Chyet (Detroit: Wayne State University Press, 1975), 438–39, quotation on 439.

3. Arlington National Cemetery, www.arlingtoncemetery.org/visitor_information/Confederate_Memorial.html. This description, in turn, is drawn from James Edward Peters, *Arlington National Cemetery: Shrine to America's Heroes* (Kensington, MD: Woodbine House, 1986), 253.

4. Vernon R. Padgett, "Did Black Confederates Serve in Combat?" Rebel Gray, www.rebelgray.com/blacksincombat.htm. "A section of the monument depicts a black Confederate soldier marching with white Confederates. Ezekiel, a veteran himself, knew as well as anyone the racial makeup of the army he served in." See http://members.tripod.com/~GA60th/links.html.

5. H.C. Blackerby, *Blacks in Blue and Gray: Afro-American Service in the Civil War* (Tuscaloosa, AL: Portals Press, 1979); Richard Rollins, ed., *Black Southerners in Gray: Essays on Afro-Americans in Confederate Armies* (Murfreesboro, TN: Southern Heritage Press, 1994); Charles Kelly Barrow, J.H. Segars, and R.B. Rosenburg, eds., *Black Confederates* (Gretna, LA: Pelican Publishing 2001 [1995]). The last volume originally appeared under the title *Forgotten Confederates.*

6. Address delivered by the Reverend Father Alister C. Anderson, chaplain (colonel), U.S. Army (ret.), and chaplain in chief of the Sons of Confederate Veterans, at Arlington National Cemetery, June 6, 1999, www.arlingtoncemetery.net/anderson-address.htm.

7. Terrell's 37th Texas Cavalry, www.37thtexas.org/html/MsnStat.html.

8. Eddie Dean, "A Memorial to Black Troops That Fought for the Union Finds a Place on

U Street This Weekend, but a Group of Historians and Re-enactors Thinks It's Time to Recognize the Black Soldiers Who Wore Gray," *Washington City Paper,* July 17, 1998, Terrel's 37th Texas Cavalry, www.37thtexas.org/html/Wshcitypaper.html; Tony Horwitz, "Shades of Gray: Did Blacks Fight Freely for the Confederacy?" *Wall Street Journal,* May 8, 1997; Scott Williams, "On Black Confederates," www.37thtexas.org/html/BlkHist.html; Vincent F. A. Golphin, "Black Confederates Have Their Own Lesson to Teach," *About . . . Time Magazine,* Nov. 1998, www.abouttimemag.com/nov98story2.html.

By one account, "black southerners participated in the Confederate war effort at all levels to a greater extent than in the Union war effort." Charles W. Harper, "Black Loyalty Under the Confederacy," in Barrow, Segars, and Rosenburg, eds., *Black Confederates,* 28. It is commonly acknowledged that some two hundred thousand blacks served as either Union soldiers or sailors.

9. Ulysses S. Grant, *Personal Memoirs* (New York: Konecky and Konecky, n.d. [1885]), 629–30.
10. Sons of Confederate Veterans, www.scv.org/directory/atm.asp.
11. Dean, "A Memorial to Black Troops."
12. Maria Sanminiatelli, "Blacks Join Confederate Group to Honor Heritage," Associated Press dispatch, July 13, 2002, at Know Southern History, www.knowsouthernhistory.net/Articles/Minorities/blacks_join_confederate_group.html.
13. Blackerby, *Blacks in Blue and Gray,* i.
14. Ibid.
15. Ibid., 40.
16. Harper, "Black Loyalty Under the Confederacy," 28.
17. P. Charles Lunsford, "The Forgotten Confederates," in Barrow, Segars, and Rosenburg, eds., *Black Confederates,* 97.
18. Edward C. Smith, "Calico, Black and Gray: Women and Blacks in the Confederacy," *Civil War* 23 (1990): 10–16, quotation on 13.
19. So, concludes one contribution to *Black Confederates,* "let it never again be said that the war was fought to free the slaves." James L. Harrison, "A Tribute to Loyal Confederates," adapted from the June 1992 edition of *Dispatch,* a membership newsletter of the Confederate Historical Institute, Little Rock, AR, in Barrow, Segars, and Rosenburg, eds., *Black Confederates,* 62.
20. Rebel Gray, www.rebelgray.com/BlacksForced.htm.
21. Smith, "Calico, Black and Gray," 12.
22. Rev. Edward C. Raffetto, "Facing the Reality of Southern History," in Barrow, Segars, and Rosenburg, eds., *Black Confederates,* 154–55.
23. James Ronald Kennedy and Walter Donald Kennedy, *The South Was Right!* (Gretna, LA: Pelican Publishing, 1999), 116.
24. Kennedy and Kennedy, *The South Was Right!,* quotations on 83, 116, 91, 89.
25. Blackerby, *Blacks in Blue and Gray,* 6.
26. The Confederate Memorial Chapel, display advertisement in the *Richmond Times-Dispatch,* Apr. 19, 1998, clipping courtesy of the Eleanor S. Brockenbrough Library, The Museum of the Confederacy.
27. Kennedy and Kennedy, *The South Was Right!,* 115.
28. Wayne R. Austerman, "The Black Confederates," in Barrow, Segars, and Rosenburg, eds., *Black Confederates,* 54, 49.
29. Arlington National Cemetery, www.arlingtoncemetery.net/anderson-address.html.
30. League of the South, www.dixienet.org.
31. League of the South, www.dixienet.org/spatriot/vol6no4/notes30.html.
32. League of the South, www.dixienet.org/ls-bod/kennedy.html.
33. Kennedy and Kennedy, *The South Was Right!,* 307, 309.
34. An example of this outlook may be found in Thomas J. DiLorenzo's fantasy-ridden

book, *The Real Lincoln: A New Look at Abraham Lincoln, His Agenda, and an Unnecessary War* (New York: Three Rivers Press, 2003).

35. Walter Williams, "Black Confederates," Jan. 26, 2000, George Mason University Department of Economics, www.gmu.edu/departments/economics/wew/articles/archives/2000arc hive.html.

36. Walter E. Williams, "Why the Civil War," Nov. 18, 1998, George Mason University Department of Economics, www.gmu.edu/departments/economics/wew/articles/98/civil-war.htm.

37. Sanminiatelli, "Blacks Join Confederate Group to Honor Heritage."

38. Linda McNatt, "Black Confederate Honored in Suffolk," *Virginian-Pilot* (Norfolk), Oct. 24, 1999.

39. Edward C. Smith, "In Defense of General Lee," *Washington Post,* Aug. 21, 1999, also available at http://users.erols.com/va-udc/lee-defense.html. Lee's most admiring modern biographer flatly acknowledges that Lee owned quite a few slaves. When two of them attempted to flee to the free state of Pennsylvania, "Lee sent them to labor in lower Virginia, where there would be less danger of their absconding." Douglas Southall Freeman, *R.E. Lee: A Biography* (New York: Charles Scribner's Sons, 1934), 1:390.

40. Edward C. Smith, "Opinion: U.S. Racists Dishonor Robert E. Lee by Association," Sept. 7, 2001, *National Geographic News,* National Geographic Society, http://news.nationalgeographic.com/news/2001/09/0907_smithgenlee.html. In fact, after the war Lee repeatedly expressed opposition to federal attempts to elevate the condition of former slaves and especially to federal enfranchisement of black males. His resentment of the political role that southern blacks played in the Civil War era boiled over in March 1868, when he advised his son not to employ black farm laborers. "You will never prosper with the blacks," he advised Robert, "and it is abhorrent to a reflecting mind to be supporting and cherishing those who are plotting and working for your injury, and all of whose sympathies and associations are antagonistic to yours." Robert E. Lee, *Recollections and Letters of General Robert E. Lee by His Son* (New York: Doubleday, Page, 1904), 305–7.

41. When urged to replace his slaves with wage workers, South Carolina's James Henry Hammond replied in 1845 that if he could obtain wage workers as cheaply he "would, without a word, resign my slaves. . . . But the question is, whether free or slave labor is the cheapest to use in this country, at this time, situated as we are. And [that issue] is decided at once by the fact that we cannot avail ourselves of any other than slave labor. We neither have, nor can we procure, other labor to any extent on anything like the [inexpensive] terms mentioned." James Henry Hammond, *Letter to an English Abolitionist,* reprinted in Drew Gilpin Faust, ed., *The Ideology of Slavery: Proslavery Thought in the Antebellum South, 1830–1860* (Baton Rouge: Louisiana State University Press, 1981), 184–85.

42. Kenneth M. Stampp, *The Peculiar Institution: Slavery in the Ante-Bellum South* (New York: Alfred A. Knopf, 1956); Paul David, Herbert G. Gutman, Richard Sutch, Peter Temin, and Gavin Wright, *Reckoning with Slavery: A Critical Study in the Quantitative History of American Negro Slavery* (New York: Oxford University Press, 1976).

43. Roy P. Basler, ed., *The Collected Works of Abraham Lincoln* (New Brunswick, NJ: Rutgers University Press, 1953), 2:461.

44. Dunbar F. Rowland, ed., *Jefferson Davis, Constitutionalist: His Letters, Papers and Speeches* (Jackson: Mississippi Department of Archives and History, 1923), 5:72–73. See also Charles B. Dew, *Apostles of Disunion: Southern Secession Commissioners and the Causes of the Civil War* (Charlottesville: University Press of Virginia, 2001); James Oliver Horton, "Confronting Slavery and Revealing the 'Lost Cause,' " *CRM: Cultural Resource Management* 21 (1998): 14–20.

45. *Journal of the Senate at an Extra Session of the General Assembly of the State of Georgia, Convened Under the Proclamation of the Governor,* Mar. 25, 1863 (Milledgeville, GA: Boughton, Nisbet and Barnes, 1863), 6.

46. Bell Irvin Wiley, *Southern Negroes, 1861–1865* (Baton Rouge: Louisiana State University Press, 1965 [1938]), 130–33; James H. Brewer, *The Confederate Negro: Virginia's Craftsmen and Military Laborers, 1861–1865* (Durham: Duke University Press, 1969).

47. *Southern Confederacy* (Atlanta), Jan. 24, 1865.

48. Arthur W. Bergeron Jr., "Free Men of Color in Grey," *Civil War History* 32 (Sept. 1986): 247–55, quotation on 255.

49. Joseph T. Wilson, *The Black Phalanx: A History of the Negro Soldiers of the United States* (New York: Arno Press, 1968 [1890]), 483.

50. Blackerby, *Blacks in Blue and Gray,* i.

51. "Uncle Gilbert Is Dead," reprinted from the Covington (GA) *Enterprise,* Jan. 18, 1907, in Barrow, Segars, and Rosenburg, eds., *Black Confederates,* 103.

52. Reprinted from the Huntsville (AL) *Times,* Aug. 31, 1929, in Barrow, Segars, and Rosenburg, eds., *Black Confederates,* 105–6.

53. Notice in the Columbia (SC) *State,* reprinted in Barrow, Segars, and Rosenberg, eds., *Black Confederates,* 105.

54. Barrow, Segars, and Rosenburg, eds., *Black Confederates,* 63–67.

55. Letter from George L. Christian in the *Richmond Times-Dispatch,* Mar. 19, 1913, in scrapbook C6, p. 48, Eleanor S. Brockenbrough Library, Museum of the Confederacy. Thanks to John Coski for showing me this and other items and for allowing me to read his own unpublished manuscript, "Black Confederates: A Skeptical View."

56. Blackerby, *Blacks in Blue and Gray,* 27; *The War of the Rebellion: A Compilation of the Official Records of the Union and Confederate Armies* (Washington, DC: Government Printing Office, 1898), ser. 1, vol. 49, pt. 1, 818. Hereafter cited as OR.

57. Blackerby, *Blacks in Blue and Gray,* 5.

58. Clipping in the Eleanor S. Brockenbrough Library, Museum of the Confederacy.

59. Rollins, *Black Southerners in Gray,* 21.

60. See James M. McPherson, *The Negro's Civil War* (Urbana: University of Illinois Press, 1982 [1965]), 26–28, quotation on 26.

61. Rollins, "Black Southerners in Gray," 27; R.J.M. Blackett, ed., *Thomas Morris Chester: Black Civil War Correspondent* (New York: Da Capo Press, 1991 [1989]), 248–49.

62. A.T. Bledsoe, chief of the Bureau of War, to W.S. Turner, Aug. 2, 1861, Letterbook, Confederate War Department, Letters Sent, ch. 9, vol. 1, 732–33, Record Group 109, National Archives.

63. Tasker Gantt to Henry Hunt, May 19, 1886, Henry Jackson Hunt Papers, Library of Congress; Jefferson Davis to Campbell Brown, June 14, 1886, George Washington Campbell Brown Papers, Manuscript Division, Library of Congress.

64. OR, ser. 4, vol. 1, p. 1020; Arthur W. Bergeron, *Confederate Mobile* (Baton Rouge: Louisiana State University Press, 1991), 105.

65. OR, ser. 4, vol. 1, 1087–88, 1111.

66. James A. Seddon to Hon. E.S. Dargan, Dec. 18, 1863, War Department, Letters Sent, ch. 9, vol. 14, 289, Record Group 109, National Archives; OR, ser. 4, vol. 2, 941.

67. *Public Acts of the State of Tennessee, Passed at the Extra Session of the Thirty-third General Assembly* (Nashville: J.O. Griffith, 1861), 49, ch. VIII, vol. 2782, Record Group 109, National Archives.

68. James A. Seddon to Hon. E.S. Dargan, Dec. 18, 1863.

69. "DeVere, M. Schele," Unfiled Papers and Slips, D-626, and James A. Seddon to M. Schele De Vere, Esq., Oct. 20, 1863, vol. 14, ch. IX, War Department, Letters Sent, both in Record Group 109, National Archives. Thanks to Michael Musick for copies of these documents.

70. James M. McPherson, e-mail message to author, Sept. 13, 2004.

71. R.K. Krick, unpublished memorandum, Sept. 2004, copy in author's possession.

72. Maria Sanminiatelli, "Descendants of Slave Join Ranks for Confederate Turning Pain into Pride," Associated Press, July 13, 2002, available at Know Southern

History, www.knowsouthernhistory.net/Articles/Minorities/blacks_join_confederate_group.html.

73. William R. Blair et al. to Maj. P.H. Nelson, n.d., and accompanying notations, copy in Eleanor S. Brockenbrough Library, Museum of the Confederacy; see also Bergeron, "Free Men of Color in Grey," especially 250–53.

74. Richard Rollins, "Servants and Soldiers: Tennessee's Black Southerners in Gray," in *Black Southerners in Gray*, 77.

75. Blackerby, *Blacks in Blue and Gray*, 31.

76. General Nathan Bedford Forrest Camp #469 of the Sons of Confederate Veterans, "The Black Confederate," www.scvcamp469-nbf.com/theblackconfederatesoldier.html. Forrest was a former slave trader, the commanding officer during the massacre of black U.S. troops at Fort Pillow, and the first Grand Wizard of the Ku Klux Klan. Of course, neo-Confederates have their own version of all of these facts, too.

77. Keisha Stewart, "Confederate Groups Honor Black Soldiers," *Roanoke Times*, Sept. 8, 2002, available at www.scvcamp469-nbf.com/memorailfor3slaves.html.

78. Bernard Nelson, "Confederate Slave Impressment Legislation, 1861–1865," *Journal of Negro History* 31 (Oct. 1946): 392–410.

79. Stewart, "Confederate Groups Honor Black Soldiers."

80. Norfolk *Virginian-Pilot*, October 19, 1993; *Richmond Times-Dispatch*, Oct. 22, 1993.

81. Bernard H. Nelson, "Legislative Control of the Southern Free Negro, 1861–1865," *Catholic Historical Review* 32 (Apr. 1946), 43–47.

82. *Public Acts of the State of Tennessee*, 49; Nelson, "Legislative Control of the Southern Free Negro," 46n; Wilson, *Black Phalanx*, 483.

83. Wilson, *Black Phalanx*, 487.

84. Quoted in Benjamin Quarles, *The Negro in the Civil War* (New York: Da Capo, 1988 [1953]), 275.

85. Sally E. Hadden, *Slave Patrols: Law and Violence in Virginia and the Carolinas* (Cambridge, MA: Harvard University Press, 2001), 167–202; Gregg D. Kimball, *American City, Southern Place: A Cultural History of Antebellum Richmond* (Athens: University of Georgia Press, 2000), 248; Nelson, "Legislative Control of the Southern Free Negro," 28–46; J.H. Unthank and Geo. S. Hebb, *A Digest of the Militia Laws of Tennessee Now in Force* (Memphis: Hutton and Freligh, 1861), quote on 49.

86. As this brief notice in the Macon *Telegraph and Confederate* of Nov. 11, 1864, reminds us: "A negro man was recently hung by the citizens near Duck Hill, Carroll county, Mississippi. He was raising a company of negroes to go to Memphis. When he was overtaken he resisted so defiantly that he had to be shot before surrendering. He was then tried and hung. Many other negroes were implicated in the move."

87. Letter to the editor signed "Q," Macon *Telegraph and Confederate*, Jan. 6, 1865.

88. J.H. Stringfellow to Jefferson Davis, February 8, 1865, S-WD-57, documents printed in *The War of the Rebellion*, Record Group 109, National Archives.

89. See Robert F. Durden's splendid documentary collection on this subject, *The Gray and the Black: The Confederate Debate on Emancipation* (Baton Rouge: Louisiana State University Press, 2000 [1972]). The discussion that follows is based upon my book *Confederate Emancipation: Southern Plans to Free and Arm Slaves During the Civil War* (New York: Oxford University Press, 2005).

90. Sons of Confederate Veterans Education Committee, "Black History Month, Black Confederate Heritage," www.scv.org/education/edpapers/blackhst.html.

91. Scott Williams, "On Black Confederates," www.37thtexas.org/html/BlkHist.html; also see members.tripod.com/~GA60th/links.html.

92. J.H. Segars, *In Search of Confederate Ancestors: The Guide* (Murfreesboro, TN: Southern Heritage Press, 1993), 97.

93. Even militant defenders of the black Confederate legend find it hard to evade this truth when they get to this point in the war's history. Thus H.C. Blackerby noted tersely that

"relatively few blacks bore arms until the final year." Blackerby, *Blacks in Blue and Gray,* 22.

94. OR, ser. 1, vol. 52, pt. 2, 587–88, 590.
95. Robert E. Lee to John C. Breckinridge, Mar. 14, 1865, Army of Northern Virginia Headquarters Papers, R.E. Lee Papers, Virginia Historical Society.
96. Howell Cobb to James A. Seddon, Jan. 8, 1865, in OR, ser. 4, vol. 3, 1010.
97. Lee to Andrew Hunter, Jan. 11, 1865, in OR, ser. 4, vol. 3, 1012–13, emphasis added.
98. Lynchburg *Virginian,* Feb. 13, 1865.
99. Judah P. Benjamin to Frederick A. Porcher, Dec. 21, 1864, in OR, ser. 4, vol. 3, 959–60, emphasis added.
100. Campbell Brown, "Notes on the Campaign before Richmond, 1864–1865," in *Campbell Brown's Civil War: With Ewell and the Army of Northern Virginia,* ed. Terry L. Jones (Baton Rouge: Louisiana State University Press, 2001), 272, emphasis added.
101. Edward A. Pollard, *Life of Jefferson Davis with a Secret History of the Southern Confederacy* (Atlanta: National Publishing, 1869), 456.
102. The passage comes from Faulkner's 1951 novel *Requiem for a Nun.*

Epilogue: Reflections (Edward T. Linenthal)

1. See "For the Union Dead," in Robert Lowell, *Selected Poems* (New York: Farrar, Straus, and Giroux, 1977), 135–37. See, as well, Steven Axelrod, "Colonel Shaw in American Poetry: 'For the Union Dead' and Its Precursors," *American Quarterly* 24 (Oct. 1972): 523–37, and Helen Vendler, "Art, Heroism, and Poetry: The Shaw Memorial, Lowell's 'For the Union Dead,' and Berryman's 'Boston Common': A Meditation upon the Hero," in Martin H. Blatt, Thomas J. Brown, and Donald Yacovone, eds., *Hope and Glory: Essays on the Legacy of the Fifty-Fourth Massachusetts Regiment* (Amherst: University of Massachusetts Press, 2001), 202–14.
2. See, for example, John W. Dower, *Embracing Defeat: Japan in the Wake of World War II* (New York: The New Press, 1999); Ian Buruma, *The Wages of Guilt: Memories of War in Germany and Japan* (New York: Farrar, Straus, and Giroux, 1994); Laura Hein and Mark Selden, eds., *Censoring History: Citizenship and Memory in Japan, Germany, and the United States* (London: M.E. Sharpe, 2000). Quoted material from the introduction to Omer Bartov, Atina Grossmann, and Mary Nolan, eds., *Crimes of War: Guilt and Denial in the Twentieth Century* (New York: The New Press, 2002), x.
3. Denis Byrne, "The Ethos of Return: Erasure and Reinstatement of Aboriginal Visibility in the Australian Historical Landscape," *Historical Archaeology* 37, no. 1 (2003): 83.
4. John Hope Franklin in "The National Park Service and Civic Engagement," National Park Service, 2001, 5.
5. Oklahoma Commission to Study the Tulsa Race Riot of 1921, *Tulsa Race Riot: A Report* Oklahoma City, OK: The Commission, 2001), 8.
6. Michael H. Cottman, *Spirit Dive: An African-American's Journey to Uncover a Sunken Slave Ship's Past* (New York: Three Rivers Press, 1999), 165. The monument reads "In memory and recognition of the courage, pain and suffering of enslaved African people. 'Speak her name and gently touch the souls of our ancestors.' "
7. Nathan Irvin Huggins, *Revelations: American History, American Myths* (New York: Oxford University Press, 1995), 29.
8. Ibid., 34–35; Kathleen Stewart, *A Space on the Side of the Road: Cultural Poetics in an "Other" America* (Princeton: Princeton University Press, 1996), 3–4.
9. Adam Goodheart, "The Bonds of History," *Preservation: The Magazine of the National Trust for Historic Preservation,* Sept./Oct. 2001, 40. There is nothing new about controversy regarding African American monuments. Historian Dennis P. Ryan informs readers that in 1887 the Massachusetts General Court decided to erect a memorial to

the King Street Martyrs (those killed in the Boston Massacre, including, of course, Crispus Attucks). "Over the next eighteen months," writes Ryan, "historians, politicians, newspaper editors, clergymen heatedly debated the worthiness of the monument proposal. . . . Participants accused one another of racial prejudice, historical distortion, and political opportunism." Dennis P. Ryan, "The Crispus Attucks Monument Controversy of 1887," *Negro History Bulletin* 40, no. 1 (Jan./Feb. 1977): 656.

10. Jon Nordheimer, "A Creek, Negro Run, Is the Source of Debate," *New York Times,* Nov. 3, 1994; Peter H. Wood, "Slave Labor Camps in Early America: Overcoming Denial and Discovering the Gulag," in Carla Gardina Pestana and Sharon V. Salinger, eds., *Inequality in Early America* (Hanover and London: University Press of New England, 1999), 234; Laura (Souillière) Gates, "Frankly, Scarlett, We Do Give a Damn: The Making of a New National Park," *The George Wright Forum* 19, no. 4 (2002): 41.

11. Denis Byrne, "Segregated Landscapes: The Heritage of Racial Segregation in New South Wales," *Historic Environment* 17, no. 1 (2003): 16.

12. See Lewis's introduction to Jim Carrier, *A Traveler's Guide to the Civil Rights Movement* (Orlando: Harcourt, 204), ix; Robert Weyeneth, "Historic Preservation and the Civil Rights Movement," *CRM: Cultural Resource Management,* 19, no. 2 (1996): 26–28; Carrier, *A Traveler's Guide,* 264.

13. The Medgar Evers home was also used for a reenactment of the assassination during the filming of *Ghosts of Mississippi* in 1994. Willie Morris reports, "Black families from the adjoining houses stood watching on their front lawns, beyond the range of the cameras. These spectators . . . were hushed and respectful, the atmosphere almost funereal. A number of older people among them had been here on the night of the murder." Willie Morris, *The Ghosts of Medgar Evers: A Tale of Race, Murder, Mississippi, and Hollywood* (New York: Random House, 1998), 187. I am very grateful to Stacy White, the reunion coordinator for the Ruleville/Sunflower County Black Historical Society, for sending me materials about the commemorative events in Indianola, and to Todd Moye, director of the Tuskegee Airmens' Oral History Project, for telling me about these events.

14. Richard Rubin, *Confederacy of Silence: A True Tale of the New Old South* (New York: Atria Books, 2002), 11 and passim.

15. Ibid.

16. Ibid. For a brilliant and moving meditation on "touching" evil in a physical manner, see Pumla Gobodo-Madikizela's *A Human Being Died That Night: A South African Woman Confronts the Legacy of Apartheid* (Boston: Houghton Mifflin, 2004).

17. Paul Hendrickson, *Sons of Mississippi* (New York: Alfred A. Knopf, 2003), 6, 9.

18. Edward Ball, "One Man Living with the Past," *History News,* winter 2001, 8.

CONTRIBUTORS

Ira Berlin is Distinguished University Professor at the University of Maryland and a Fellow at the W.E.B. Du Bois Institute for African and African American Research at Harvard University. He is the founding director of the Freedmen and Southern Society Project and chief editor of the first four volumes of the Project's *Freedom: A Documentary History of Emancipation*. His books include *Slaves Without Masters: The Free Negro in the Antebellum South, Many Thousands Gone: The First Two Centuries of Slavery in North America,* and *Generations of Captivity: A History of American-American Slaves.* He was the 2002–2003 president of the Organization of American Historians.

David W. Blight is Class of '54 Professor of American History and Director of the Gilder Lehrman Center for the Study of Slavery, Resistance, and Abolition at Yale University. His books include *Race and Reunion: The Civil War in American Memory, Frederick Douglass' Civil War: Keeping Faith in Jubilee,* and *Passages to Freedom: The Underground Railroad in History and Memory* (editor). He is completing *Rowing to Freedom: The Emancipation of Wallace Turnage and John Washington,* based on two newly discovered slave narratives.

James Oliver Horton is the Benjamin Banneker Professor of American Studies and History at George Washington University and Historian Emeritus at the National Museum of American History, Smithsonian Institution. He was Senior Advisor on Historical Interpretation and Public

Education for the Director of the National Park Service in 1994–95, chair of the National Park System Advisory Board in 1996, and president of the Organization of American Historians in 2004–2005. His books include *Free People of Color: Interior Issues in African American Community, The Landmarks of African American History,* and *In Hope of Liberty: Free Black Culture and Community in the North, 1700–1865* (co-authored).

Lois E. Horton is Professor of History at George Mason University and serves on the faculties of Cultural Studies, Women's Studies, and the Honors Program. She serves on the advisory board of the Gilder Lehrman Center for the Study of Slavery, Resistance, and Antislavery at Yale University. She was contributing author to *City of Magnificent Intentions: A History of the District of Columbia,* and her co-authored books include *Slavery and the Making of America, Hard Road to Freedom: The Story of African America, Von Benin nach Baltimore,* and *Black Bostonians: Family Life and Community Struggle in the Antebellum North.*

Bruce Levine is Professor of History at the University of California, Santa Cruz. His books include *The Spirit of 1848: German Immigrants, Labor Conflict, and the Origins of the Civil War; Half Slave and Half Free: The Roots of Civil War; Confederate Emancipation: Southern Plans to Arm and Free Slaves during the Civil War; Work and Society* (co-editor); and *Who Built America* (co-author, first edition).

Edward T. Linenthal is Professor of History at Indiana University and editor of the *Journal of American History.* He has worked on the National Park Service's Civic Engagement and Public History project since 2002 and is a member of the Flight 93 Federal Advisory Commission. His books include *Preserving Memory: The Struggle to Create America's Holocaust Museum, Sacred Ground: Americans and their Battlefields,* and *The Unfinished Bombing: Oklahoma City in American Memory.*

Joanne Pope Melish is Associate Professor of History at the University of Kentucky. She is the author of *Disowning Slavery: Gradual Emancipation and "Race" in New England, 1780–1860* and several articles on race and slavery in the early republic. She is working on a study of evolving racial language and what it reveals about the changing racial order in New England through 1880.

Gary B. Nash is Professor of History at UCLA, where he has taught for the last thirty-nine years, and Director of the National Center for History in the Schools. He was the 1994–95 president of the Organization of American Historians. His books include *Red, White, and Black: The Peoples of Early America; The Urban Crucible: Social Change, Political Consciousness and the Origins of the American Revolution; Forging Freedom: The Formation of Philadelphia's Black Community, 1720–1840; History on Trial: Culture Wars and the Teaching of the Past* (co-author); *First City: Philadelphia and the Forging of Historical Memory; Landmarks of the American Revolution;* and *The Unknown American Revolution: The Unruly Birth of Democracy and the Struggle to Create America.*

Dwight T. Pitcaithley is Adjunct Professor of History at New Mexico State University. In 2005 he retired as Chief Historian of the National Park Service, a position he held for ten years. During his thirty-year career with the National Park Service, he worked in Santa Fe, Boston, and Washington, D.C. He has published articles related to historic preservation and the interpretation of historic sites and visited 220 of the 388 natural and cultural places that comprise the National Park System.

Marie Tyler-McGraw is an independent scholar currently working as a consultant and contractor for public history projects. She was a historian at the National Park Service and the Valentine Richmond History Center. She worked for the National Endowment for the Humanities, taught American history and American studies in several colleges and universities, and held a postdoctoral fellowship at the Smithsonian Institution. She has recently completed a book manuscript on the American Colonization Society, *Crossing Over: Virginia and Liberia.*

John Michael Vlach is Professor of American Studies and Anthropology and Director of the Folklife Program at The George Washington University. His museum exhibitions on the material aspects of African American life and history include the "The Afro-American Tradition in

Decorative Arts," "Before Freedom Came," and "Raised to the Trade: Creole Building Arts in New Orleans." His many books include *Back of the Big House: The Architecture of Plantation Slavery, By the Work of Their Hands: Studies in Afro-American Folklife,* and *The Planter's Prospect: Privilege and Slavery in Plantation Paintings.*

INDEX